CREATIVE EXCHANGE

innovations
African American religious thought

Anthony B. Pinn and Katie G. Cannon, editors

Innovations publishes creative and innovative works in African American religious thought and experience. The series highlights creatively progressive projects in Womanist and Black theology and ethics. It also encourages interdisciplinary discourse that expands understanding of African American religion and religious experience as well as the manner in which African Americans have envisioned and articulated their religiosity.

Titles in the series—

Enfleshing Freedom: Body, Race, and Being
   M. Shawn Copeland

Creative Exchange: A Constructive Theology
   of African American Religious Experience
   Victor Anderson

Making a Way Out of No Way: A Womanist Theology
   Monica A. Coleman

Plantations and Death Camps: Race, Sin, and Human Dignity
   Beverly E. Mitchell

CREATIVE EXCHANGE

A CONSTRUCTIVE THEOLOGY
OF AFRICAN AMERICAN RELIGIOUS EXPERIENCE

VICTOR ANDERSON

FORTRESS PRESS
MINNEAPOLIS

CREATIVE EXCHANGE
A Constructive Theology of African American Religious Experience

Howard Thurman, *The Creative Encounter* (Richmond, Ind.: Friends United, 1972), 117, 123. Used by permission.
Howard Thurman, *The Inward Journey* (Richmond, Ind.: Friends United, 1971), 135,138. Used by permission.

Cover image: Jacob Lawrence, *Through Forests, Up Rivers, Up Mountains*, 1967. Hirshhorn Museum and Sculpture Garden, Smithsonian Institution, The Josseph H. Hirshhorn Bequest, 1981. © 1967 The Estate of Gwendolyn Knight Lawrence / Artists Rights Society (ARS), New York. Photo © Art Resource, NY. Used by permission.
Cover design: Diana Running
Book design: Carolyn Banks

Library of Congress Cataloging-in-Publication Data

Anderson, Victor, 1955–
  Creative exchange : a constructive theology of African American religious experience
/ Victor Anderson.
      p. cm. — (Innovations: African American Religious Thought)
  Includes bibliographical references and index.
  ISBN 978-0-8006-6255-4 (alk. paper)
  1. African Americans—Religious life. 2. Black theology. I. Title.
  BR563.N4A534 2008
  277.3'08308996073—dc22

                              2007048842

The paper used in this publication meets the minimum requirements of American National Standard for Information Sciences—Permanence of Paper for Printed Library Materials, ANSI Z329.48-1984.

Manufactured in the U.S.A.
12   11   10   09   08   1   2   3   4   5   6   7   8   9   10

I dedicate this book to the memory of my friend, teacher, and mentor Malcolm L. Diamond. The openness of his spirit continues to inspire me toward the cultivation of creative exchanges that substantiates for me an ethics of openness. Standing together silently at his office window at Princeton University in 1879 Hall on October 11, 1988, Mal pointed to the sunset. As tears fell from our faces, we encountered the setting sun that afternoon, no longer as an "it" but a "thou" in the creative exchange of our religious experience.

I also dedicate this book to the memory of my friend, colleague, and confidant at Vanderbilt Divinity School, Howard L. Harrod. I miss him daily.

CONTENTS

FOREWORD

African American theological discourse has changed over the course of the late twentieth century and early twenty-first century. From a rather strict preoccupation with race/racism, it has grown to include a much richer understanding of the "web-like" nature of oppression and the various ways in which we encounter the world. Scholars participating in this discourse have struggled with the nature and meaning of their work, the proper audience for their writings, and the meaning of their commitments for life in the academy. Much of this wrestling has centered on the substance of black life—the described details of this existence. Less attention, however, has been given to the theoretical underpinning and methodological commitments that shadow the work of these scholars: What is the nature and meaning of the experience that centers publications, lectures, and conversations on African American religion, and how does one theologize regarding this experience? Several works hint at such questions, but full attention has been wanting.

This book has been a good number of years in the making, but it is well worth the wait. Beginning to outline a necessary shift in the theological and ethical sensibilities informing African American theology in particular and African American religious studies in general through his earlier *Ontological Blackness*, Anderson here presents the next logical step—a theological program that interrogates the messy and complex nature of religious experience. Yet the book you hold is not simply a consequence of Anderson's interrogation of black theology's inner logic, its primary concerns and structures. Rather, it also owes a debt to his comment to pragmatism, particularly his concern with a "monistic conception of experience." For Anderson, theology is a way to interpret the complexities and thickness of religious experience—pointing all the time toward relationality and a longing for a richness of life as the "Beloved Community." *Creative Exchange* unpacks the ambiguities of experience in ways that celebrate its unresolved tensions and paradoxes.

Creative Exchange is not simply the title of this book. Rather, it also captures the process, the manner in which theology does it work, the way in which theology provides rich interpretation of religious experience, keeping our focus on the "unresolved ambiguities" of life, as Anderson puts it.

In spite of what one might think after reading his earlier books, race is not removed as a category of investigation. Rather, consistent with his earlier work, Anderson understands race as a deep symbol that must not be flattened or rendered ontological in nature, but understood as simply one dimension of experience. Such a stance opens *Creative Exchange* to a wide array of source materials and perspectives that challenge black and womanist theologies. Yet it is a challenge that also calls for conversation, for dialogue, and such an appeal frames each chapter of this splendid book.

This book suggests the strengths and capacity of theological inquiry to wrestle in productive ways with the nature and meaning of African American religious experience. While respecting and insightfully presenting earlier takes on the topic, this book suggests a cartography of deep thinking that exposes new perspectives and alternate approaches.

It is the creativity of this book that appealed to us first, and it is because of the manner in which Anderson so brilliantly pushes scholarship on African American religion forward that we are delighted to have it as the first book in this new series, "Innovations: African American Religious Thought." In his writing, Anderson captures the concern for innovation, for new approaches, new perspectives, and new possibilities for the study of African American religious thought and life that shape this series.

We are certain you will be challenged and inspired by the sharp scholarship that marks this book.

Anthony B. Pinn
Katie Geneva Cannon

PREFACE

CREATIVE EXCHANGE: A Constructive Theology of African American Religious Experience is written to clarify the relation between my previous books, *Beyond Ontological Blackness* (1995) and *Pragmatic Theology* (1998). The latter was based on my doctoral dissertation, *The Legacy of Pragmatism in the Theologies of D.C. Macintosh, H. Richard Niebuhr, and James M. Gustafson* (Princeton, 1992). Yet my constructive theology of African American religious experience is not only the result of reading those classical American pragmatists. It is also derived from a course of life. From my youth, I have been a student of theology, raising many questions and puzzlements about the Bible that I rambunctiously put to my pastor during youth retreats. Who wrote it? If God is good, why does he scare people with the threat of hell? Will I see my mother and father in heaven? Will they remember me? Why did God create the devil? If God is eternal or everlasting, how did he get to be so old? At fifteen, I read my first book on the Pentateuch and learned a very strange new set of symbols called JEPD. I did not understand all that I was reading, but its impact stayed with me even as it was later clarified for me at Calvin Theological Seminary.

Theology and Bible study were not my only youthful intellectual passions. I also read every book in my high school library that I could find on the history and art of the Renaissance. There I had my first encounter with humanism and skepticism. While cutting high school to sit and draw at the Art Institute of Chicago, I became fascinated by religiously inspired paintings and other arts. These and more of my early curiosities have contributed to my academic preoccupation with "religious experience."

It was in the sphere of worship, however, that my fascination with religious experience was most centered. There I witnessed such things as demonic possessions, exorcisms, ecstatic worship, shouting, exuberant praying, and speaking in tongues. I asked myself and others why some people experienced such things and others did not. Throughout most of my childhood and youth, however, I reflected most on the power of prayer in faith healing services and in testimonies to miracles. These early experiences continue to inform my sense of humility when confronted by questions of African American religious experience. I learned to respect the lived practices of such religious experience, even if I had no intellectual stake in affirming the theologies that supported them. The possibility of error hovers over all, says Josiah Royce, one of my greatest influences. This also includes my own judgments. For me, such experiences are the stuff of religious experience performed in the everyday and ordinary lives of African American people. I hope that I have been faithful in my appreciation of such experiences in this book.

My aforementioned dissertation was a critical exploration of the relevance of traditional American theology after the critique of metaphysics and classical theism by American pragmatists. Although Charles Sanders Peirce had always been of interest to me, the dissertation focused on the pragmatisms of Royce, William James, and John Dewey. The influences of these three American philosophers are present throughout this book in a constructive manner. It was James and Dewey who most informed my understanding of experience. They provided me with a monistic conception of experience that helped me make sense of the complexities of how the world is experienced. Our experiences are not compartmentalized or dichotomized into just so many world- and life-views. Rather, experience is a holistic unity of purposes and actions, thought and life, that begs for interpretation. This is a central theme in this book.

It was Royce who made metaphysical thinking lively for me. Through his great essay, "The Possibility of Error," Royce made possible my understanding of just how fragmentary all knowledge claims are—specifically, the understanding that we know in part and that those parts are increased by enlargement with other knowers. In this accumulative manner, we construct our various pictures of the whole. Royce's *whole* he called the "Absolute Knower"; in this book, I call it the *World*. It was Royce's conception of God as the world in all its concreteness and ideal potentiality that became the basis for my pragmatic theology, which I develop here into a constructive theology of African American religious experience. Studying Royce's book *The Problem of Christianity* also helped me to see that the ideals of the "Great Hope" and the "Beloved Community" are not only regulative ethical ideals. They are also actual events that are concretely manifest in communities of interpretation that are supportive of loyalty to a cause that transcends every particular cause. For Royce, that cause was "Loyalty to Loyalty." For me, it is "Creative Exchange" that maximizes not only the flourishing of human good but also the good of nonhuman others.

Theology thus became for me interpretation of religious experience both as discursive and nondiscursive practices. My study of the early Chicago School of Shailer Matthews, G. B. Foster, G. B. Smith, Edward Scribner Ames, and Henry Nelson Wieman deepened my understanding of theology as a constructive or, I should say, a reconstructive enterprise. Folks today call this revisionist theology. From these pioneers of the Chicago School, I came to understand Christian theology in a historical manner, as borne out of human needs, the social dynamics of the historical past, and as responsive to the moral world of the first Christians. From these indirect teachers, I came to see that theology is relative to historical change and that the task of theology is to make relevant the Christian faith in contemporary times just as Christian predecessors did for their times, revising doctrine for the sake of the "glory of God" or the "kingdom of God." This is an awesome and profoundly ethical task that contemporary theologians owe to predecessors of the Christian faith.

From these theologians of the early Chicago School I came to see that the task of the theologian is to do in and for our times what the apostles did in and for their times—namely, making sense of the revelation of God in their historical moments. It is in this sense that we stand, in our historical moment, where they once stood. In this manner I came to understand and appreciate the doctrine of the communion of saints and the symbol of Beloved Community. Beloved Community is the concrete actualization of creative exchange with the past, present, and future of Christian faith in community. Readers will note that throughout this book I resist putting the definite article before my own use of the symbol *Beloved Community*. It is my attempt to keep the concept active, not passive and inert; open, not reified; always forming and anticipated as a concrete event in experience and not only a regulative ideal.

In graduate school I continued my interests in the tradition of American religious empiricism. As the subtitle of my dissertation indicates, D.C. MacIntosh, H. Richard Niebuhr, and James M. Gustafson are major influences on my pragmatic theology. Their influence has been mostly epistemological. They share a basic insight that is central to my thinking—namely, that all theology is interpretation of human experience and that the relevance of theology is in its expressive capacities to take hold of human experience and the world experienced by all. The theological task is to give the best interpretation that we can of the widest ranges of human experience and to regulate our moral thinking responsively to the ways of the world, human needs and goods, and seek the good in ways most fitting the requirements of human flourishing. Such a position makes me suspect of what George Lindbeck calls an "experiential expressivist," which in these days of postliberal theology, is not a good thing. It is longhand for the "L" word: Liberal!

To some of my readers, the approach I take in this book will smack of theological liberalism. I confess that they are right. If doing theology is a matter of holding a preference for one tradition over another and if it is a matter of finding oneself within a community's narrative, then I am well at home in the tradition of theological liberalism. No, I neither embrace ideas like the inevitable progress of history nor do I have exuberant optimism in human cooperation to bring into existence the kingdom of God on earth through ecumenical cooperation. But I am committed to human betterment by human endeavors, however momentary such events arise in our life together. I am committed to interpreting and reinterpreting and perhaps even jettisoning many of our long-standing cherished beliefs (the divinity of Jesus, the afterlife, final judgments, virgin birth, bodily resurrections, nature miracles, and the like) in light of our growing knowledge about the universe we inhabit and whether such beliefs support exclusionary modes of social discourse that threaten social peace. In good liberal fashion, from Albrecht Ritschl and Walter Rauschenbusch to Wieman and Gustafson, I also hold that the worth of Christian doctrine is appraised by its ethical consequences and by whether those doctrines comport with the world as it is experienced by all. That's pretty liberal.

Finally, the pragmatic theology of African American religious experience developed in this book is committed to a liberal, ethical vision of the great hope and Beloved Community that was so basic to the social ethics of Howard Thurman and Martin Luther King Jr. For them, Beloved Community was not only a regulative ideal. It is a human possibility. Unbridled optimists? I think not. They were very aware that social experiences of white supremacy and Jim Crow segregation, race violence and genocide, and that the rape and torture of black bodies undermine the persuasiveness of their great hope.

Like Thurman and King, I also am aware that contemporary social experiences (such as our culture wars over family values, same-sex marriage, the war on terror, the war on drugs, the indifference of government agencies to rush to the aid of victims displaced by Hurricane Katrina—indeed, that the war on terror can trump concern for the least advantaged throughout the Gulf Shore states) may tempt people to chide, "Anderson! Where is your Beloved Community?" As it was for Thurman and King in their times, so Beloved Community seems in our times a joke to the powerful machinery of Western-driven economic globalization that expands the gap between the rich and powerful and brings to near-bankruptcy African states devastated by HIV/AIDS. *Anderson! Where is Beloved Community?* Is it only a regulative ideal owing to a Kantian moral imperative that in all our relations to one another that we regard each not only as a means but as a kingdom of ends? Is my hope for Beloved Community, in our so-called postmodern moment, the last residue of modern, liberal ethics?

Yes, it is a regulative ideal. But it is also concretely actualized wherever genuine creative conflict opens to creative exchange. I see signs of it wherever racial, gender, sexual, and class identity politics are no longer totalizing but transcended—not negated—in creative exchange with other communities. I see it where our loyalties to homes, families, and our churches are qualitatively enlarged by a loyalty to the flourishing of human needs and human goods beyond gender, sexuality, class, and race. Where these possibilities are actualized in creative exchange, there are signs of Beloved Community. On Christmas Eve, 1967, the Reverend Dr. Martin Luther King Jr. preached these words, which were broadcast beyond Atlanta, Georgia, to the world:

> I have a dream that one day men will rise up and come to see that they are made to live together as brothers: I still have a dream this morning that one day every Negro in this country, every colored person in the world, will be judged on the basis of the content of his character rather than the color of his skin, and every man will respect the dignity and worth of human personality. I still have a dream that one day the idle industries of Appalachia will be revitalized, and the empty stomachs of Mississippi will be filled, and brotherhood will be more than a few words at the end of a prayer, but rather the first order of business on every legislative agenda. I still have a dream today that one day justice will roll down like water, and righteousness like a mighty stream. I still have a dream today that in all of our state houses and city halls men will be elected to go there who will do justly and love mercy and walk humbly with their God. I still have a dream today that one day war will come to an end, that men will beat their swords into plowshares and their spears into pruning hooks, that nations will no longer rise up against nations, neither will they study war any more. I still have a dream today that one day the lamb and the lion will lie down together and every man will sit under his own vine and fig tree and none shall be afraid. I still have a dream today that one day every valley shall be exalted and every mountain and hill will be made low, the rough places will be made smooth and the crooked places straight, and the glory of the Lord shall be revealed, and all flesh shall see it together. I still have a dream that with this faith we will be able to adjourn the councils of despair and bring new light into the dark chambers of pessimism. With this faith we will be able to speed up the day when there will be peace on earth and good will toward men. It will be a glorious day, the morning stars will sing together, and the sons of God will shout for joy.[1]

Dreams and dreaming are also the stuff of African American religious experience. Such a dream also informs my understanding and hope for Beloved Community not only as a regulative ideal but also a concrete moment in creative exchange. It is a creative event. I have written this book to conceptualize the possibility and actuality of Beloved Community. In the end, I hope that all that I have written in *Creative Exchange: A Constructive Theology of African American Religious Experience* is faithful to this confession.

ACKNOWLEDGMENTS

The doctoral dissertation that informs this and my previous books was directed by my advisor and friend Jeffrey L. Stout. As I think about the matters discussed in this book, I think not only of Jeff with great fondness but also of others who cultivated within me the love of creative exchange while in graduate school. It was Jeff and Cornel West who made American philosophy, particularly pragmatism, a lively discourse and option for my dissertation. William "Bill" Werpehowski deepened my appreciation for the theology and ethics of H. Richard Niebuhr. Mal Diamond and Victor Preller enriched my appreciation for traditional matters in the philosophy of religion. It was my privilege to study with each of these thinkers.

While in graduate school, I received an exchange fellowship to study at Yale University for one year, where I was privileged to immerse myself in the study of American philosophy and religious thought with Professor John Edwin Smith during his last year of full-time teaching. It was with Smith that I feverishly read American religious thought from Jonathan Edwards to Josiah Royce and American pragmatism. Harry "Skip" Stout, who sponsored me while at Yale, enriched my understanding of American religious history. I also worked with professors Gene Outka and David Kelsey on American empirical theology and ethics. I learned much from my association with all of these thinkers, and I am grateful for their influence upon my work.

Unfortunately, while performing the many duties of my profession— teaching, advising, committee work, directing dissertations, maintaining regular publishing responsibilities, and sheer intellectual burnout—work on this book was often simmering on the back burner but not forgotten. I owe much to friends, colleagues, and especially my students who constantly encouraged me to complete it after rehearsing chapters in seminars and lectures. More than anyone, my friend Anthony B. Pinn relentlessly pushed me toward completing this volume, constantly offering commentary. I was privileged to have worked with him as a coeditor of the Trinity Press International series on African American Religious Life and Thought. Rarely did we have a phone call when he did not chide me for not completing this book. Other friends provided me a community of interpreters by responding to my work also by way of commentary; their camaraderie has been indispensable. They include Monica Coleman, Barbara Holmes, Chandra Taylor Smith, and Cory B. D. Walker.

I owe a great debt to all of my students who endured my use of them as sounding boards. Their gracious attentiveness and criticisms I have taken to heart. However, two doctoral students deserve special thanks: Christopher D. Ringer served as my research assistant and a discerning critic while working on this book for publication and David Cox provided the indexing of the book. Other doctoral students in ethics and society sat for hours in my office willingly reading out loud with me chapters of this book in order to gain a critical audience: Amy E. Steele, Natasha Coby, Monique Moultrie, Charles Bowie, Keri Day, and Albert Smith. Colleagues and friends such as Lewis V. Baldwin, William D. Hart, Eddie S. Glaude Jr., Forrest Harris, and Brad Braxton have all enlarged my respect for genuine interdisciplinary conversation on the relationship between African American religious studies and black church studies. Those conversations are reflected throughout this book. Theologians Edward Farley and Paul DeHart have been genuinely supportive of my interests in American empirical theology and other matters dealing with the processes of thinking theologically. Vanderbilt Divinity School has been most gracious in providing me a sabbatical to work on this book to move it toward publication. I am grateful to Dean James Hudnut-Beumler and Associate Dean Alice Hunt for their constant encouragement of my work.

The Reverend Dr. William F. Buchanan and members of my adult classes in Basic Christian Theology and Basic Christian Ethics at Fifteenth Avenue Baptist Church, Nashville, helped me most to discern whether what I have written can be communicated beyond the academy. As always, my sisters and family have been a hovering cloud of witnesses that never tire of sending up prayers on my behalf. While moving this book toward publication, my grandmother (Mama), Flora Helen Anderson (1912–2007) departed this life to be in beloved community with her God and loved ones. I miss her most. Since moving to Nashville, friends such as Dwayne Jenkins, Nathaniel Mitchell, Samuel Wyatt, and Tamyron McGirt have provided me a new sense of home and family. They have enlarged my understanding of what it means concretely to live within beloved community, and for them I am thankful. To all those at Fortress Press who helped me bring this book to the public I am very grateful: Michael West, David Lott, and Carolyn Banks.

Finally, although he cannot read this acknowledgment, Sebastian, my black Labrador Retriever, is my constant source of comfort and my reason for coming home at night rather than hanging out with friends. He greets me every morning and evening with jubilant excitement, a slashing tail, and affectionate licking even when I am not particularly pleasant. I am thankful for the creative exchange I have with him, my nonhuman family.

From Human Experience to Creative Exchange

Benchmarks of a Pragmatic Theology of African American Religious Experience

> It is absurd to say that religion is a mere belief. You might as well call
> society a belief, or politics a belief, or civilization a belief. Religion
> is a life, and can be identified with a belief only provided that belief
> be a living belief—a thing to be lived rather than said or thought.
> —Charles Sanders Peirce, "What Is Christian Faith?"

THIS BOOK HAS BEEN A long time coming. One significant delay was that
as I laid out the plan for these chapters, I found myself greatly dissatis-
fied with the approach that I was taking—an approach I had learned from
my studies in Western philosophy and the philosophy of religion. I initially
thought that I would write a philosophical theology more in line with traditional modes of argument on problems: the problem of religious knowledge,
the problem of evil and suffering, the problem of God, and the problem of
human meaning—the usual line-up. I would then set up figures as straw
men and women only to topple them by counterarguments to show just
how much they all went wrong and how mine was the better argument. It's
a mean reading strategy when you stop to think about it. Yet I continue to
think and teach in this manner.

It is the *one–upmanship* game. It goes like this: Plato did "one-up" the
talkative Sophists; Aristotle's materialism "up-turned" Plato's idealism;
Augustine's sacred theology "took out" the pagans, until St Thomas did
Augustine one better, by baptizing Aristotle. The game goes on until Nietzsche knocks them all out, including Kant and Hegel. The one–upmanship

game is quite convenient if one has a taste for the idea of progress in the way of thinking. Yet William James cites one Professor John Grote of Cambridge regarding this manner of thinking: "I wish that people would consider that thought—and philosophy is no more than good and methodical thought—is a matter *intimate* to them, a portion of their real selves . . . that they would *value* what they think, and be interested in it. . . . I can conceive of nothing more noxious for students than to get into the habit of saying to themselves about their ordinary philosophic thought, Oh, somebody must have thought it all before."[1] James himself comments: "Yet this is the habit most encouraged at our seats of learning. You must tie your opinion to Aristotle's or Spinoza's; you must define it by its distance from Kant's; you must refute your rival's view by identifying it with Protagoras's. Thus does all spontaneity of thought, all freshness of conception, get destroyed. Everything you touch is shopworn."

As I began to apply the one–upmanship strategy to African American religious thought, however, I realized that I was not locked into an intellectual contest with strangers or historical figures. Rather, I was engaged in conversations with many contemporary friends and colleagues. I *know* the people I was planning to topple; many are my intellectual cohorts. From the context of intimate conversation partners, the one–upmanship game felt like intellectual snootiness. Therefore, I decided that I wanted to write a different kind of book, one that genuinely reflects the character of my ongoing conversations both in African American religious studies and African American theology. *Creative Exchange* reflects conceptual conversations with partners, some now departed, like Howard Harrod, and many still living. It also displays my own reflexive engagement within African American religious experience.

In writing this book, I could not easily put on the mask of the disinterested critic who enjoys nothing more than carving up concepts and figures for intellectual consumption. I found myself deeply interested in and affected by the materials making up the book's content. This is a critical book insofar as it takes seriously the ways that African American religious thinkers conceptually frame the meaning of race and religious experience; however, it is also constructive insofar as I put my own thinking into the hermeneutics of African American religious experience. This book is a constructive theology. It is not historical research on black religion such as Charles H. Long has offered in his *Significations: Signs, Symbols, Images in the Interpretation of Religion*,[3] although the influence of his hermeneutical phenomenology permeates much of this book. Furthermore, *Creative Exchange* is not a comparative study on the variety of African American religious traditions such as

Anthony B. Pinn's *Varieties of African American Religious Experience*.[4] However, I am greatly indebted to Pinn's theological interest in making difference a controlling logic in his account of African American religious traditions. Like Pinn, I am also committed here to enlarging the account of African American religious experience beyond near totalizing interpretations bound by the black church tradition and black liberation theology. Moreover, this book is not a comprehensive study of the material, ritual, and performative practices of conjuration in black religion such as Theophus H. Smith brilliantly offers in *Conjuring Culture: Biblical Formations of Black America* (1994).[5] Yet the intersections of black religion and culture studies provide a background condition for my constructive theology.

Rather, the following quote by Tyron Inbody best captures the basic logic running throughout this book:

> Experience is never "pure experience" (individualistic, subjective, original, underived, autonomous, and foundational). It is always derived from, shaped, and interpreted in a social context, both a natural environment of interrelationships and interdependence (nature) and a cultural environment of language, symbol, and myth (tradition). Neither exists without the other and each is reciprocal with the other. Language arises and develops in the context of an organism encountering a complex environment in experience, and tradition shapes and reshapes the experience of an organism in its (natural, social and cosmic) environment through language, symbol, and myth. The organism does not have a world without experience and culture interacting to construct a world of organism and environment. The resources of faith convey through the interaction of experience and culture the depth of relationships within the natural environment which create, judge, redeem, and fulfill the individual and the society.[6]

At its deepest level of insight, this book is about relationality constructed through the lens of a pragmatic theology. Through this lens thought and action, organism and environment, experience and culture refract a unity of interdependence and creative exchange that keep life open to the event of Beloved Community.

More strictly, then, *Creative Exchange* is a philosophical approach in which the constructive, innovative deployment of concepts themselves—such as experience, ambiguity, the grotesque, creative exchange, creative conflict, difference, race, God, world, community, and more—do the work of interpretation, criticism, and directing possibilities toward openness. Although organized around typical themes in the philosophy of religion (sources of religious insight, evil and suffering, God and faith, and community and fulfillment), these topics are interpreted under the symbolic force that race creates in the religious experiences of African American people.

Drawing on Edward Farley's *Deep Symbols: Their Postmodern Effacement and Reclamation*,[7] I understand race to be a deep symbol that arises from the interhuman depth structures of human communities and functions as a deeply rooted category in the stock of knowledge that contributes to social meaning in Western culture. As a deep symbol, race has the *feel* of being a priori, but in reality it is a historical construct that regulates our interhuman relations, though not always toward malicious forms of racism. Indeed, race may also enable forms of community bound by filial care and interests. As with all our deep symbols, race too is fallible because it is vulnerable to historical change and corruptibility. As Long, Pinn, and Smith show, the representational force of race is located in a master narrative that identifies and defines social action in human communities. *Creative Exchange* conceives of forms of relations in African American religious experience that are resistant to any essentialist strategy for reading the modes of difference that constitute African American life.

Although this book draws heavily on the insights of African American religious thinkers, I make a wide use of philosophical resources from American philosophy and religious thought and American empirical theology for the construction of a pragmatic theology of African American religious experience. *Creative Exchange* is consistent with what I put forward in my earlier book, *Beyond Ontological Blackness*, as a religious criticism that is both iconoclastic and emancipatory. The basic insight of this present book may be stated thus: When African American religious experience is fundamentally understood as relational, processive, open, fluid, and irreducible, creative exchange keeps our interpretations and understandings of the meaning and significance of our particular religious experiences open to forms of enlargement that transcend the limits of our particular faith communities and actualizes in the here and now concrete instances, moments, or creative events of what Martin Luther King Jr. and Howard Thurman called "the Beloved Community." Beloved Community is concrete in every event where creative exchange is realized.

THE AUTOBIOGRAPHICAL IMPULSE

After reading a draft of this book, a friend told me that in doing so she came to know me more intimately than in all the personal conversations we have had over ten years of friendship. I think her comment reflects what others have told me in the decade since I published *Beyond Ontological Blackness*. At its most dismissive, the comment has been something

like this: "Who is . . . Victor Anderson?!" —as in, "Who is this upstart?!"—
reflecting the reader's dismissal of my criticism of black theology as auda-
cious. Others, trying to find ways to situate my work, asked me, "Who is
your audience?" Still others asked, "Where is your voice in the argument?"
However such questions were raised, readers noted that absent from my
work was the autobiographical impulse. If this is a criticism of my prior
works, it's a fair one.

Two things may account for the absence of any autobiographical impulse
in my previous books. First, I was trained in the classical tradition of Western philosophical arguments where the argument itself carries the weight of
persuasion. In general I am still deeply committed to this way of thinking
and writing, though many of my readers have shown frustration with such
commitment. Anthony Weston's *A Rulebook for Argument* and P. T. Geach's
Reason and Argument have guided my reading and writing—short books that
underscore my concern whether our propositions and conclusions have
good, valid, and sound reasoning supporting them. So I suspect that it is this
philosophical account of rigor that lies behind my silencing the autobiographical impulse in my own writings.

Second, I have always been suspicious of folks who require some articulation of an author's social location as a basis for judging effective scholarly
writing. I have not always been sure just what kind of work these kinds of
confessions are supposed to do. They may be a way of couching arguments
against anticipated ideological charges that the argument is patriarchal, elitist,
or displays racial privilege. In this way, the writer acknowledges the charges
and can now get on with the argument. On a benign level, one's social location
may establish solidarities with particular pockets of readers whose identities are
defined by race, class, sex, or sexual orientation loyalties. Yet I also suspect that
the reader requires my social location in order to determine whether I have
anything to offer her or him before the argument is dismissed on ad hominem
(or circumstantial ad hominem) grounds. For example: "His privileged elite
education is why he says the things he says." "He's been around all them white
folks and all he reads are mostly dead white philosophers and theologians."
"He's an angry black gay male and that is why he *comes out* [pun intended] the
way he does." Whatever requires the social location of the writer as a basis for
judging effective academic writing, every writer has to determine for himself
or herself just what he or she owes the reader or the audience. As I see it, too
much information is as much a turn-off as is too little.

Now that I have articulated my suspicions, I think that when it comes to
matters of experience, and religious experience in particular, the autobiographical impulse has a legitimate place. In the case of this book, the nature

of the topic itself and my intention to establish intersubjective understanding between my conversation partners or interlocutors and myself warrant autobiographical exchanges. In other words, my use of autobiographical exchanges throughout the various chapters is a reflexive requirement of my attempt to critique pragmatically African American religious experience. I regard experience to be a unity before it is ever differentiated by categories or ideas. This means that human beings are entailed in that unity as a subject with a biography, a subject developing into a personality with its interests, goals, loves, desires, and basic needs. This is the narrative quality of experience.

Although experience is not reducible to its narrative quality, there is no account of experience that is biographically free if, as I argue in this book, a pragmatic theology of African American religious experience is committed to modes of interpretation that are open to the widest ranges of human experience. This includes the narrative structure of experience. In his discussion on the narrative constructions of individual and collective identities, Kwame Anthony Appiah suggests that narratives "provide loose norms or models, which play a role in shaping our plans of life. Collective identities, in short, provide what we might call scripts: narratives that people can use in shaping their projects and in telling their stories."[8] However, Appiah does not want to reduce individual experience to the structural force of narrative. He says:

> So we should acknowledge how much our personal histories, the stories we tell of where we have been and where we are going, are constructed, like novels and movies, short stories and folktales, within narrative conventions. Indeed, one of the things that popular narratives (whether filmed or televised, spoken or written) do for us is to provide models for telling our lives. At the same time, part of the function of our collective identities—of the whole repertory of them that a society makes available to its members—is to structure possible narratives of the individual self.[9]

Experience is disclosed by basic irreducible yet complexly integrating structures of physicality, temporality, spaciality, sociality, and basic human senses or affectivities. This ontological schema is not meant to be exhaustive. Nevertheless, it leaves our interpretations of African American religious experience open to the widest ranges of our *experiencing* of the world, as both collective and individual identities, by resisting interpretations of identities that are oriented toward reductivism and antithetical to ambiguity. Ambiguity keeps experience itself open to what William James called the

MORE (the conception of which I retrieve here) beyond its narrative qualities. In what follows in the remainder of this introduction, I want to focus
on certain intellectual benchmarks or unit ideas on which I construct my
pragmatic theology of African American religious experience. First, I reflect
on the relationship between experience and the grotesque or ambiguity.
Second, I reflect on pragmatic naturalism and religious experience. Last, I
discuss the concept of creative exchange.

EXPERIENCE AND THE GROTESQUE

It was my own interest in the concept of experience in black theology that
motivated me to write this book. I became invested in this concept when I
first read James H. Cone's *Black Theology and Black Power* as an undergraduate student in history and theology at Trinity Christian College. Cone made
black experience the point of departure for the black liberation theology
movement, saying:

> Black Theology must take seriously the reality of black people—their
> life of suffering and humiliation. This must be the point of departure
> for all God-talk which seeks to be black-talk. When that man is black
> and lives in a society permeated with white racist power, he can speak
> of God only from the perspective of the socio-economic and politi-
> cal conditions unique to black people. Though the Christian doctrine
> of God must logically precede the doctrine of man, Black Theol-
> ogy knows that black people can view God only through black eyes
> that behold the brutalities of white racism. To ask them to assume a
> "higher" identity by denying their blackness is to require them to
> accept a false identity and to reject reality as they know it to be.[10]

The quotation is striking not only for what it says about the meaning of
black theology and black experience, but also for what it does not say. For
instance, is black experience fundamentally suffering and humiliation? What
is it about these two aspects of experience that make them prolegomena to
"all God-talk"? What are we to make of this little word *all*? Is black experience unique with respect to socioeconomic and political conditions? What
does it mean to say that black people *can only* view God through black eyes
turned on white supremacy? If black experience transcends *blackness,* is this
really to accept a false identity or a rejection of reality as it is known by black
people?

Behind such questions are my deep suspicions about the meaning of
experience itself in black theology. As I read it, experience is used as a cultural signifier in which culture itself achieves a totalizing effect. In *Beyond*

Ontological Blackness, I questioned what I saw as a reductivist conception of black experience typified as *ontological blackness*. My argument was this:

> Most of Cone's problems center around the category of symbolic blackness. Cone's problems are matters of internal contradiction. First, black theology, as Cone formulated it, risks self-referential inconsistency when it sees itself radically oppositional to white racism and white theology. Because Cone collapses metaphysics into ontology, blackness is reified into a totality or a unity of black experience. At the same time, blackness is regarded as symbolic; so that anyone who can participate in its meaning can be said to be black. However, black theology exceptionally circumscribes the meaning of symbolic blackness in terms of black oppression and suffering.
>
> The difficulty arises here: (a) Blackness is a signification of ontology and corresponds to black experience. (b) Black experience is defined as the experience of suffering and rebellion against whiteness. Yet, (c) both black suffering and rebellion are ontologically created and provoked by whiteness as a necessary condition of blackness. (d) Whiteness appears to be the ground of black experience, and hence of black theology and its new black being. Therefore, while black theology justifies itself as radically oppositional to whiteness, it nevertheless requires whiteness, white racism, and white theology for the self-disclosure of its new black being and its legitimacy. In this way, black theology effectively renders whiteness identifiable with what is of ultimate concern. "Our ultimate concern is that which determines our being or not being," says Tillich. . . . In black theology, blackness has become a totality of meaning. It cannot point to any transcendent meaning beyond itself without also fragmenting.[11]

More than a decade of dialogue has occurred since I made this argument, during which I have benefited from conversations and debates with self-identified black liberation theologians regarding it. In hindsight, I may have overstated my criticism for the sake of foregrounding forms of difference that render any essentialist conception of race or blackness problematic by distorting the richness and worlds of difference that make up the lives and purposes of African Americans. A decade later, however, I remain rather suspicious about the ways African American experience is typified in black and womanist theologies. To be sure, I have witnessed great attention among black liberation theologians and womanist theologians to move beyond any ontologizing strategies that essentialize black experience. Yet I am still suspicious of their persistent defining of black experience as the experience of suffering, humiliation, struggle, survival, and resistance. I argue in this book that the manner in which we take up the concept of experience itself will determine what gets emphasized as defining aspects of African American religious experience, and that experience itself has all too often been the unexamined language controlling African American theology, the exception being perhaps African American process theologians.

Readers will note that as I talk about experience and religious experience I show a preference for the signifier *African American* over *black* (although I will sometimes slip into the latter). My preference is for a signifier that connotes contexts of experience that are structured by the ambiguities of difference over sameness. The signifier entails great realms of ambiguity that have historically defined the consciousness of African American history as it is based on the historical reality of the transatlantic slave trade and cross-cultural pollinations by conquest and contact between North Atlantic slave traders and missionaries and African peoples. The signifier points to forms of ambiguity that were shaped by the broken promises of the reconstruction and the bifurcation of consciousness that W. E. B. Du Bois called a twoness, a double consciousness maintained by racial segregation. A century after being first penned, Du Bois's rhetoric has not lost its existential bite:

> Why did God make me an outcast and a stranger in mine own house? The shades of the prison-house closed round about us all: walls strait and stubborn to the whitest, but relentlessly narrow, tall, and unscalable to sons of night who must plod darkly on in resignation, or beat unavailing palms against the stone, or steadily, half hopelessly, watch the streak of blue above.
>
> After the Egyptian and Indian, the Greek and Roman, the Teuton and Mongolian, the Negro is a sort of seventh son, born with a veil, and gifted with second-sight in this American world—a world which yields him no true self-consciousness, but only lets him see himself through the revelation of the other world. It is a peculiar sensation, this double consciousness, this sense of always looking at one's self through the eyes of others, of measuring one's soul by the tape of a world that looks on in amused contempt and pity. One ever feels his twoness—an American, a negro; two souls, two thoughts, two unreconciled strivings; two warring ideals in one dark body, whose dogged strength alone keeps it from being torn asunder.[12]

The signifier *African American* leaves my interpretation of African American culture and religious experience open to forms of freedom (political, social, moral, spiritual, and expressive) that arise from the worlds of difference (class, family, educational, regional, religious, sexual, political, and more) that make up the African American community.

In my understanding of experience in general and African American religious experience in particular, the grotesque or ambiguity is a controlling unit idea or benchmark.[13] In *Beyond Ontological Blackness*, I offered an aesthetic critique of racial essentialism by the disrupting significations of the grotesque over the simple, fixed, singular, and unchanging. There I was drawing on Friedrich Nietzsche's understanding of the concept, in his description of the Dionysian personality, which he describes this way:

> It is impossible for the Dionysian man not to understand any suggestion of whatever kind, he ignores no signal from the emotions, he possesses to the highest degree the instinct for understanding and divining, just as he possesses the art of communication to the highest degree. He enters into every skin, into every emotion; he is continually transforming himself.[14]

The grotesque ought not to be thought of as an opposition between two diametrically opposed sensibilities. Yet it has to do with sensibilities that are apparently oppositional, such as attraction and repulsion or pleasure and pain. However, the grotesque seeks neither the negation nor mediation of these sensibilities. It leaves them ambiguous and unresolved by negation or mediation. Philip Thomson describes the grotesque thus:

> The most consistently distinguished characteristic of the grotesque has been the fundamental element of disharmony, whether this is referred to as conflict, clash, mixture of the heterogeneous, or conflation of disparates. It is important that this disharmony has been seen, not merely in the work of art as such, but also in the reaction it produces and (speculatively) in the creative temperament and psychological make-up of the artist.[15]

The disharmony or ambiguity may be compared best to the optical games "Duck or Rabbit," "Man's Face or Nude," or the infamous "Wife or Mother-in-Law" drawings. Consider these optical games: duck or rabbit and girl's face or saxophonist.[16]

In the grotesque, consciousness and judgment are a play of the imagination. They are the play of senses, contour, tactility, detail, shades, light, and the mechanics of focusing the eye one way or another to bring to judgment the resolution of disjunctive reasoning. One is asked to decide either/or, this or that, one way or another. In the two drawings here, one is invited into the play, a certain dance between the eyes, the movement of the head, physically placing oneself in different relations to the image. Each move of the dance, including staring and rocking one's head side to side or back and forth, brings into focused decision the resolution of the ambiguous image. In reality, however, the images are not reducible to disjunctive judgments: duck or rabbit, face or saxophonist. The grotesque leaves each image an unresolved ambiguity that resists such reductive reasoning and judgment. As Frederick Burwick says, "The grotesque, then, involves an elaborate multistability of manner and matter. This was Friedrich Schlegel's reason for defining the grotesque as a mode of irony, for he recognized in the grotesque a challenge to the mind's instinctive endeavor to synthesize."[17]

In a schematic manner, first, the grotesque recovers and leaves unresolved prior and basic sensibilities such as attraction/ repulsion and pleasure/pain differentials. Second, the nonresolution of these aesthetic and cognitive senses renders the objects perceived and our perception of the object confused or ambiguous as in the two drawings. Third, these unresolved ambiguities may leave possibilities open for creative ways of taking an object or subject; for in the grotesque, an object is,

at the same time, other than how it appears when one contour or another is accented. Fourth, the grotesque disrupts the penchant for cognitive synthesis by highlighting the absurd and sincere, the comical and tragic, the estranged and familiar, the satirical and playful, and normalcy and abnormality.[18] It is profoundly oriented toward the interplay or creative interchange of difference.

What work does the grotesque play in the context of this book? The unresolved ambiguities of African American experience leave interpreters open to the creative interplay of an undifferentiated unity of experience that comes into focus only by the activity of squeezing the eye one way or another. It sees African American experience as being open to the *feel* of unresolved joys and laughter; open to the experiencing of the comedic and tragic in experience; open to the interplay of sameness and difference. Ambiguity is *the feel of experience* before it is captured, frozen, and domesticated by our clear, distinct, exceptional racial descriptions and our totalized frames of reference for understanding and interpreting African American religious experience.

The pragmatic concept of experience has been most determinant in my interpretation of African American religious experience.[19] Experience is a complex environmental unity in which nature and logic, thought and life, purpose and action are together embedded in creative exchange. William James discusses the unity of experience this way:

> Experience is a process that continually gives us new material to digest. We handle this intellectually by the mass of beliefs of which we find ourselves already possessed, assimilating, rejecting, or rearranging in different degrees. Some of the apperceiving ideas are recent acquisitions of our own, but most of them are common-sense traditions of the race. There is probably not a common-sense tradition, of all those which we now live by, that was not in the first instance a genuine discovery, an inductive generalization like those more recent ones of the atom, of inertia, of energy, or reflex action, or of fitness to survive. The notions of one Time and of one Space as single continuous receptacles; the distinction between thoughts and things, matter and mind; between permanent subjects and changing attributes; the conception of classes with sub-classes within them; the separation of fortuitous from regular caused connections; surely all these were once definite conquests made at historic dates by our ancestors in their attempts to get the chaos of their crude individual experiences into a more shareable and manageable shape. They proved of such sovereign use as *denkmittel* [thought materials] that they are now a part of the very structure of our mind. We cannot play fast and loose with them. No experience can upset them. On the contrary, they apperceive every experience and assign it to its place.[20]

Like the ambiguities of the grotesque, the unity of experience is also an antireductivist principle in my pragmatic theology. John Edwin Smith's account of the unity of experience is helpful:

> Experience, understood as the funded result of many encounters with what is presented, is too rich and varied in content to be adequately described by any one predicate. There is no descriptive term comprehensive enough in meaning to express the entire content of experience as such. Experience is of events and things, of hopes and fears, of disappointments and expectations, of persons and places; in short, experience must be open to everything that is, and we are never justified in anticipating its content by assigning to it some specific and differential character purporting to express the sort of thing it must contain.[21]

This conception of experience in my pragmatic theology of African American religious experience keeps interpretive judgments open to play, to the dance, within the grotesqueries or ambiguities of experience itself.

PRAGMATIC NATURALISM AND RELIGIOUS EXPERIENCE

Inasmuch as the unit ideas of ambiguity and the unity of experience fund my pragmatic theology, pragmatic naturalism frames my metaphysical point of view. In *Pragmatic Theology*,[22] I proposed that pragmatic naturalism is the *metaphysical* aspect of pragmatism. By metaphysical thinking, I simply mean the ways that we picture the world, and for a pragmatic naturalist such as myself, the picture is one in which parts of experience are related to other parts and then related to wholes that are then related to larger wholes within a comprehensive picture of the world. For instance, our galaxy is related to other galaxies. Our construal of observable galaxies enters into our latest theories of what holds things together or what gives us the appearance that things are held together. Pragmatic naturalism takes the widest ranges of human experience and relates them to larger, expansive wholes. Pragmatic naturalism will not rest well with any radical positivistic mandate to relegate human subjectivities to the unknowable while making reality of only the physical fields and properties of experience. As Maurice Blondel puts it so well in his classic book, *Action* (1893):

> The field of becoming is without assignable limit; and new perspectives will always open up, with new theories that will not exhaust the object to be known since they constitute it in part. What seems chimerical to claim becomes scientific truth; external finality itself recovers once again the characteristic of definite certitude that only internal finality had maintained. Man [*sic*] is a "microcosm," *summa mundi et compendium* (a summation of the world and a compendium), the summary of experiences, of all the inventions and of all the ingenuities of nature, an extract and an original product of the whole; the universe concentrates all its rays in him [*sic*]. Subjective life is the substitute and the synthesis of all other phenomena whatever they may be.[23]

From the point of view of its internal subjectivity, the world is organic, processive, open, unfinished, and open to novelty. In chapters 1 and 4, this metaphysical picture is constructed in the context of African American relational theology. Eugene Fontinell's account of pragmatic naturalism is helpful here:

> The new always emerges from or grows out of what is already in
> existence; however, it cannot be understood as simply a particular-
> ization of an essence that is eternal or absolutely permanent. The
> processive world [is] envisioned by radically novel events and realities
> . . . which are not simply the actualization of pre-existence potentiali-
> ties whether such realities are ultimately located in something called
> nature or in the reality of God.[24]

The world ought not to be thought of as only a signification of our small
planet, Earth. World is the naming of God as radically inclusive, relational,
interdependent, interactive, and an interfunctional whole. The principle of
enlargement is my way of coming to terms, quite literally, with the world. This
principle forms a basic tenet in *Creative Exchange* as it defines the end, goal,
good, and value of creative exchange throughout each chapter. The principle
has a nonreductive emphasis in our reflections on the world, its processes,
patterns, and powers. It "seeks to account for human experience with no
reference to the otherworldly and to discover the meaning available within
human experience itself."[25]

It was this insight into pragmatism and religious thought that led me to
the works of two American empirical theologians, Henry Nelson Wieman
and James M. Gustafson. Through them I sought to relate constructive theology to pragmatic naturalism. It was Gustafson's pragmatism and account of
theocentric piety that most influenced my account of religious experience.
And it was Wieman's notion of God as creative interchange that influenced
my normative commitments. Together they brought balance to my pragmatic theology.

Gustafson thinks of experience as a unity that is prior to theological
reflections. He says: "Whatever claims are made for reason, theological arguments for the existence of God are based upon human experiences of other
persons, of nature, and of society. Both revelation and reason are human
reflections on human experiences."[26] Experience is a holistic background
condition. Whatever experiences we claim, they are given as a whole web
of relations before they are conceptually isolated, catalogued, and become
the subject of discourse. This is what Gustafson means when he insists that
general human experience is prior to distinctions.[27]

Gustafson is in agreement with John Edwin Smith when he conceives of
the unity of experience as basic but not some sort of "transcendental limit."
The unity of experience has a critical immanence within the context of
social and historical understanding. Although a holistic background condition of meaning, experience is always social and historical. In agreement
with Smith, Gustafson says: "It is a process of interaction between persons,

between persons and natural events, and between persons and historical events."[28] The social is the interaction of a self with an other and others in experience. The meaning and significance of human experience is continually being assessed in communities that share common objects of interests and common concepts, symbols, and theories. Human experience is immanently intersubjective and communicative so that if there is knowledge of God at all, it is human knowledge. It is knowledge mediated through human experience of one's own, of a community, or of another person.[29]

The process of differentiation immediately arises in talk about the unity of experience. Gustafson acknowledges that the process is often exaggerated so that hierarchies are created out of human experience and experience itself becomes fragmented and compartmentalized. What result are theories of experience that are radically reductionistic, atomistic, strictly utilitarian, and individualistic. Socially such theories result in anthropocentrism and individualism. Such theories of experience that bifurcate and compartmentalize experience and reality are to be rejected because they fail to take into themselves the reality of finitude that meets us at every turn in our experiencing of the world.

Gustafson offers a grotesque account in which the experience of God may well be perceived as a religious experience, but it may just as well be perceived as an aesthetic or moral experience. Unlike disjunctive reasoning, moral experience may not be strictly differentiated from religious experience; however, this does not mean that there are no possibilities of isolating any genuinely distinctive discourses on the various aspects of human experience. For theology is based on the possibility that genuine religious experience can be isolated in terms of natural piety. The word *piety* denotes the *senses*, the affectivities, through which the overwhelming power(s) that persons meet in their experiencing the world are apprehended and relate human beings to those powers. Gustafson says that "our 'senses' are senses *of*; what they are senses of stems from our relation to others, the world around us, and in the religious context, to God."[30] It is through social interaction that the senses gain specifically religious meanings.

Religious experience is social, and the affections that are associated with it are prior to our naming them. They are first evoked by human relationships with others. Others are not to be taken as designating only human persons but also as including nonhuman others. The religious affections are grounded in the experiences of nature, of human communities, and of human culture and actions.[31] They are deeply relational.

In human experience with others, certain senses are evoked and sustained, and from these senses we give theological interpretations. Gustafson identifies basic senses that frame his theology. They are the senses of dependency and trust, obligation, remorse and repentance, possibility and hope, and the sense of direction from which we project our future ideals. Each of the senses is relational, and each relates to the other, evoking them in terms of an awareness of another, a disposition to act in particular ways, an attitude of adjustment in line with the dignity of the object, and affection toward the object.[32] These religious senses are not unnatural or supernatural but are interrelated with many other aspects of human experience. Although these senses are natural and exhibit a certain universality, they are not perceived immediately to be religious. They are understood to be religious as a consequence of the social interactions of persons in communities of shared experience.

In particular religions, shared experiences are explained and interpreted by means of the internal resources of languages and symbols that a community uses to communicate the meaning and significance of its experiences of some one or complex of overwhelming presences, powers, processes, and patterns. In chapter 3, Gustafson's perspective of the relation of shared meaning within communities to the interpretation of faith and suffering will be most central in my defense of redemptive suffering in African American religious experience. A pragmatic theology is based on the possibility of identifying genuine religious experiences that correlate to the whole of human experience. Theology is always a community affair. "From a variety of communities, information necessary for individuals and groups to engage properly in ethical reflections is derived. In these communities, mutual understandings are gathered, differences in points of views are expressed, perspectives and interpretations from a broad range of gifted members are enlisted, and consciences are formed when informed reasoning is brought to clarity."[33] These possibilities are what Wieman calls *creative interchange* and I refer to as *creative exchange*. Theology relates the religious affections to the power(s) bearing down on us and sustaining us and the ways in which human life is ordered within the nexus of natural and social processes and patterns, says Gustafson.[34] God simply is the world—its powers, processes, and patterns into which we have our being and to which we are all related in creative exchange.

CREATIVE EXCHANGE

Wieman is one of the more significant figures of the twentieth century to advance the prospect for an empirical account of religious experience. Yet it is his construal of the world as the source of human good that informs the normative vision of my pragmatic theology. Wieman's theology and ethics are complex, not so much in terms of difficulty but with respect to the many turns they take through experience. In the most simple terms, Wieman thinks of God as that structure that sustains and promotes the maximization of value, that increases, enlarges, and progressively integrates human good. God is the infinite possibility and concrete actuality of value in experience. Gustafson's theology emphasizes finitude and human limits within the world. Wieman's theology emphasized radical transcendence within the world. For him, every relation entails values, goods, and goals. God maximally relates our goods, ends, purposes, and values toward insuring their mutual support and enhancement.

If it is the case that only our instrumental and extrinsic goods or ends are satisfied, then our lives cannot be said to be maximally fulfilled. All of our attempts at fulfilling these values issue in conflict. As I argue in chapter 5, the values internal to our homes and churches enter into conflict with other members of our society who also seek to actualize values internal to their homes and churches. There is nothing intrinsic in our instrumental and extrinsic values that make them the goods of all. For as Aristotle suggests, even in what we consider to be evil acts, the agent has some good or end in mind. In Wieman's ethics, conflict is also a good; it is an intrinsic value in our experiencing the world. Conflict is necessary for the clarifying of goods, ends, and values that enlarge our horizons of meaning in order to make for a life that is livable with others, including nonhuman others. God is the source of this human good. This processive integration of good, Wieman names *creative interchange*. He says:

> What makes for the greatest good when required conditions are present? Is it God? That is a word I shrink from using because it carries so many different meanings for different people. But there is a creativity in human experience. It begins with the newborn infant, expanding the valuing consciousness to the widest and deepest range of values which conditions permits. But what are values? As I use the word, I mean goal-seeking activities expanding in range and mutual support, both in the life of the individual and in mutual support between individuals and peoples. No individual can expand the range of his goal-seeking activities of his associates and his culture and transforming them to fit the demands of his own unique individuality. This absorbing of the goal-seeking activities of others and transforming them to meet the demands of the unique individuality of each participant, I call creative interchange. It does three things all at the same time. It expands the valuing consciousness of each. It widens and deepens mutual support between individuals and peoples. It develops the unique individuality of each person.[35]

God is the naming of creative interchange. God names the conditions of its possibility as concrete actuality and the processes, patterns, and powers that make for the maximization of all relative values and goals. Creative interchange is the basis for the forms of enlargement that relativize the instrumental goods that define our particular communities. As I argue in this book, creative interchange also substantiates, in however limited ways, Beloved Community. Wieman says: "Creative interchange is the only ultimate and valid basis of community because it is the one ultimate source of our humanity, also the way leading to the greatest good to be attained by human kind. It makes possible disagreement and diversity without hate or fear, without retaliation or estrangement, because the demands of creative interchange, are contributory to the good of each."[36] Creative interchange is not only the source of human good; for Wieman, it is also an ultimate human commitment.

> The human race cannot long survive on this planet with the increase of power and complex interdependence unless the ultimate foundations of community be shifted from culture, race, class, nation or alliance of nations and from any one or all of the world religions and is firmly established on that creative interchange which has created the humanity in every individual, from the first days of infancy, no matter to what culture, race, class, nation, or traditional religion he may belong. Creative interchange cannot save us unless we make a religion of it. That means to give our ultimate commitment to it, accept it as the sovereign good of our lives, the source, guide and goal of our existence.[37]

Both Gustafson and Wieman bring a sense of balance to my pragmatic theology. Gustafson provides a sobering sense of reality to my understanding of human possibilities and actualities. He installs on my pragmatic theology the conviction that, at every turn, we are met with finitude and limits. The world—its powers, processes, and pattern—may not cooperate with our human endeavors to satisfy our wants and needs. Here, however, Gustafson and Wieman greatly differ. While admitting the reality of transcendence into his theology, Gustafson emphasizes the sense of limits. He warns that humility may be the most appropriate sense of piety before the powers bearing down on us, perhaps conditioning our own demise.

Gustafson's position is not without either its problems or critics.[38] I am not as bothered as some critics have been concerning whether his account of experience smacks of some kind of transcendental phenomenology or an ever-receding into the background condition against which to ground religious claims against the relativity of historical formations of theology within particular religious communities.[39] In what I have said above and elsewhere, such a reading does not square with a close reading of Gustafson's position.[40] Moreover, I am not particularly worried that Gustafson appears to be overly dependent on the empirical and natural sciences in revising traditional understandings of God in his theocentric ethics.[41] Although he draws heavily on the empirical sciences for his constructive theology, Gustafson insists that the relation between theology and the empirical sciences is a critical one and not one of dependency. He also acknowledges that the empirical sciences are as socially contested in theories and findings as are Christian theologies. Gustafson's position to the empirical sciences is far more nuanced than critics may allow.[42]

It is Gustafson's theory of consent that I find most problematic, however. While I appreciate his radical critique of anthropocentrism in theology, Gustafson's theory of consent proposes that we consent to the power(s) bearing down on us, powers that may also bring about our own demise, and consent to the claim that God may not always have human flourishing as God's end. Such a theory profoundly confounds the meaning and significance of worship, adoration, but especially prayer in the Christian tradition. In his attempt to minimize anthropocentrism, he says too little concretely about the place, goods, and ends of human flourishing in his theocentric ethics. In chapter 4, I try to resolve this problem of prayer within my own pragmatic theology of African American religious experience. However, Gustafson's realism regarding the place of the human in his theocentric ethics and his account of ethics as mostly an intellectual, deliberative activity left me turning to Wieman for a more concrete appreciation of human possibilities to effect creative exchange and contribute to substantive forms of flourishing and fulfillment within community.

Wieman's account of creative interchange balances Gustafson's piety of pessimism. He provides me with a normative outlook in my interpretation of our interhuman encounters. Like Gustafson, he is also a theologian of radical immanence. God is no wholly transcendent reality, much less a person. Rather, God names the sources of all those concrete moments in experience in which the limits of our self-descriptions, immediate situations, of our attempts to satisfy our particular goals, are enlarged toward forms of community that increase our sense of human purposes beyond the race, family, and nation, and beyond group interests. The world concretely—its processes, powers, and patterns—makes for these possibilities.

Wieman's position also is problematic in a number of ways. Besides an overly optimistic account of human possibilities toward the enlargement of value, his relational value theory is itself rather reductionistic. Here, value itself just might as well be equated with God, since it is the maximization of value that is of supreme commitment. The American empirical theologian Tyron Inbody reported to me that while Wieman was at Chicago, when referring to his doctrine of God as creative interchange, the standing joke among students and colleagues was, "Henry, which is it this time?" This is a criticism that has long plagued Wieman since H. Richard Niebuhr first charged it in a 1931 critical essay:

> The American theologian or philosopher appears to abstract indi-
> vidual experience unduly from its historic context and to be inad-
> equately aware of the cultural matrix out of which his experience
> is born. Abstracting the experiencer from his cultural conditions, he
> ascribes to the content of experience a universal availability and valid-
> ity which it does not possess since it is in fact relative to a particular
> historical nexus. The result is either the universalization of Christian
> theology, which is regarded as available for all rational human beings
> because they are rational and human, or . . . the reduction of the
> content of theology to that which is abstracted from all particular
> historical connection to the consensus of all religions or to a natural
> theology gained by a process of inference from man's universal expe-
> rience of nature, thought and morality.[43]

Value appears to be a projection of the subjectivity of human subjects. How, then, does one render value universal beyond subjective forms of appraisal? Again Niebuhr:

> Being inadequately critical and relativistic in its analysis of religious
> experience, American realism appears to discover the absolute within
> the relative more readily than seems permissible; hence it fails to rec-
> ognize the urgency and difficulty of discovering the absolute and to
> appreciate the peculiarity of Christianity as revelation or of faith as a
> divine *tour de force* by which the relative is transcended.[44]

From Niebuhr's position, it is the relativism of values that raises questions about Wieman's relational value theory.

Closely tied to this problem is that Wieman's theology and ethics appear radically anthropocentric, especially when compared to Gustafson's. Here, value holds for human purposes, goods, ends, flourishing, and fulfillment. Wieman's locus of creative interchange is human good, and he is optimistic that when human good has become a matter of humans' ultimate com-mitment, then humans will maximally flourish. Given this moral vision of creative interchange, one has to wonder, Why use God-talk at all?—for it is value itself that maximizes and enlarges value. There is something greatly unsatisfying in Wieman's relational value theory that, as in the case of Gustafson, raises questions about the meaning and significance of worship, adoration, praise, and thanksgiving in religious experience. I am left to ask just how satisfying such a minimal account of divine transcendence communicates in its own exchange with normative, aesthetic, and practical performances in religious experience. Notwithstanding the importance of these questions, I nevertheless find both Gustafson's and Wieman's theologies and ethics attractive in our contemporary context of theological ethics so preoccupied with or nearly totalized by power and identity politics and the particularity of tradition, story, and narrative. In both theologians, I find the kindred spirit of unrepentant liberals. Together, they substantiate my belief in the possibility of and concrete actualization of Beloved Community.

CONCLUSION

To conclude, *black* experience as I first read it in black theology and then in womanist theology has remained a major basis for my critical reflections on African American religious experience. I realized early in my college and seminary years that I could not be a black liberation theologian if it meant bracketing the grotesqueries, the unresolved ambiguities, of black life for a picture of black experience defined by the blackness that whiteness created. I could not suppress the worlds of difference that keep African American experience open to more than struggle, more than survival, more than resistance, and more than suffering. I needed a pragmatic theology of African American religious experience. This is what I have attempted to construct in this book.

Beyond this introduction, *Creative Exchange* contains five chapters. Chapter 1, "Beyond Dichotomies: Toward a Relational Concept of Race in African American Religious Experience," first appeared in part as a journal article in celebration of Charles H. Long's contribution to the study of black religion.[45] It has been significantly revised and expanded. Based on Edward Farley's book, *Deep Symbols*, I develop a relational concept of race as a deep symbol. I then place the symbol in conversation with two very different views of race in black philosophy, drawing on Lucius T. Outlaw's *Race and Philosophy* and Kwame Anthony Appiah's *In My Father's House: Africa in the Philosophy of Culture*. I use these thinkers in order to disclose the grotesqueries of race discourse in African American experience. I then connect race relationally to African American religious experience by drawing on Long's hermeneutical phenomenology and Hans–Georg Gadamer's conception of the *sensus communis* (community sense). I close by showing how the relational concept of race meaningfully comes to expression in traditional African ways of religious and moral thinking as well as in contemporary African American religious thought. When race is understood as a deep symbol, but one that is radically ambiguous, it enters into creative exchange with difference. Race and difference are then relationally united into a picture of the world in which mutuality concretizes the event of Beloved Community.

Chapter 2, "We See Through a Glass Darkly: Slave Narrative Theology and the Opacity of African American Religious Thought," was tested as a chapter in Anthony B. Pinn's and Benjamin Valentin's *The Ties That Bind*.[46] It has also undergone significant revisions. This chapter is a critique of slave narrative theology as developed in Dwight N. Hopkins and George C. L. Cummings's *Cut Loose Your Stammering Tongue: Black Theology in the Slave Narratives* (1991, 2005). Here I identify several interpretative problems that arise when theologians seek, in the world of slave culture and slave religion, a protoblack theology. I retrieve Long's concept of "opacity" to move the discussion of black sources of religious insight into modes of interpretation that are grounded on difference and oriented toward forms of enlargement in which creative exchange keeps African American theology open to internal criticism and a truly interdisciplinary discourse. In creative exchange, all of our sources of religious insight are irreducible wells from which to draw vibrant interpretations of the worlds of difference that make up African American religious experience.

Chapter 3, "Faith on Earth: A Defense of Redemptive Suffering in African American Theology," is an apology in defense of redemptive suffering in African American religious experience. My argument is set in relation to the critique of redemptive suffering given by Anthony B. Pinn in *Why Lord? Suffering and Evil in Black Theology* and Delores S. Williams in *Sisters in the Wilderness: Womanist God-Talk*. Mine is a critical reading of their positions on theodicy and sins of servanthood and surrogacy. My defense of redemptive suffering is derived from my reading of H. Richard Niebuhr's phenomenology of faith in *Faith on Earth: An Inquiry into the Structure of Human Faith*. I argue that redemptive suffering is not inherently a theological symbol but an economic symbol of exchange. At its very root is the experience of creative exchange. Redemptive suffering symbolizes creative exchanges of human possibilities of faith, hope, and love concretely actualized within our experiences of evil and suffering. These possibilities are not derived benefits or goods from suffering and evil. Rather, they are possibilities copresent or creatively exchanged in the experiences of suffering and evil. I argue that such an account of redemptive suffering adequately meets the religious demands of those who sing and pray that "God will make a way out of no way."

Chapter 4, "The Smell of Life: A Pragmatic Theology of Religious Experience," brings together the major unit ideas of experience, the grotesque and pragmatic naturalism, and creative exchange and shows how they can enliven and enlarge our understanding of African American religious experience. In this chapter, Howard Thurman is my principle interlocutor with whom I engage in creative exchange. The second half of the chapter addresses the problem of prayer in my pragmatic theology when God is no longer pictured as a person but as the world—a plenitude of being—characterized by finitude and transcendence. In creative exchange, a pragmatic theology of African American religious experience connects us by memory and lived experience to the pains, sorrows, sufferings, and closures of the world. Yet it looks beyond these realities to the surprising joys of life that find expression in our songs of adoration and praise and our prayers of gratitude.

Chapter 5, "Home and the Black Church: Centers of Value in a Pragmatic Theology of African American Religious Experience," concludes the book. I have dedicated this chapter to the memory of my mother, Flora H. Anderson, who died on June 18, 2007, while I was preparing this book for publication. The most autobiographical, this chapter is a reflexive engagement of myself with the ambiguities, the grotesqueries, of two of the most powerful centers of African American religious experience. In both centers, I show how they can be simultaneously centers of harm and care. This is their grotesquery. Through commitment to creative exchange, however, I also argue that they may be concrete actualizations of that creative event that thinkers such as Howard Thurman and Martin Luther King Jr. called Beloved Community. The ethical position that I explicitly put forward in this concluding chapter is this: If the Beloved Community that thinkers such as Howard Thurman and Martin Luther King Jr. envisioned is concrete and not only a regulative ideal, then our particular families must enlarge themselves in creative exchange with other families and homes in which the filial bonds of kinship increase the plurality of goods connecting all our families. Moreover, when it seeks to maximize those goods and desires that make life qualitatively good, fulfilled and flourishing for all its members, the black church also concretely actualizes, however fragmentarily, the creative event of the Beloved Community. Beloved Community is not only a regulative ideal, it is also a creative event arising within the creative exchanges of the home, family, church, and by enlargement the world.

CHAPTER 1

Beyond Dichotomies

Toward a Relational Concept of Race in African American Religious Experience

> After this I looked, and there was a great multitude that no one could count, from every nation, from all tribes and peoples and languages, standing before the throne . . . (Rev 7:9a)

My INTEREST IN WHAT IT means to belong to a race is deeply rooted in the make-up of my family, its formation, and its profound sense of difference. For instance, the members of my family have striking differences in our hair textures and colors. One of my brothers had kinky, short hair, so we called him *pea head* because its texture was like a mass of curly green pea shoots. Some of my sisters had thick, smooth, braided hair, rich in hues of brown, red, auburn, and dark brown or black. My brother Barry and I would chide them, calling their hair "doo-doo braids."

Our table was a mosaic of skin colors; we ranged from the darkest of browns to the palest of whites. And in our home in the Englewood district of the South Side of Chicago where I was reared, my siblings and I constantly fought our way back home from school (sometime the fights were fist fights and other times just cussing) as we defended ourselves against neighborhood kids who ridiculed us by calling us "white kids." We were yellow and tan, but not white. It was nothing to go to Hamilton Park to play on a Saturday morning and return home bearing the wounds of our fights for our black identities.

When I was a teen, one night Grandfather left for work at his usual time, heading for his midnight shift at the post office. Suddenly, he returned home.

He had been attacked and severely beaten, his jaws so broken they had to be wired shut for months afterward. At the time of the assault, he was not even a block from the house where we had lived for nearly thirteen years. He was beaten because boys not from our neighborhood thought he was a white man. To be sure, his skin was a pale olive tone, his nose long, his ears big and wide, and his hair straight and black. We would say that he reminded us of Bing Crosby. It was all right for my brother and me to joke about his apparent whiteness; after all, he was our grandfather. However, the anguish of this event remained on my consciousness as a real, felt experience of the demonic. That race should spawn such internal contradictions within the black neighborhood of my youth has shaped my preoccupations with race theory in culture and theology ever since.

This chapter is a return to that unresolved itch of unforgotten ambiguity that marked the development of my racial consciousness as a youth. It seeks to come to terms with race in black philosophy and African American religious thought in a creative exchange that takes up the ambiguities of race while forging a constructive place for it in African American religious experience. Race symbolically participates with other deep symbols in constructing a relational, pragmatic theology of African American religious experience. Although Edward Farley does not himself make this connection, I argue that race might be best understood in line with his notion of "deep symbols." I then discuss the views of Kwame Anthony Appiah and Lucius T. Outlaw Jr. on the symbolic role that race plays in African American philosophy. In the final section, I turn to Charles H. Long's hermenutical phenomenology to suggest that the grotesqueries of "race" in black philosophy are compatible with the relationality of religious experience displayed in African traditional religion and contemporary African American religious thought. The task of a pragmatic theology of African American religious experience is to understand its relativity, map its grotesquery, and integrate race into a larger unity of life within the creative exchange.

RACE AS A DEEP SYMBOL

What is this "black" in black theology and black philosophy? The question is not one peculiar to our recent times concerned with strategies that affirm racial significations and those that reject any value at all to "race-ing." Writing in Gina Dent's collection of essays, *Black Popular Culture*, Stuart Hall foregrounds one of the enduring questions of African American studies: "What is this 'black' in black popular culture?"

> I begin with a question: what sort of moment is this in which to pose the question of black popular culture? These moments are always conjunctural. They have their historical specificity; and although they always exhibit similarities and continuities with other moments in which we pose a question like this, they are never the same moment. And the combination of what is similar and what is different defines not only the specificity of the moment, but the specificity of the question, and therefore the strategies of cultural politics with which we attempt to intervene in popular culture, and the form and style of cultural theory and criticizing that has to go along with such an intermatch.[1]

Indeed, this question has had a perennial effect in the development of two insurgent movements in African American studies and American intellectual history, both of which have profoundly shaped my own interests in race and religion: black theology of liberation and black philosophy. Both discourses have now become well documented by Gayraud Wilmore and James Cone in a their multivolume series *Black Theology: A Documentary History*.[2] In 1979, an entire volume in the journal *Philosophical Forum* was devoted to black philosophy.[3] Drawing on William R. Jones, a primary contributor to the volume, the volume represented an initial recognition of black philosophy as a legitimate and necessary philosophical discourse by the American Philosophical Academy. Since then, black philosophy has gained wider recognition through publications such as Fred Lee Hord (Mzee Lasana Okpara) and Jonathan Scott Lee's *I Am Because We Are: Readings in Black Philosophy* (1995), Lewis Gordon's *Existence in Black: An Anthology of Black Existential Philosophy* (1997), and James A. Montmarguet and William H. Hardy's *Reflections: An Anthology of African American Philosophy* (2000). Between the two discourses, forming a creative exchange of cultural significance is Cornel West and Eddie S. Glaude Jr.'s monumental collection, *African American Religious Thought: An Anthology* (2003).

For black theology and black philosophy, the historical moment that fueled their discourses, providing them with historical and cultural content is the cultural milieu of the black power movement and the new black aesthetic movement. For over thirty years, each discourse had a significant impact on the constructions of religious and philosophical thinking in universities, colleges, and seminaries not only in the United States but globally. The relation between black philosophy and black theology has been a creative exchange that radically exploded long-standing discursive standards and practices that determined "great scholarship." Great scholarship had been defined by disciplinary uniqueness or specialization in substantive or material content and characterized by methodological distinctiveness. Black theology and black philosophy opened African American studies and African American scholars to genuine "internal criticisms" that enriched, enlarged, enlightened, and emancipated the creative imaginations, energies, and critical consciousness of African American scholars of history, religion, literature, social sciences, philosophy, culture studies, and medical arts sciences.

In their internal critiques, black philosophy and black theology often allowed each discipline to gain clarity on its own distinctive contributions to African American cultural experience. To be sure, the exchange highlighted continuities but also differences. For instance, referring to pre-black power developments in African American religious thought, characterized by thinkers such as Carter G. Woodson, E. Franklin Frazier, Benjamin E. Mays, Howard Thurman, and Martin Luther King Jr., some black philosophers viewed these discourses as inadequately critical of Western oppressive ideologies, especially Christian theology. Some philosophical critics also extended this criticism to black theology of liberation, requiring a more rigorous Marxist critique of ideology. Others turned to black existentialism or black humanism for critically assessing the meaning and value of "the black experience."[4] Yet some black theologians rejected the scrutiny of their projects by black philosophers. They insisted that black philosophers themselves had not emancipated themselves sufficiently from the oppressive canons of rationality inscribed on black academic minds by the white philosophical canon. Notwithstanding the back and forth of such internal criticisms, both communities of scholars grounded their legitimacy and necessity as critical intellectual movements on the critique of white supremacy and the social, political, economic, educational, and religious conditions that had a negative impact on black experience on a global scale.

The moment that defined black philosophy and black theology was not the moment that legitimated and made necessary the ideologues of the Beloved Community. Indeed, conscious of the brutal effects of racism, slavery, and African colonization, many African American religious thinkers tried intellectually to transcend the demonic legacies of white supremacy by a philosophy of religion constructed on the abstract universality of a Christian humanism. Thinkers such as Mays, Thurman, and King raised to critical consciousness, in a Jim Crow society, the "impossible possibility" of the Beloved Community as the regulative symbol for guiding our understanding of human experience beyond particular experience.[5] Through this symbol, these thinkers sought to disempower race as an ontological symbol in understanding religious experience. Their moment was crucial, and it remains critical to my pragmatic theology of African American religious experience. As a critical principle in African American religious thought, however, the symbol is now challenged, but not negated, in our postmodern moment by the ascendancy of the symbol of difference and its new cultural politics.

The new cultural politics of difference points toward the rejection of "the monolithic and homogeneous in the name of diversity, multiplicity and heterogeneity; a rejection of the abstract, general, and universal for the concrete, specific and particular; and it signifies commitment to writing that privileges the historic, contextual, and plural by emphasizing the contingent, provisional, variable, shifting, and changing."[6] In thinking about culture, the new cultural politics of difference points toward the celebration of tradition, but it also celebrates multiculturalism. It recognizes that no adequate account of the self can be gained from a grand narrative about the nature and destiny of humanity in general. Rather, the new cultural politics of difference privileges the historical, cultural context as the locus for self-understanding and meaning. Politically, it sets itself in opposition to the politics of domination.

It is enabled by the openings in our political culture that provide the vocabulary and vision for the self-determination, self-realization, and self-conscious reflection of the situated subject. Therefore, the new cultural politics of difference is not satisfied with the cultivation of a critical consciousness that only sets itself to the task of disclosing the dark side of modernity. Rather, it proposes a political praxis that results not only in critical enlightenment but also emancipatory practices that celebrate the potentialities of situated subjects. In the new cultural politics of difference, multiplicity of cultural expressions contributes to a transformation of our life together and explodes our preoccupation with the so called "Other" while celebrating difference: racial, gender, sexual, cultural, national, political, and religious. Here, a word of caution is in order for those of us who make the symbol of *difference* controlling in our constructive projects. I agree with Appiah that, when associated with identities, even difference itself can dangerously slip over into reifications. He rightly cautions that "as it is mobilized within the discourse of ethnography, it can harden into something fixed and determinate, a homogeneity of Difference. But I don't know what to do about such perils, aside from pointing them out, and trying to avoid them."[7]

I am profoundly appreciative of those thinkers who, in their historic moment, sought to untangle race as a defining category that frames religious experience by metaphysical categories of abstract universality, unity, and an abstract human community. As they knew all too well, however, race remained an unavoidable symbol in their critical religious thinking about African American religious experience. For instance, King says:

Racism is the myth of an inferior race, of an inferior people, and I think religious institutions, more than any other institutions in society, must really deal with racism. Certainly, we all have a responsibility—the federal government, the local government, our educational institutions. But the religious community, being the chief moral guardian of the over-all community should really take the primary responsibility in dealing with this problem of racism, which is largely attitudinal.[8]

I suggest that *race* may be understood as a "deep symbol" in African American religious experience. But what does this mean? In responding to this question, I am indebted to my friend Edward Farley for conversations with him over the years and his insightful book, *Deep Symbols: Their Postmodern Effacement and Reclamation.*[9]

Farley's talk of deep symbols is located within the currents of postmodern life. For him, the postmodern signifies a social context in which many traditional, societal norms, values, and institutions are in disarray, lacking contemporary consensus on regulative ideals that may function today as deep symbols. By deep symbols, Farley means words of power that "constrain and guide" persons in their various negotiations with postmodern life.[10] To be sure, Farley is aware that such words or symbols are not the conventions of any one institution such as religion, law, politics, science, and so forth. Nevertheless, they are conventions. They arise from the intersubjective and inter-human depth structures of human communities. They function as deeply rooted categories of social meaning within our increasing, changing and developing stock of knowledge.

Deep symbols are so basic that one almost always *feels* them to be a priori, or at least one is tempted to regard them as such. But they are historical constructs. Farley warns that they are so basic that their taken-for-granted qualities often conceal their more elusive qualities and ambiguities.[11] Deep symbols have at least four characteristics, says Farley: (1) They function normatively insofar as they are regulative ideals. (2) They enchant insofar as they keep society open to mystery. (3) They are fallible insofar as they are vulnerable to historical change and corruptibility. And (4) they are located in a master narrative that reflexively identifies and defines social action in human communities.[12] Deep symbols are historical and as such they "arise within and express the historical determinacy of a community. The community's particular character, tradition, and situation are the locus of deep symbols. This means that deep symbols are historical, and hence relative, to a particular community, and thus are changeable. They can rise and empower, and they can lose their power and disappear."[13]

Among Farley's candidates for deep symbols are education, beauty, reality, rights, nature, freedom, community, and justice. Noticeably absent are nation and race. The absence of these symbols is curious given Farley's formal account of deep symbols. For to qualify as a deep symbol, the word must formally have the quality of signifying a value or a set of values "by which a community understands itself, from which it takes its aims, and to which it appeals as canons of cultural criticism."[14] Surely, both nation and race meet these formal requirements. Race certainly seems to meet these requirements in African American philosophical and religious thinking. As a deep symbol, race has a duplicity that signifies cultural solidarity among groups of people, provides conceptual possibilities for social self-definition, as well as possibilities for individual transcendence within the community.

I think that the omission of race from Farley's constellation of deep symbols is no oversight. Rather, I take it that some precommitment on his part to a set of humanistic assumptions prohibits race from functioning as a deep symbol in his philosophical and theological construction. I suspect that the erasure lies in Farley's respect for the interhuman encounter where

> . . . human beings relate to each other, not merely as functionaries in a preprogrammed bureaucracy, but in mutual perceptions of their vulnerability, needs, pathos, possibilities, and mystery. In the sphere of relation human beings continue to experience mutual obligation, guilt and resentment, gratitude, limitations on their autonomy, and mutual activities of creativity. From such relations are born notions of personhood, justice, mutual obligation, and even truth and reality.[15]

Here one notes that it is not so much Farley's humanism that precludes race from functioning as a deep symbol. Rather, the omission is an inference Farley draws from his insight into the interhuman sphere. He finds race to be dangerously oriented toward forms of totality in which "death camps, genocidal policies and events, malicious torture, and cynical nihilism" cut off the interhuman appeal.[16]

I am sympathetic to Farley's judgment about such symbols as nation and race. Indeed, they are among the most idolatrous symbols in human cultures. For African American thinkers, however, any suggestion of bracketing these symbols is a cognitive feat near unimaginable. From my point of view, it is in embodied relations signified by race and nation that recognition arises not only of semblances but also of differences among human beings encountered in the interhuman relation. Moreover, such recognition of others is trained and nurtured in human communities through myths, stories, lore, songs, and genealogies of ethnic and racial descent. Descent symbols, therefore, contribute to the stock of knowledge by which the symbolic universe of human situated lives is understood and negotiated. For instance, in the Western Christian theological tradition, the universal appeal of divine grace, redemption, love, and peace is not made to bodiless humans or to faceless, deracial, or nonethnic others (if such things were imaginable). According to this religious tradition, these divine gifts are extended to the nations, to the peoples of the earth, and to the kingdoms of this world. For Christian theologians, the power of the divine to transform the miseries of the human condition arises among situated subjects who are embodied spatially, temporally, historically and culturally.

I am aware of the ways in which descent symbols such as race and nation can distort our understanding of the many ways that human identities are influenced by a constellation of other symbols—individuality, freedom, and openness. Therefore, keeping a critical eye on the idolatrous and totalizing tendencies of these symbols is crucial. Nevertheless, I cannot escape the facticity of human relations, practices, and cultural activities that are signified by symbols such as race, nation, and peoples. I regard race to be a grotesquely ambiguous symbol. Again, the grotesque recovers and leaves unresolved basic ambiguous sensibilities, attraction and repulsion or pleasure and pain, which are evoked by the symbol. In creative exchange, the unresolved tensions render the symbol ambiguous, for the unresolved tensions may also leave open creative possibilities for reclaiming the symbol in our postmodern moment.

It can occasion innovation while resisting essentialist reductions. When race is grasped as a grotesquely ambiguous symbol, the symbol itself occasions —in our racialized social practices within our racialized culture—a play on the absurd and sincere, the comical and tragic, the estranged and familiar, and the satirical and playful. It is this interplay of possibilities evoked by the symbol that leaves race open to creative exchanges within the social life-world. It keeps the symbol oriented toward openness and not closure. Although race may not be necessarily a malicious symbol, the symbol nevertheless falls under Farley's fallibility principle.

As a deep symbol, race is relative and open to corruption. Inasmuch as deep symbols creatively constrain and guide human practices, they may also condition the possibility of totality. In this regard, Farley writes:

> As instruments of corrupted power, deep symbols can mirror the society's stratification of privilege. . . . Thus, the deep symbols can be so framed as to advance the privileged members and suppress the voice of the unprivileged. They still may function as deep values and ideals, but in those ideas lurk racism, the disenfranchising of women, and the maintenance of social policies that favor an existing social elite.[17]

Farley's caution about the power of a symbol such as race to orient communities toward malicious social practices that totalize the "other" is well taken. Still, the question of race as a deep symbol, like the other social symbols that Farley wants to reclaim in our postmodern moment, is whether race can be understood and appreciated in a manner that orient our social practices away from forms of closure and toward what Jerome A. Stone calls "an ethics openness." According to Stone, "the basic moral principle of this philosophy is that we should be critically open to situationally transcendent resources and critically open and committed to challenging ideals. In short, we should adopt and continually nurture a stance of critical openness and commitment."[18]

For my purposes, I am not interested in defining race—indeed, the very idea of defining or explaining a symbol! Here, I am mindful of Ludwig Wittgenstein's disdain for Frazer's *The Golden Bough* and his admonition that when confronted by the mysteries of religion one would do better to describe them and not explain away their power. Witttgenstein scholars G. P. Baker and P. M. S. Hacker say:

> "Every explanation is a hypothesis" ([*Golden Bough*] 30). *A propos* Frazer's explanation of magic, Wittgenstein remarks, 'I think one reason why the attempt to find an explanation is wrong is that we have only to put together in the right way what we know without adding anything, and the satisfaction we are trying to get from the explanation come of itself.' This holds true for philosophy too. There is nothing more dangerous than employing the word "explanation" in logic (philosophy) in the sense in which it is used in physics.[19]

The risk of explanation is reductivism and hermeneutical violence to the ones whose religious experience calls us to theological and philosophical inquiry in the first place. The task is not to explain the deep symbol of race but to describe its power. Thus, my tasks here are to disclose the ambiguities of this symbol, track its effects on black philosophy, and construct its possibilities for a pragmatic theory of race in African American religious experience within the creative exchange of African *traditionary* and African American religious sources.

Two Assessments of Race in Black Philosophy

In the United States, the debate over black philosophy has been going on for approximately thirty years.[20] Behind the debate are a number of historical provocations. What is black philosophy? Who are its representatives? What is its canon of literature? What are its constitutive problems? A number of African and African American philosophers have discussed both historical and contemporary denials of black philosophy. From a historical perspective, many European philosophers have argued that people of African descent are intellectually incapable of producing philosophical discourse. Here one only has to recall the judgment of David Hume, Immanuel Kant, Thomas Jefferson, and G. W. F. Hegel.[21] A few instances from Kant and Jefferson will suffice. In *Observations on the feeling of the Beautiful and Sublime* (1763), Kant presents a comparative ethnography that, drawing on Hume, "challenges anyone to cite a single example in which a Negro has shown talents, and asserts that among the hundreds of thousands of blacks who are transported elsewhere from their countries, although many of them have been set free, still not a single one was ever found who presented anything great in art or science or any other praise worthy quality . . ."[22] In "Notes on the State of Virginia," Jefferson writes concerning the rationality of blacks that, when compared to whites, they are in memory equal to whites but in reason inferior, in imagination dull, tasteless, and not worth mentioning, and not able to "utter a thought above the level of plain narration."[23]

As African and African American intellectuals responded critically to sentiments expressed by these thinkers, many did so in terms provided by white philosophers themselves. This has led more contemporary thinkers to argue that even if people of African descent were capable of producing a black philosophy, their thinking appears to mirror Western European thought rather than enunciating anything distinctively "black." As stated above, negative objections to black philosophy are instances of question begging. They make sense only if one already operates with an unquestionable definition of what philosophy is and agrees on what the "essence" or "nature" of philosophical thinking entails. Here, given the terms provided by white philosophers of what philosophy is, critics of black philosophy deny the very idea of a "black philosophy."

I think that the more serious and interesting questions surrounding black philosophy come from African and African American thinkers themselves who operate out of the postmodern recognition of difference, where philosophy is by nature particular. Therefore, if there are any appeals to universal standards, they are, at best, to be understood as generalities based on the particulars of the particular, barring generalities being set aside altogether in light of difference. The particulars of the particular capture the gaze of the postmodern critic. In this regard, two philosophers are worth discussing at some length: Kwame Anthony Appiah and Lucius T. Outlaw Jr. I am aware that as Appiah and Outlaw have developed their positions, their overall differences are more mitigated than my strong reading might suggest. However, I focus on their discussion because of the substantive differences they exhibit on what I shall call, for heuristic purposes, a strong and weak conception of race in black philosophy. A strong view of race foregrounds race as a socio-biological or sociocultural signifier of collective black experience.[24] A weak view of race rejects any ontological standing for the concept but understands the symbol as holding only a weak connection for establishing collective colonial experiences of subjugation among peoples of African descent. Race is symbolic in meaning and resists any reification into a collective identity.[25]

In *In My Father's House,* Appiah puts forward a weak conception of race in which race is an illusion, predicated on categories invented by the European mind to serve only European intellectual purposes. As a symbol, Appiah understands race to signify no simple, concrete social relation. It can mean almost anything to any number of people. It can signify biological determinants, social arrangements, a shared ancestry, or cultural specificity. He faults African American thinkers such as Alexander Crummel and W. E. B. Du Bois for making race an empirical fact—that is, something that can be understood historically. But what is the historical reality that race brings to light? It cannot be color—there are just too many shades. Not tribe—there are just too many families to try to come to terms with. The historical reality cannot be language—there are too many languages. And it cannot be a common culture—there are just too many differences among African people and people of the African diaspora.

According to Appiah, race may exist, but only as a rationalization of European cultural particularisms; it exists for ideological purposes. All that Appiah means here, however, is that the category *race*, when properly under-stood, is as arbitrary as are signs of Europe, Africa, Asia, and the like. Each sign designates a land mass that shows essential or pervasive "traits" among those who inhabit these geographical spaces. Appiah thinks that such talk flies against any honest empirical study of human societies. When he exam-ines Du Bois's great essay, "The Conservation of the Races," he suggests that there is nothing to conserve except Du Bois's own wishes, desires, and situ-ated cultural longings. The problem is that Du Bois is trying to make race an essential quality of human existence. Rather, it is only a concession to a sociobiological ontology that falls apart when its propositions are tested by genuine difference. In an important passage, Appiah explains:

> No doubt we can find generalizations at a certain abstract level, which hold true of most black Africa before European conquest. It is a familiar idea in African historiography that Africa was the last conti-nent in the old world with an "uncaptured" peasantry, largely able to use land without the supervision of feudal overlords and able, if they chose, to market their product through a complex system of trading

networks. . . . But if we could have traveled through Africa's many cultures in those years—from the small groups of Bushman hunter-gatherers, with their stone-age materials, to the Hausa kingdoms, rich in worked metal—we should have felt in every place profoundly different impulses, ideas, and forms of life. . . . To speak of an African identity in the nineteenth century—if an identity is a coalescence of mutually responsive (if sometimes conflicting) modes of conduct, habits of thought, and patterns of evaluations; in short, a coherent kind of human social psychology—would have been "to give to aery [e.g., eerie] nothing a local habitation and a name."[26]

Appiah recognizes that racial ideology exists. He also recognizes that it is a complex ideology that with every critical challenge expands its differentiating postulates from mere physicalism to include moral and cultural differentials. He does not think that all who appeal to race are themselves malicious in intention. However, he suggests that many have in mind some form of moral and social solidarity that are worth pursuing in and for themselves. Nevertheless, he argues that because such moral actions are hard to garner agreement among people without some external constraint, many feel compelled to coerce or harness their moral affiliations and social sympathy by appealing to race. In his argument, no matter what moral intentions one may have in arguing for the conservation of the races, Appiah thinks that race ideology not only distorts the real particulars of particular people, it is also cognitively unsuccessful. He says that "the truth is that there are no races; there is nothing in the world that can do all we ask race to do for us."[27]

Appiah suggests that the intellectual energies of African thinkers would be better served by attending to the shared ecological problems that plague African people and states; to the ways that African nations are related to a world economy, to the invidious forms of racism that bring about more death, harm, and exclusions; to the possibilities of more development through local and regional cooperation; as well as to the contingencies of various histories.[28] However, Appiah concludes that in a world characterized by categorical logics such as gender, ethnicity, sexuality, and the like, race is a category that we would all do well to negate for the sake of "conserving" the particularity of African cultures. Appiah's argument on the conservation of African cultures has some sympathetic hearers among black philosophers. I find it quite compelling when I reflect upon the development of my own racial consciousness in my youth. But others resist it. Lucius Outlaw puts forward a position that foregrounds a social ontology of race in black philosophy. In several important works, Outlaw advances a defense of Du

Bois's "The Conservation of the Races," which is the essay against which Appiah posits his own critique of race ideology.

Like Appiah, Outlaw begins *On Race and Philosophy* with an account of his social location. However, Outlaw's situation is focalized by his experience as an African American, living in the South, educated under Jim Crow, and trained in professional philosophy at Fisk and Boston College in the sixties and early seventies. Having had his own racial consciousness awakened by the black power movement and its new black aesthetic rationalizations, he was led to question the relevance of black philosophers to these movements.

> In not one of my classes in philosophy at Fisk (nor in graduate school, it would turn out) did I *ever* read a text written by a Negro, a Black person, an African. And since the quest for Black Power! required, first, the transformation of Negro minds [into Black consciousness] as a necessary condition for Black liberation, what was I to do? . . . the core foundation of my strength of conviction, my sense of self, was now under *radical* challenge.[29]

As were many African American intellectuals trained in American humanities departments, Outlaw also adopted the Enlightenment's liberal humanism that values freedom, self-autonomy, and moral action justified by the weight of uncompromising justice and reason and not the coercion of race. However, he also suggests that such philosophical thinking is highly unrealistic in a social-cultural life-world defined by vicious racism and all of its absurdities in American life and thought. He came to see black philosophy as a systematic discipline that tries to make sense of America's racist realities. The Black Philosophy Project was launched by African American philosophers to establish a place for themselves professionally, socially, and intellectually in ways that take account of their new black consciousness. It also required the forming of a black philosophical canon and providing norms for how black philosophers would respond to and focus on the concerns and interests of black people. For the project, philosophy is not just a task of reading a canon but also an active engagement with the concerns of black life. Outlaw would come to see the task of black philosophy as thinking "carefully and clearly about how we might resolve America's most persistent dilemma."[30]

As he situates the idea of black philosophy, Outlaw's is not the situation where recognized differences are part of the "taken-for-granted" conditions of social life as was Appiah's father's house. Rather, he says that race and ethnicity are two of the most pervasive aspects of life in America: "That there are different races and ethnic groups, that each person is a member of

one or more races and ethnics, is taken for granted by most people."³¹ However, as a black philosopher, Outlaw is also prepared to take race as "a real,
constitutive aspect of determinate populations of human beings."³² What he
means by "constitutive" is the "about which" or the "facticity" on which
black philosophical discourse turns. It is here, then, that he returns to an old
argument for an evolutionary, sociobiological account of the races, indeed,
returning to Du Bois's "The Conservation of the Races."

I do not want to rehearse the complexities of either Du Bois's or Outlaw's
discourse on race, here. In summary statements, however, Outlaw argues that
we need not reject the old notion of race as signifying "social-natural kinds"
of populations; we need not accept the view that there are pure races, populations whose biological, moral, and social traits are absolutely determinate
of a particular population so that a group is essentially differentiated from
others. Nevertheless, he suggests that black philosophers may still be warranted in using race as "a group-identifying or group-characterizing term."³³
However, Outlaw continues: "It is not biology . . . that determines the cultural productivity of any group or that determines the moral significance of
racial groups: that is to say, determines the regard we should have for racial
and ethnic groups and their members, in themselves and in relation to one
another."³⁴ Rather, it is in the fundamental associations, affections, loyalties,
and attachments that bind groups of populations together that race functions
positively in our social stock of knowledge and participates in the construction of our social and cultural realities.

According to Outlaw, recognizing that race is a social symbol that contributes to a social ontology requires some biological determination on
which to ground its cognitive significance. That is, without such a facticity,
race, like gender, is rendered only a social fiction, an illusion, or a social desire
that is incapable of justifying the kinds of loyalties, affections, and obligations
groups of people owe to each other because they hold "natural" affiliations.
Outlaw then grounds his defense of race discourse on the evolutionary and
human sciences. Reflecting on Du Bois's essay, race ideology for Outlaw
is a social and political necessity. In a passage worth quoting at length, this
necessity crystallizes:

> The unit of focus, for Du Bois, if one is to understand human his-
> tory and attempt to structure the making of the future through orga-
> nized effort, is the racial group, the "vast family" of related individuals.
> Individuals are necessary, but they are neither sufficient nor self-
> sufficing, the political philosophy of modern Enlightenment liberalism
> notwithstanding. Whether or not an individual can enjoy a relatively
> unrestricted and flourishing life is tied to the well-being of the group;

the well-being of the group requires concerted action predicated on self-valorization within the context of a shared identity without succumbing to chauvinism. Further, the racial and/or ethnic life-world provides the resources and nurturing required for the development, even, of individual talent and accomplishment such that distinctive contributions can be made to human civilization.[35]

To be sure, Outlaw would have to show more substantively than he has here how racial identity leaves open individuality while forging group loyalty, affections, and kinship for political success. However, this is a problem endemic to any social ontology that makes race a constitutive feature of human description.

Appiah and Outlaw disagree on the cognitive status of race and their moral expectations for race. Both thinkers recognize that race is a social symbol and both argue that, notwithstanding its cognitive structure, as a social symbol race functions as an ambiguous symbol. It can elicit social behaviors and patterns by a group that the group desires to conserve in religious and mundane ritual practices. Such practices may include telling the group's history or story in myths and folklore and educating the generations in the group's way of life. Appiah and Outlaw also see race as signifying a group's identity beyond physical traits; however, each theorist also sees race as a potentially dangerous symbol or, as Farley would have it, a poisonous symbol.[36] Both thinkers hold no illusions about the harms, evils, and atrocities perpetuated in the name of this symbol. Rather, each thinker holds high a moral imperative to eliminate malicious kinds of racializations. Still, each position is as persuasive as it is assessed in light of the cognitive structure of race. On this criterion, Outlaw and Appiah are worlds apart.

As each theorist turns to the taken-for-granted conditions of his social world, each comes to see things differently. In the world of African particulars, Appiah sees no empirical basis for justifying the cognitive standing of race. It is rendered a valuational proposition and not a fact of life for African peoples. For Outlaw, race is entailed in the taken-for-granted social world of human relations in the United States. For the one, the world of African differences makes race a cognitively unintelligible ground for establishing the legitimacy of black or African philosophy. For the other, the world of racist social politics makes race a philosophical necessity if black philosophers and theologians are to make sense of life in America.

It is at the pragmatic level that Appiah and Outlaw enter into a creative exchange on the meaning of race in black philosophy. Each theorist thinks that whatever positive potential race may have as a social symbol, it is likely to be most effective as a conceptual tool for mobilizing the social and political interests of Africans and people of African descent. It can syndicate the interests of those whose social realities have been defined by European colonizing effects, mass poverty, underdevelopment, negative prejudices that result in the degradation of a people's social image, and other systemic effects of white supremacy.

Defining blacks' social and political interests is something quite capable of being taken up under racial ideology; however, whatever more the symbol may elicit is widely open to debate and disagreement among African American philosophers and religious thinkers. This unifying potential of race for forging social and political solidarity circumscribes the content and task of black philosophy. For Outlaw, the task of black philosophy is first hermeneutical: "[to] aim at the full disclosure of the life-worlds of black people, our life praxes, and help us in formulating our projects."[37] The second task is moral: "to increase the degrees of freedom, happiness, and well-being that blacks might enjoy, to be in solidarity with them in these struggles in our own life-practices and our own struggles."[38]

For Appiah, black philosophy is about truth seeking and truth telling, discerning the truths of our lives in the first instance—all else that black philosophy might mean is subordinated to this task. In a summary statement, he says: "If an African identity is to empower us, . . . what is required is not so much that we throw out falsehood but that we acknowledge first of all that race and history and metaphysics do not enforce an identity: that we can choose, within broad limits set by ecological, political, and economic realities what it will mean to be African in the coming years."[39] From my point of view, when race is recognized as a social symbol, the social bonds formed by this symbol display unresolved ambiguities. Yet the creative exchange between racial identity and social reality makes the meaning of race ambiguous and not absolute, relative and not simple, open to difference and particularity and not closed, and cognizant of both the light and dark potentials of race in our social experience.

A RELATIONAL CONCEPTION OF RACE IN AFRICAN AMERICAN RELIGIOUS EXPERIENCE

In this last section, I want to place the discussion of race and its significations within the hermeneutical phenomenology of Charles H. Long. I turn to Long's hermeneutics to deconstruct—or in Long's language, to "demythologize"—race in a way consistent with Appiah's position. However, I also ask whether the symbol might be reoriented in a manner consistent with Outlaw but in the context of African American religious experience.

Any attempt to reclaim the concept of race under the symbol of difference involves the critic in the practice of deconstructing the symbol. In a section on "Primitive/Civilization," Long argues that to understand the power of these symbols, one has to come to terms with their internal ambiguities or doublings. The power of civilization lies in "othering" effects that require the "other" in all its significations for structuring the cultural and empirical realities signified by the symbol. In this case, the meaning of civilization cannot be disclosed without the primitive being copresent both culturally and empirically. Long says:

> The self-conscious realization of the Western European rise to the level of civilization must be seen simultaneously in its relationship to the discovery of a new world which must necessarily be perceived as inhabited by savages and primitives who constitute the lowest rung on the ladder of cultural reality. The sociogenesis and psychogenesis of this formation are equally formed by the explorers, adventurers, merchants, and literary artists whose field of opportunity and expression are the brave New World of savages and primitives beyond the Atlantic sea.[40]

On Long's argument, in the process of conceptualizing race in African American religious thought, we must realize that the symbols *race* and *races* are entailed in the cultural logic of the West. When put in Farley's understanding of deep symbols, the intentionality of race is fundamentally oriented toward "othering" and structuring a hierarchy of cultural, economic, historical, and religious differences that is maintained by domination. In this sense, the figures discussed in this essay are warranted in maintaining a hermeneutic of suspicion about the power of race as a symbol, just as Long holds suspicion about the concepts *primitive* and *civilization*. Likewise, one wonders whether race can be reclaimed for a pragmatic theology of African American religious experience without maintaining symbolic meanings that are totalizing rather than oriented toward an ethics of openness. Long drives home this point in his discussion of *primitive/civilization*:

> The problem surrounding the usage of the term "primitive" as a proper designation for certain cultures, histories, and religions must therefore be seen as a crisis of the term "civilization." Other terms have been forthcoming to replace the term "primitive"—noncivilized, nonliterate, cold culture, and so on. These changes will not suffice, for the cultural language of civilization that brought forth the structure of the primitive has not changed.[41]

Long's criticism certainly seems appropriate when discussing the concept of race. Still, he argues that the process of demythologization leads to a hermeneutical reorientation by which we might ask "whether we are able to discern a structure of symbols and meanings that will establish a new integrity for the status of the primitive religions, on the one hand, and demonstrate the proper place for this study within the history of religions, on the other."[42] Drawing on the dynamics of signs, symbols, and signification as developed by Long, this is exactly what I attempt to do in this chapter on race.

In agreement with Outlaw, I hold that blackness is a social sign; however, I am also in agreement with Appiah that it is as arbitrary a sign as is any other linguistic convention by which persons negotiate their environment; signs such as, stop, go, caution, exit, enter, blue lights, red lights, ten miles vs. ten kilometers, white, black, and so forth. Independent of discrete social contexts and actions such signs are arbitrary markings. However, placed within a cultural context of social action, movement, travel, traffic, and the like, the signs signify matrices of human behavior, commands, admonitions, and guidance. Together they form a whole scene of human activity from stopping at red lights while traveling ten miles to being pulled over to the curb by blue-lighted police cars for disregarding caution. Similarly, as a sign, race has no self-evidential meaning. When the sign is evoked, however, it refracts individuated modes of behavior, wishes, desires, preferences, actions, and expressions of persons. In its travel from a sign to symbol, such behaviors, habits, desires, preferences, expressions, and actions are what Long calls significations, and the significations of race are open to religious interpretation.

On Long's account, when one asks what "black religion" is, one is not looking for an essence or a formal abstraction from the concrete practices and historical reality of religious life. Black religion signifies discrete ritual, cognitive, and moral practices disclosed in the historical life-worlds of people of African descent. Whatever unities prevail among such communities, they may properly be understood as associational or family resemblances without evoking essentialist notions of meaning and value. In the same manner, white theology, religion, or philosophy could mean nothing other than commonalities in thinking, language, and religious practices among North Atlantic intellectual communities and associated with persons of European origins (Irish, French, Italian, English, German, Dutch, and so on). To understand what black religion signifies, then, theologians and religionists need to first describe, as thickly as possible, the religious life-worlds of African and African American peoples before they inscribe religious meaning and value on different black societies. In an important passage, Long states the complexity of such a movement from symbolism to interpretation:

> Reflection proceeding from religious symbolism has the merit of correlating the interpreter on a search for inner being of self and humanity with a level of historical expression commensurate with this intention. As the interpreter moves from symbolism to rationality, another movement will become necessary—a movement back into the shadows of one's ego and history—for the interpreter will discover that one's being is mirrored in the reality of life and history and simultaneously created in the moment of interpretation.[43]

As the sign travels toward symbol, race constructs not only a social ontology; it may also express religious intentions within a people's historical self-understanding; however, racial significations need not determine malicious dichotomies, hierarchies, or domination. For instance, the symbol may signify a relational perspective in which African and African American communities, societies, lives, bodies, and cultures are understood as religiously connected by webs of significance and circles of relations.

This relational concept of race that I have developed here finds expression hermeneutically in Hans-Georg Gadamer's retrieval of Shaftsbury's *sensus communis*. The *sensus communis* ought not to be translated as the "sense of community" with all the vagaries of other phrases like the "sense of life," or a "sense of joy." It is neither a feeling of community nor a mystical, subjective longing for community. It was Gadamer's intention to move the notion completely out of the romantic conception of feeling and desire. In the context of this essay, *sensus communis* will not signify a "feeling for the black race" or a "sense of my blackness" as a subjective longing. Rather, for Gadamer, the *sensus communis* is "community sense."

Shaftsbury says: "A public spirit can come only from a social feeling or sense of partnership with human kind."[44] *Sensus communis* is not a subjective appreciation for one's community. It signifies an acquired understanding of and appreciation for a community's ways: its public, social, cultural, political, economic, and moral practices. For Shaftsbury, the term refers to a community's manners, customs, and virtues. Shaftsbury elucidates the meaning of *sensus communis* in the social practices of wit and humor. When one learns a language that is not one's own, one learns the grammar and the vocabulary and speaks in an intentional manner, usually according to its proper grammatical form. However, one has not truly acquired a sense of the language until one can laugh at the jokes and recognize a pun without asking for an explanation. In this way, then, my relational understandings of race signifies an understanding of the symbol as its meaning is formed or cultivated (*Bildung*) by the community's ways, its manners, customs, wit, humor, and virtues. Such a conception of relationality comes to expression in what Francis Hutcheson called *social sympathy*. Gadamer describes it thus:

> By *sensus communis*, according to Shaftsbury, the humanist understood a sense of the common weal, but also "love of the community or society, natural affection, humanity, obligingness." They adopt a term from Marcus Aurelius, *koinonoemosune*—a most unusual and artificial word, confirming that the concept of *sensus communis* does not originate with the Greek philosophers, but has the Stoical conception of harmonic. The humanist Salmasius describes the content of this word as "a customary, and regular way of thinking in a man, which as it were looks to the community and does not refer everything to its own advantage but directs its attention to those things with which it is concerned, and thinks of itself with restraint and proper measure." What Shaftsbury is thinking of is not so much a capacity given to all men, part of the natural law, as a social virtue, a virtue of the heart more than of the head. And if he understands wit and humor in terms of it, then in this respect too he is following ancient Roman concepts that include in *humanitas* a refined *savoir vivre*, the attitude of the man who understands a joke and tells one because he is aware of a deeper union with his interlocutor. (Shaftsbury explicitly limits wit and humor to social intercourse among friends). Though the *sensus communis* appears here mostly as a virtue of social intercourse, there is nevertheless a moral even metaphysical basis implied.[45]

Both the metaphor of "web" and "circles" of relation and the moral meaning of *sensus communis* are hermeneutical ways of signifying the concept of race that moves beyond any essentialist construction of the term and reconstitutes this deep symbol within the natural and social affections and forms of sympathy that substantively fund the idea of community (*comunitas*) itself. Indeed, such a reconstitution of the symbol, I think, is more than adequately enriched by the *traditionary* wealth of African traditional folklores, riddles, and proverbs and is therefore not alien to but enters into creative exchange with African American religious experience.

Some African folklores address moral connectedness by explaining why certain practices must be done one way and not another, but other stories express traditional moral values and attitudes toward the realities of traditional African experiences. For example, the African concept of "others" includes not only human beings but also heavenly bodies, the sky, the sun, the moon, and the stars. "Others" may also include seasons, birds and fowl, animals of prey, and domesticated animals.[46] And "Others" may include experiences of deities and of spirit ancestors.[47] The Congolese folktale, "How the Crocodile Lost His Case," reveals how these "others" can be personified, unified, and morally interconnected in attitudes toward such questions as blame and innocence.

In the old days, animals could speak. On the island of Mateva ("Borassus"), the people told the following history:

One day all the animals foregathered with the purpose of discussing the crisis in the animal world. They soon began to accuse one another. Some blamed the Nkanka-fua, the armadillo:

K'aka, K'aka,
sleeping in the thickest shrubs.
To which the latter replied:
I sleep in the thickest foliage,
is that a forbidden act?
Look rather at the weaverbird,
he eats the people's corn!
To which the accused retorted, in the same tune:
I eat the people's corn, I do
but only just a grain or two.
Look rather at that bird of prey,
who eats a chicken every day!
The accused harrier, replied:
I eat no chicken every day,
Perhaps a chick that went astray,
Look rather at the crocodile,
Who eats man's children all the while!
The crocodile too, defended his case by blaming another:
Perhaps I kill a man sometimes,
but only out of self-defense.
No, blame the hippopotamus,
who overturns the people's boats!
The latter had his answer ready:
If men hunt me, I sink their boat,
and if they drown, do not blame me!
I neither eat nor kill those men,
it is the crocodile who does!
The crocodile was now almost cornered:
If I eat people, blame not me,
do not accuse me lyingly!
I did not make myself like this,

no, it was God who made me so!
To this, God himself answered from Heaven:
I did create you, but for peace.
I never destined you for evil![48]

Not all African traditional stories have such morally weighty relational conclusions. In no small measure, some may center on the creative exchange of children, the world, and elders. Some stories use comforting images, humor, and irony to teach, while others evoke a feeling of moral dread. They emphasize the moral consequences of disobeying the wisdom of the elders. Consider the story of Halandi and Mayindana and "The Vindictive Fruits."

> Halandi and Mayindana, a boy and a girl, wanted to go and visit their grandmother, but their mother forbade them. She had not seen grandmother herself since they were born. So she told them: "Children, there is something terrible on the road to Grannie's: the big-head Salas! "Do they kill people?""Oh yes they do, especially children like you are killed by them."
>
> Remember that children care little about what they are told. Halandi and Mayindana did not care much, and so they just walked away from home one morning when their parents were working in the fields.
>
> Soon, they arrived in the forest and after a long time they felt hungry and thirsty. Looking up, they saw big, round, colorful fruits dangling from the lowest branches. They could just reach them with their hands. Those were the forbidden fruits, the big-head Salas. On the ground there lay a small Sala, not yet ripe. It looked so tempting that the girl persuaded her brother to break its shell so that she could suck the juice. No sooner had he done so, than all the big-head Salas dropped their branches to the ground, with their little feet extended they landed, their little arms holding spears and shields. Soon there were a dozen armed Salas who came running for the children, singing angrily:
> We Halandi! Mayindana!
> You have eaten little brother!
> You knew better, still you did it,
> Smashed his skull and drank his blood up.
> The children were surrounded, speared to death and eaten by the angry Sala fruits.[49]

Myths and folklore, along with the other oral practices such as riddles and proverbs, socially connect everyday life to human limits as well as to transcendent meanings. Among the Masai people of eastern Africa, primarily a herding culture, myths closely connect the life of herds-people and domesticated animals in such a manner that a descent story and the principle of difference explains how the Masai are distinguished from their relational other:

> In the beginning of things the Masai had no cattle. Only the Dorobo people had cattle.
>
> Naiteru-kop, a lesser god, came down one time and spoke to a Dorobo, saying, "Meet me early tomorrow morning. I have something for you."
>
> The Dorobo answered, "Very well." Then he went to his house and slept.
>
> A Masai named Le-eyo overheard the conversation. He arose during the night and went to the place where Naiteru-kop had spoken. He waited. When the day dawned he approached Naiteru-kop.
>
> Naiteru-kop said to him, "Who are you?"
>
> The Masai said, "Le eyo."
>
> Naiteru-kop asked, "Where is the Dorobo?"
>
> Le-eyo said, "I do not know."
>
> Naiteru-kop then began lowering cattle down from the sky with a leather thong. One by one he let the cattle down until there were many and the Masai told him to stop. In this way the Masai received their cattle from the demigod Naiteru-kop. The cattle wandered off, and as they did so the cattle of the Dorobo mingled with them. The Dorobo were unable to recognize which cattle were theirs and so they lost them.
>
> The Dorobo people were angry. They went to where the leather thong hung from the sky, and they shot it down with arrows. Seeing this, Naiteru-kop went away from there to a distant place.
>
> After that it was the Masai who owned all the cattle. The Dorobo had to hunt wild beast for their food.[50]

While the Masai story of descent entails the interaction of the deity, the Ronga tale of Halandi and Mayindana mentions no deities at all. Yet, the oral traditions—including stories, proverbs, riddles, and other oral practices—can be constructed in a cumulative way to establish a certain relational outlook on life. Proverbs "taken one by one, their cumulative impact may transform one's vision and life and teach a poise or stance on life that may be said to be the chief fruit of religion," says Benjamin Ray.[51] Some African traditionalists also use riddles to communicate generative social values to future generations. Consider the following Zulu riddle:

> A pumpkin plant: it is single, and has many branches; it may be hundreds; it bears many thousand pumpkins on its branches, if you follow

the branches, you will find a pumpkin everywhere. You cannot count the pumpkins of one branch; you can never die of famine; you can go plucking and eating; and you will not carry food for your journey through being afraid that you will find no food where you are going. No, you can eat and leave, knowing that by following the branches you will continually find another pumpkin in front; and so it comes to pass. Its branches spread out over the whole country, but the plant is one, from which springs many branches. And each man pursues his own branch, and all pluck pumpkins from the branches.

[The other Zulu replies]: A village and the paths which pass from it are the branches, which bear fruit; for there is no path without a village; all paths quit [at] homesteads and go to homesteads. There is no path which does not lead to a homestead. The pumpkins are villages from which the paths go out.[52]

African traditionalists use riddles, proverbs, and a variety of other oral arts to transmit moral norms, customs, and manners from the elders to future generations. In this way, the ancestors who lived long ago continue to be effective sources for revitalizing today's postcolonial Africa. For instance, the Ashanti people of what is now Ghana express this connection in their typically proverbial way: "When a child learns to wash his hands before he eats, then he dines with his elders."[53]

The stories, proverbs, and riddles elicited above are but only a few among thousands within the rich folk materials of African traditional societies. Yet in these sources of religious insight, our identities as human beings are understood within ever widening circles of relations that are integrated into an irreducible whole symbolized by the word *World*. In creative exchange, this relational understanding of religious experience renders human actions interconnected, dynamic, and fluid. It also keeps our imaginations open to determinate powers on which all our lives depend and from which all beings proceed and return. As a deep symbol, race is understood as a signification of the *sensus communis* and comes to signify forms of affection and sympathy for the community's manners, ways, customs, and social, cultural, public, and moral practices that solidify a community. And thus by way of creative exchange opens it up to wider ranges of human experience and flourishing. This is Beloved Community.

In this regard Alice Walker commends such a construal of race and the *sensus communis* in her "womanish" trope. Here, she sees the self-understanding of African American women's identities in creative exchange and Beloved Community when their identities are open to relational circles that circumscribe their self-interpretations: openness to men and women, sometimes sexually, openness to the world of sun, moon, stars, openness to the world of social responsibility and generative care, openness to the wide expansion of sight and color, openness to the opaque qualities of purple and lavender.[54] Barbara Holmes also suggests such an appreciation for creative exchange and Beloved Community when she writes:

> From our own experiences we know that reality is not a seamless whole. Multiple realities rise, recede, and eclipse on the cognitive horizons as subuniverses that we inhabit from time to time. These worlds are available to us and characterized 'by peculiar modifications of the basic categories of thought, namely, space time, and causality.' The portals to these universes are not always cognitive. Perhaps they can be entered through dance and song and story.[55]

The pragmatic relational theory of religious experience I have put forward envisions the whole world as a network of emanating life-forces and creative possibilities that in creative exchange condition limits and finitude as well as forms of transcendence. Following Long, sometimes these networks, forces, and possibilities are given religious interpretation—but they need not; they also may be understood, appreciated, and interpreted through symbols of aesthetic and moral experience where beauty and virtue may be equally illuminating of creative exchange and Beloved Community. Although she does not use the language of creative exchange, commenting on Zora Neale Hurston's great novel, *Their Eyes were Watching God*, Karen Baker-Fletcher eloquently describes the novel as a relational interpretation of the World.

> In that novel, the stormy, powerful clouds and winds of a hurricane symbolize God for the ordinary black folk of a Florida town. The power of God is experienced in nature, and it is not always comforting. Sometimes nature's beauty is fierce, its power frightening, because it reminds us that it is larger than our small bodies and the puny homes we build to shelter ourselves. At such times, one feels less ecstasy and more awe, even terror. Hurston's novel reminds us of the respect that African ancestors had for nature and of their belief that God acts in nature. She calls to remembrance elemental understandings of God as moving in wind, rain, sky, and earth.[56]

Unlike Baker-Fletcher, my pragmatic theology does not require a picture of God as doing anything in and through nature. For me, such a description requires a maximal kind of divine transcendence. Nevertheless, as a relational theological interpretation of the World (as the processes, patterns, and powers that maximize the concrete actuality and ideal potentiality of human good in creative exchange), Baker-Fletcher's interpretation is powerfully expressive of the religious imagination turned toward lived human experience. Her account approaches the pragmatic understanding of religious experience as a felt quality of the world, its limits and possibilities, or the sense of finitude and transcendence in creative exchange:

> While Emerson's essay *Nature* emphasizes what I would call nature's awesome side, we humans are also confronted with nature's awful side. Nature affects us with these two experiences of awe: the first form of awe is often euphoric while the second form can be terrifying. Both forms of awe lead to questions about God and theodicy—the problem of evil and why God allows it. Is God in the hurricane, the tornado, the earthquake? Or is that just nature living on its own life, doing what it must do to exist, to live, to express the fullness of its life-force? Is God in nature or not? Perhaps God is in nature, but nature is not God. Nature reveals God, because God is present in all that lives, in all that is. But God is larger than any part of Creation as the power of creativity itself, the life force of life in and beyond all others.[57]

Baker-Fletcher's account of religious experience connects well with the principle of enlargement that I discussed the introduction. That is, all experiences enlarge our understanding of the World and our place in the World. Both limits and transcendence contribute to an enlargement—cognitive, aesthetic, and moral—of our understandings of the World beyond finite particular moments of actuality and possibilities. Insofar as race contributes to such religious significations of enlargement, it contributes powerfully toward a pragmatic theology of African American religious experience. As a deep symbol, race may signify a relational moral attitude toward the world and human life beyond one's preoccupation with his/her own group. Among all the particulars that encompass the lives of African and African American peoples, race entails circles of relations. And when the symbol is reconstituted under the *sensus communis*, it signifies sympathetic filiations between families, villages, provinces, cultures, and by greater enlargement, humanity.

In creative exchange, a pragmatic theology of African American religious experience then connects these relations and affiliations to powers qualitatively felt as transcendent in experience or to communities of others—ancestors and saints long absent from us and those recently departed. It sees connections between people's social lives and their valuations of power in the land and sea, in the beloved country, in the diaspora, in sacred trees and haunts, sun, moon, stars, plants, and animals with whom we share the earth and those whose lives are contingent on our own. The relational vision of religious meaning that I am commending will not settle with racial descriptions based on any dichotomy between thought and life, ideas and action, and meaning and art. Rather, it reflexively relates a community's understanding of art, music, dance, stories, proverbs, myth, being, life, morality, aesthetics, and social identity. It seeks to integrate these relations into a unity of meaning and value that, in creative exchange, takes hold of our experiencing of limits and openness and of finitude and transcendence.

CONCLUSION

I am not altogether sure that the autobiographical itch that led me to such a relational vision of understanding and appreciating the deep symbol of race based on creative exchange and *sensus communis* settles the unresolved ambiguities that the symbol holds for me. As an academic reflecting on the grotesqueries or ambiguities of race, I am content to play, to dance, within the ambiguities of the symbol. Sorting through the layers of disagreements that exist within black philosophy and black theology, I am aware that the disagreements are themselves inferred from the differences of social and cultural locations. I am also aware that even the most rigorous attention to our social locations does not provide us with any unambiguous agreement on the meaning of race. Still, I think that the relational perspective of religious experience developed in this chapter is useful to African American thinkers who want to transcend classical Western metaphysics based on abstract universality, hierarchy, domination, and dichotomies. This is not to say that the relational insights of African and African American thinkers should be thought of as forming any radical discontinuities between the formal cognitive standards of reasonableness that have governed Western thought.

Nevertheless, the racial and ethnic symbols that we evoke to identify ourselves, all of our deep symbols, are fallible, relative, contingent, duplicitous, and vulnerable to social change. On Farley's description of deep symbols, none is absolute. This does not mean that we can simply do without them. So we ought to find better ways of deploying these kinds of symbols. In light of its ambiguous and relative quality, race might be best grasped as a deep symbol in African American religious experience. However, it is at best a grotesque symbol. The hermeneutical task is to track its irreducible significations. This will involve both African American religious thinkers in creative exchange on the meaning, value, distortions, and cultural effects of race on our everyday lives and religious experience.

In the following chapter, I extend this relational concept of race in African American religious thought to critique the ways that some contemporary African American theologians use slave narratives to form spiritual, theological, and moral solidarity under a grand existential narrative of black religious identity and experience. In their attempts to reconcile the moral and spiritual wisdom of slave ancestors with our contemporary context, characterized by great social differentiation, near nihilism, indifference, and moral decay among African Americans, they also risk totalizing the worlds of difference that make the slave narratives themselves open to ever-increasing enlargements of meaning and significance by rendering their spiritual insights a protoblack theology of liberation.

CHAPTER 2

We See Through a Glass Darkly

Slave Narrative Theology and the Opacity
of African American Religious Thought

> For now we see through a mirror, dimly, but then we will see face
> to face. Now I know only in part; then I will know fully, even as I
> have been fully known. (1 Cor 13:12)

A FEW YEARS AGO AT THE American Academy of Religion meetings in
New Orleans a robust discussion occurred in the Black Theology Group,
focused on research methods in black theology. First, Anthony B. Pinn presented on the methodology he was using to develop a comparative basis for
"doing" black religion, focused on religions of African diaspora societies
—Santeria and Voudon and Black Islam and the black church in North
America—a method he would subsequently call "theological archeology" in
his 1998 book, *Varieties of African American Religious Experience*. Next, Linda
E. Thomas spoke about her use of ethnographic cultural studies to examine
the religious lives and spirituality of African women in African indigenous
churches. Her findings were published under the title, *Under the Canopy*
(1999).

Will Coleman was to speak next on his linguistic hermeneutics for the
study of orality in slave religion and slave narratives, which framed his book
Tribal Talk (2000); however, Coleman changed his topic in light of the sud-
den and tragic death of rap artist Tupac Shakur on September 13, 1996.
Coleman's eulogy for Shakur was prophetic and culturally sensitive to a

growing black youth culture, alienated from the black church and the black theological academy, as he called for the black theological academy to attend to the social misery, frustrations, and alienation of black youth as expressed in hip-hop culture. Coleman struck a chord with the crowd, mostly advocates of black liberation theology and womanist theology struggling with how to connect their theological discourse to black popular culture. I thought this would be the perfect context to begin serious discussion on the limitations of black liberation hermeneutics for contemporary black hip-hop culture in particular and black popular culture in general. As I raised methodological concerns Coleman's speech occasioned for me, I was quickly shut down. To some, my interest in method distracted from the existential crisis of our black youths that Coleman's presentation evoked. Since that time, I remain convinced that those black liberation theologians who ignore the methodological questions of liberation hermeneutics—or take them for granted—will continue to wrestle with how to make their ideological interests relevant to a black society and culture far alienated from those concerns.

In this chapter, I focus on two paths in theological method in contemporary African American theology for understanding African American religious experience. The one path is ideological and the other is genealogical. The ideological path enters into the slave narratives having already a clearly articulated agenda that is thematized by tenets or logia of black liberation theology. Black sources of religious insight are retrieved as a depth grammar for understanding and legitimating claims of historical continuity in black experience with the interests of black theology. In slave narratives, as well as in other sources such as songs, spirituals, and prayers, is found a protoblack theology. I give primary attention to a research project proposed in a collection of essays entitled *Cut Loose Your Stammering Tongue: Black Theology in the Slave Narratives* (1991, first edition; 2003, second edition; hereafter cited respectively as *CLST1* and *CLST2*).[1] Sometimes this path is called the Slave Narrative Theology Project. All of those who contributed to the development of this program have gone on to write substantial books based on the nascent ideas expressed in this book while maintaining a unity of agreement among themselves that has not changed substantially since its publication.

My reading of this research program isolates two concerns that I first presented in *Beyond Ontological Blackness;* namely, the black liberation theologian's alienated consciousness and a hermeneutics of narrative return. The first concern examines the slave narrative program in relation to the apparent alienation of the black theological academy from much of contemporary black cultural life. The second looks at the ways that black theologians return to historical black materials for grounding their contemporary constructive theologies. In my critique of this program, I focus on several ambiguities in the slave narrative research program that I think test its persuasiveness.

In the last part of this chapter, I propose an alternative, genealogical path for dealing with black sources of religious insight that I think is formative for a pragmatic theology of African American religious experience. The path is one of deconstruction or, better, a genealogical approach that is dependent on the phenomenological hermeneutics of Charles H. Long. This path accents the opacity of religious insight into the study of black religion and black sources of religious insight. I use Long's talk of "opaque theologies" to substantiate the grotesque ambiguity of black sources in theological method. By accenting their opacity, these sources remain resistant to being thematized into a black theology of liberation in which struggle, survival, and resistance have conjurational force to elicit meaning within black sources of religious insight. Alistair Kee refers to this force as the four mantras[2] in which: (1) the exodus most discloses God's relation to blacks; (2) Luke 4:18 establishes the mission of God (*missio dei*) as the liberation of the poor; (3) black Christian authenticity is confrontational, addressing oppression of race, gender, and class; and (4) racism is the most determinate factor of oppression among blacks. My argument is that the opacity and grotesqueries of these sources keep them ever irreducibly open in African American religious experience as a plentitude of being, meaning, and significance.

BLACK LIBERATION THEOLOGY
AND ALIENATED CONSCIOUSNESS

To a great extent, there has been little discussion or debate on theological method over the last thirty years in black liberation theology, the question of method having been subsumed under the problem of black sources for black liberation theology. Besides considerable glosses on James H. Cone's critical hermeneutics, particularly by black feminist and womanist theologians, the liberation hermeneutics he centralized has remained quite stable throughout subsequent stages of African American theology.[3] In *God of the Oppressed*, Cone rightly questions the adequacy of traditional European and Western theological methods for interpreting black religious faith. He says:

> I respect what happened at Nicea and Chalcedon and the theological input of the Church Fathers on Christology; but that source alone is inadequate for finding out the meaning of black folks' Jesus. It is all right to say as did Athanasius that the Son is *homoousia* (one substance with the Father), especially if one has a taste for Greek philosophy and a feel for the importance of intellectual distinctions. And I do

not want to minimize or detract from the significance of Athanasius' assertion for faith one iota. But the *homoousia* question is not a black question. Blacks do not ask whether Jesus is one with the Father or divine and human. . . . They ask whether Jesus is walking with them, whether they can call him up on the "telephone of prayer" and tell him all about their troubles. . . . [W]e must not forget that Athanasius' question about the Son's status in relation to the father did not arise in the historical context of the slave codes and the slave drivers. And if he had been a black slave in America, I am sure he would have asked a different set of questions.[4]

Cone's turn to the hermeneutical method of Juan Gusto Segundo and away from the crisis theology of Karl Barth made way for research programs in black religion that take black sources themselves—whether black church history, literature, or popular culture—as contributing to a fundamental canon for black theological interpretations of and religious reflections on black experience. The impact of Cone's critique of Western theological methods extended to the very meaning of history, narrative, religious identity, and moral consciousness in black religion. His was an ideological critique of the legitimation of structures of white supremacy, including race, class, and theology. Therefore, from the beginning of the black liberation theology program, history and narrative problematically burdened black constructive theology.

During the late 1980s, a group of African American scholars, particularly Dwight N. Hopkins, George Cummings, and Will Coleman, met continually to discuss the future of black liberation theology in their Black Theology Forum.[5] They exchanged papers and engaged in an exploration of slave narratives as a source for contemporary black liberation theology. Behind their explorations lay a set of problems that had plagued Cone's original formulation of theological method in black theology, centered on the strained and often alienated relation of academic black theology to the black churches and black culture. Black church theologians questioned whether black theology could be a theology of the black churches if it disentangled itself from the creeds, confessions, and liturgical practices of the traditional churches. Others asked in what sense black theology could be black if its theological method is derived from white, European theologians such as Karl Barth and Paul Tillich and philosophers such as Albert Camus and Jean-Paul Sartre. Still others who embraced the ideology of black power and associated Christianity with white oppression wondered how black theology could be relevant to a culture of black radicalism and revolution and remain theologically and morally Christian.[6]

In the preface to the 1997 edition of *God of the Oppressed*, Cone reflects on the history of criticism of black liberation theology:

> Black theologians challenged me from both a different and similar angle. Some questioned whether I had focused too little on the African Origin of black religion and too much on the white theology I learned in graduate school. They claimed that my black theology was not *black* enough, that is, not attentive to the "otherness" of black religion, particularly as revealed in non-Christian sources. . . . Other African-American scholars felt that the politics of black liberation needed to be balanced with an equal accent on black-white reconciliation. In addition, they saw my theological ethics as arbitrary and not sensitive to rational debate and responsible conclusions. This black critique reminded me of similar criticisms by white theologians. . . . Another critique of black theology sought to undermine its central claim: If God is liberating blacks from oppression, why then are they still oppressed? Where is the decisive liberation event in African-American history, which gives credibility to black theologians' claim?[7]

Cone addressed many of these questions in books such as *The Spirituals and the Blues* and *Speaking the Truth*.[8] But the historical problem of alienated consciousness still remains because of his call for a radical departure of black liberation theology from white religious sources. If black theology follows such a call, then the black theologian has a difficult time showing how black theology is the theology of the black churches, and the black liberation theologian is likely to remain an alienated theologian. If the theologian gives up his or her radical claims to black exceptionalism, then the claims that he or she wants to make for the epistemic privilege of blackness and black experience in black theological method are likely to be undercut, losing their countercritical bite. As Cone attempted to overcome this methodological dilemma, he emphasized the commensurability of black sources for the construction of black Christian liberation theology, turning particularly to the spirituals and the blues. Still, problems remained. On the one hand, the spirituals and blues have proved difficult sources from which to disclose the normal, routine, religious beliefs of African American peoples and to render them regulative theological and moral judgments. To many, the spirituals appear too otherworldly to be of much use for the purposes of black liberation theology and its claims for black radicalism, protest, and resistance.[9] On the other hand, black churches have regarded the blues as degenerative, secular, and misogynistic expressions of black hopelessness.

Decades after the beginning of his research program, as he assessed the history of black liberation theology at a conference at Vanderbilt Divinity

School on "What does it mean to be black and Christian?" Cone said that if such theology failed to connect the academic black theologian and the black churches, the failure belonged to the churches as much as the theologians. He exclaimed that the black churches continue to be governed by the creeds and confessions of white, European religious authorities and not by the indigenous sources of black life:

> Black people separated themselves in the nineteenth century from White denominations because they could not reconcile racism, slavery, and segregation with the Christian gospel. When Blacks left those White denominations, they took with them their statements of faith. They took their creeds with them, because they thought the creeds were okay. Most still have them. Why do we still have statements of faith of slave masters? It was not until the 1960s, with the emergence of Black Theology, that the Black Church felt the need to develop a self-identified Black Theology. Why did it take nearly 200 years for that? How do the Black churches explain that they still have not really devoted themselves to an understanding of the faith that they preach every Sunday? If they did, then, they would not need outside funding agencies to bring them together in order to dialogue on the meaning of our vocation in the ministry.[10]

In other words, after three decades, black liberation theology remains alien to the regular life and practices of the black churches in particular and to much of black culture in general. This alienation is what has provoked some black theologians to turn to the slave narratives.

A primary context of this alienation is the class differentiation of black theologians from others in the community. Socially, we African American theologians belong to an elite class of educated intellectuals who often exhibit bourgeois tendencies that alienate us from the underclass strata of life both in the churches and in black culture. Black liberation theologians, committed to liberation and radical ideology as regulative ideals of black Christianity, are often alienated from the churches for whom they desire to speak but whose piety is characteristically evangelical, reformist, and liberal in disposition, doctrine, and politics. Such churches are not likely to be moved by the revisionist agenda that defines the constructive theological content of much of black liberation theology. Black theologians are also alienated by class from the strata of black society, namely, the poor urban underclass, whose voices they want to evoke and whose desperation they now raise as the new rallying call for the advancement of black liberation and the mobilization of the prophetic witness of the black theological academy.

The shift from race-determined discourse to class is generational. In the early formulation of the black theology of liberation, the radical, ideological, revolutionary interests of liberation centered on the oppressive structures of United States and South African legislative discrimination and poverty that were justified by a history of racist public policy. Now black theologians are defending the cogency of their project and its justification by race in a climate of greater class differentiation among blacks themselves than was experienced in the 1960s and 1970s. From my point of view, it is quite clear that race and racism galvanized black liberation theology in the late 1960s and 1970s. Ideologically, it proved a powerful site for amalgamating the disperse interests of African American theologians around a radical, revolutionary liberation rhetoric. It forged widespread agreement among both theologians and church persons on the meaning of God, the social, political, and economic liberator of the poor; Jesus, the one who walks with the poor and disinherited in their situation; and the church, the mediating prophetic, spiritual, and political institution of social justice.

However, now it is not clear whether racial discourse can garner such agreement among the theologians. What is evident is that the fragility of black liberation theology in the United States is being tested by forms of social differentiation, including class, gender and sexual differentiations, which are ideologically irreducible to the racial dialectic of white over black. Rather, these forms of differentiations cut across the various levels of the black community itself. They raise the question of whether the black community may not be facing an incommensurability of values and interests among the various constituents whose differences now substantively define "the black community" and "black experience." Black life in the United States is differentiated by the wealthy, entrepreneurial, celebrity, and professional classes, middle- and lower-class white-collar and blue-collar workers, a desperate urban underclass constituted by the homeless, an undereducated and underemployed class of black youths, and a rising society of incarcerated young black males.

In identity politics, little agreement exists on the black community's valuations on interracial marriage, adoptions, sexual behaviors, and sexual identities, especially in light of the recent "Not on My Watch Rally" in Arlington, Texas, and the Atlanta "Reigniting the Legacy March" that was led by the Bishop Eddie Long and Bernice King.[11] These contemporary challenges to sexual difference in black communities pose a critical question to black theologians—namely, whether from their internal resources they can speak univocally for and to the forms of difference that define the black community and whether the ideology of black theology and the constructive theologies that emerge from it, including womanist theology and slave narrative theology, can adequately express the "real interests" of the black community today.

I am appreciative of the work of contemporary black liberation theologians who have addressed many of these concerns. For instance, in his systematic theology, James H. Evans proposes that the academic theologian's alienation from the religious life of black people can be transcended when "black theology is rooted in the faith of the church and the faith of the church is given intellectual clarity and expression in black theology."[12] Evans answers the alienation problem in a hermeneutical return to a common black narrative —that of African chattel slavery—which discloses values, commitments, teachings, and a wisdom that sustained blacks under such unprecedented experiences. Evans also contends that this wisdom can be brought forward into the present to challenge a black culture that is now struggling with the push and pull of a secular, materialistic, hedonistic, narcissistic, and pessimistic culture.[13] For Evans, then, the return of black theologians to slave narrative sources is sparked by the need to ground contemporary black culture in a morally nurturing mythos.

Dwight Hopkins proposes in books such as *Shoes That Fit Our Feet* (1993) and *Down, Up, and Over: Slave Religion and Black Theology* (2000) that the forms of alienation separating black liberation theologians from the black churches and much of black culture can be challenged effectively by a hermeneutical return to distinctive black sources as the basis for contemporary black theology. The hermeneutics of narrative return connects contemporary black life to a historical life of creative resistance and communal focus. Such a narrative can minimize what Hopkins sees as a rabid individualism plaguing much of black culture. From his study of former slaves' creative encounters with and resistance to their chattel-based economy, he says that "the forces of the capitalist market are replaced by viewing and interacting with people, first as people endowed by liberation within. Satisfying communal needs replaces the quest for individual profit."[14]

Cheryl Sanders's study of the slave narratives has had a sustained contemporary relevance for moral responsibility, from her 1985 dissertation to her more recent books. In *Slavery and Conversion: An Analysis of Ex-Slave Testimony*, Sanders finds that "the religious testimony of the former slaves provides an extraordinary context for exploring commitment and social responsibility."[15] Her initial study of ex-slave conversion testimonies culminated in her own theological ethics, *Empowerment Ethics for a Liberated People*. With this text, Sanders had come to understand that "it takes the testimony of the ex-slave to illustrate the meaning of the gospel of freedom in its most dramatic proportion."[16] Moreover, she proposes that the gospel of freedom embraced by the ex-slave can be transformative even for our contemporary social context.

Will Coleman's study of the symbolic-poetic universe of discourse created from African American slaves' embodied situatedness as nonhumans to their embodied creativity under slavery crystallizes the collective agreement among the original collaborators of *CLST.* Coleman says: "To place ourselves in front of slave narratives is to become exposed to their symbolic-poetic world. To appropriate this reality is to engage our imagination in the most characteristic existential possibility, the revelation of a possible world and the advancement toward a new way of being in this world."[17] *CLST* sees in the slave narratives rich moral sources for providing meaning and purpose in our contemporary black life in which the tendency toward nihilism threatens the vitality of much of black life today, and in which individualism threatens the communal logic of African American spirituality.

An internal logic pervades each of the essays constituting a slave narrative theology. Each contributor sees these sources as a moral and spiritual well from which to challenge our contemporary black culture with a collective wisdom and spirituality that may keep black culture itself open to its legacy of struggle, survival, resistance, and liberation. Three essays by Joan Martin, David Emmanuel Goatley, and M. Shawn Copeland added to *CLST2* on the efficacy of the slave narratives for grounding meaning and value in contemporary black culture also display such agreement. Consider Martin's estimation of the work ethic disclosed in her analysis of slave narratives. She says that "in relation to exploitation, work was evil and caused suffering. In relation to resistance for self, family, and community in the midst of oppression, work was a source of faithful, moral living. Work was, in this way, about living and resisting the consequences of evil."[18] And in *Tribal Talk*, Coleman reiterates the meaning and value of the slave narratives' theology for their contemporary spiritual and moral force most substantially, saying that: "Tribal Talk is committed to the future. It is a way of doing theology within a post–Christian, pluralistic, and postmodern reality. It not only looks toward the past to learn from its ancestors and elders, but also gazes into the future to seek out its children."

SLAVE NARRATIVES AS A SOURCE OF BLACK AND WOMANIST THEOLOGY

Slave narrative theology is an ambitious "ideological" program. Notwithstanding the many questions surrounding the collection of the narratives themselves,[19] there is a consensus among contributors that the wealth of folk materials contained in the slave narratives ought to have an authoritative function in the development of contemporary black liberation theologies, including womanist theology. At least, their task is to make a case for their canonical standing. On this point, Cummings writes:

> . . . the slave narratives are a legitimate source of the experiences of black oppressed people in the USA, as well as of the theological inter-pretations of their experiences of enslavement. Concomitantly, the slave narratives provide a means to return to the religious genius of the ancestors, who were forcibly taken from Africa and made to serve in the brutal crucible of chattel slavery. The narratives provide us with insight concerning the religious and cultural world-views that informed black slaves' theological interpretation of the experience and can be the basis upon which contemporary black theologians can incorporate the "thematic universe" of the black oppressed into their discourse.[20]

As Cummings sees it, the slave narratives open contemporary black theol-ogy to the ancestors' "past genius." They offer contemporary black theolo-gians religious insight into the dynamics of theological interpretation done by black slaves, and they provide contemporary black theologians with *a basic conceptual scheme* for framing black theology today. Hopkins concurs with Cummings, suggesting that the lessons slaves inferred from their experience cognitively protected them from "fall[ing] prey to a white capitalist theo-logical precept that glorifies individualism and private-property democracy." Hopkins then challenges contemporary black theologians "to promote indi-viduality and communalism, not individualism and selfish motivation."[21]

Among the collaborators of the slave narrative theology program, their hermeneutics of narrative signals a return of black theology to indigenous historical and narrative sources for religious insight and moral guidance. For them, the slave narratives evoke a great cloud of witnesses whose heroic leg-acy of survival, resistance, and hope mediates the fragility of African Ameri-can life today and binds together our present generation so much in need of a heroic black faith. Consider Hopkins:

> Since the two foundational arrivals of 1619 and 1620—markers of Protestantism and American Culture—and conceptualized by the sunup to sundown period of the slave master's religious strictures, enslaved African Americans used the space and time from sundown to sunup to constitute themselves with divine intent into a liberated racial religious formation. They hoped for and pursued a liberated humanity. They forged themselves as a new African American people

of faith embodied in an everyday practical knowledge anchored in their existential encounter with the Spirit of freedom and in their own hermeneutical reading of the biblical texts. In a word, the liberating Spirit met them and worked with them both in material experience and in textual deciphering. Yet this dynamic formation was not only a practical reconfiguration at the level of religious experience. It was also the crafting and deployment of faith—a quasi-theology from the oppressed African American perspective. From this religious occurrence and emerging, fragmenting faith statements, we can be informed in the construction of a black theology of liberation. Specifically we can learn from enslaved African American racial religious formation and biblical insights to seek the development of doctrinal statements on God, Jesus, and human purpose.[22]

Each *CLST* theologian regards the slave narratives as authentic historical representations of slave religion as it developed in the "invisible institution" of the antebellum South. According to Coleman, the invisible institution of slave religion was antecedent to the development of the independent African American churches.[23] From this premise, he then critically sets slave religion in relation to the black churches in such a way that the former, the invisible institution, "was not so much an organization as it was an organic syncretism that enabled slaves to combine their Afrocentric religious beliefs with the Eurocentric ones of their masters. The consequence of this merger was their unique form of African American Christianity."[24]

The *CLST* contributors hold that the ex-slave narratives authentically represent religious beliefs and moral practices constitutive of slave religion as it was practiced in the invisible institution. They also argue that the slave narratives exhibit a religious unity that is subject to theological formulation and moral inferences. Substantively, Hopkins has made the most of these possibilities in his books *Shoes That Fit Our Feet* and *Down, Up, and Over*. He argues:

> Enslaved Africans realized that God had created them originally with a free soul, heart, and mind. Yet white American Christians had re-created them in the demonic image of a distorted Christianity. Hence, for the slave, the purpose of humanity was to show fully the spark of God's created equality implanted deep within black breasts. To return to original creation, then, African American slaves pursued a resistance of politics and a culture of resistance.[25]

Hopkins's constructive task is to draw appropriate theological and moral inferences from the religious stories of African American slaves. He highlights Jesus—the mediator of God's agapic love, friend and mother, king and priest, provider of hope to the oppressed, and the one who directs the slave's path toward freedom and justice. Hopkins says that this narrative should challenge "the so-called secular black community representatives to dig within and rely on the same African American freedom impulse."[26] While Hopkins accentuates God, humanity, and Jesus, Cummings maps the religious utterances of the ex-slaves under the theology of the Spirit and eschatology.

While not based on slave narratives but the spirituals tradition, Goatley also discovers a basic logic running through these materials and others, such as folk songs, work songs, and blues, which is complimentary to the narrative retrievals among the other *CLST* collaborators as he tracks the concept of Godforsakenness in the spirituals. For Goatley, "Songs of communities are a vast reservoir of potentiality for theological reflection, discourse, and construction. Songs contain and convey critical theological concepts of various cultures, which is particularly true for the present study. The songs born out of experiences of antebellum and postbellum African Americans are rich sources of religious questions, convictions and insight."[27] What Goatley mines from these materials is a basic theological thread that identifies the sufferings of the enslaved and free with the suffering of Jesus and recognizes the suffering God in their sufferings (patripassionism). The result is a black theology of identity in which the preferential option for the poor and oppressed is established in their identification with the suffering God.

> The theology of antebellum African Americans has implications for the question of whether God suffered with Jesus and consequently whether God suffers with God's creatures who endure the inhumanity of humanity. Three essential elements present in this theological construction are: (1) God is both transcendent and immanent; (2) God is present in the midst of the existential experience of absence encountered by suffering humanity; and (3) there is no evidence that antebellum African Americans made an ontological distinction between God as Father and Jesus Christ as God's beloved Son. This theological conception includes the implication that as Jesus suffered in his death and as humans go through the extremities of human suffering, God suffers with God's creation. In contemporary theology, the concept of Godforsakenness is generally represented by three models: (1) Jesus was forsaken, and God did not suffer; (2) Jesus was forsaken, but God did not suffer; and (3) Jesus was forsaken, and God did suffer. Antebellum African American theology agrees with the third model.[28]

M. Shawn Copeland discovers in the slave narratives the roots of a womanist theology of suffering. "A womanist theology of suffering is rooted in and draws on black women's accounts of pain and anguish, of their individual and collective struggle to grasp and manage, rather than be managed by their suffering," says Copeland.[29] Derivative from these narratives, Copeland discovers basic resources of resistance, the power of their living witness, worship, memory, and language, which are then correlated with basic elements of a womanist theology of suffering. The resources of the enslaved women's confessions or living witness of divine grace, which turned their victimization into Christian triumph and their biblical faith that mediated their pain as they sang spirituals, are correlated with the first element in womanist theology that "seeks, on behalf of the African American community whose lives and struggles it honors and serves, to understand and clarify the meaning of the liberating Word and deed of God in Jesus of Nazareth for all women and men who strive against" evil and suffering.[30] This living witness was displayed in the forms of worship in which, as Copeland puts it, "the enslaved African sang because they saw the result of the cross—triumph over the principalities and powers of death, triumph over evil in this world."[31]

In their liturgical expressions, enslaved women contributed to a second element of womanist theology of resistance the power to "repel every tendency toward any *ersatz* spiritualization of evil and suffering, of pain and oppression," forming a second basic element of womanist spirituality.[32] The resource of memory provided the enslaved women with the power of "'naming, placing, and signifying' and thus the recovery, the reconstitution of identity, culture, and self. Memory then was an essential source of resistance."[33] This power of memory is correlated with a third basic element in womanist theology that remembers and retells the lives and sufferings of those who "came through" and those who have "gone on to glory land." It "honors the sufferings of the ancestors, known and unknown, victims of chattel slavery and its living legacy."[34]

And with the powerful resource of language, "enslaved black women used sass to guard, regain, and secure self-esteem; to obtain and hold psychological distance; to speak truth; to challenge 'the atmosphere of moral ambiguity that surrounds them' and sometimes to protect against sexual assault."[35] This powerful resource of resistance is correlated with a fourth element in a womanist theology of resistance in which "motherwit, courage, sometimes their fists, and most often sass, black women resisted the degradation of chattel slavery. Sass gave black women a weapon of self-defense."[36] Copeland says further that "in their resistance, black women's suffering redefined caricatured Christian virtues" in which forbearance, long-suffering, patience, love, hope, and faith cannot be the ideological tools of white supremacy in the oppression of black women.[37] Indeed, a theology of resistance takes the master's tools and revaluates them.[38]

For Copeland, then, the slave narratives of enslaved women yield resources for the "basic elements" of a contemporary womanist theology of suffering that "grows in the dark soil of the African American religious tradition and is intimate with the root paradigms of African American culture, in general, and African American women's culture, in particular."[39] With Coleman this African American cultural value system (or as Copeland puts it, "root paradigms") constitutes a symbolic universe through which the slaves created their own black existence, religion, and reality through the power of their interpretations, symbols, and metaphors. "Historically, the oral tradition of African American slaves placed a high value upon the power of speech. It was evocative, driving internal mental, emotional, and spiritual experiences into the exterior reality of the African American slave," says Coleman.[40] In other words, through their speech-acts, slaves created a social ontology of religious significance, "reality making" of their subjective experience.

Finally, Sanders explores the ethical aspects of the ex-slaves' religious utterances. According to her, "the ex-slave interviews provide day-to-day moral data that can be used to analyze the ethical perspectives of the ex-slaves. Many of them testified of the experience of conversion, understood here as a conscious moral change from wrong to right, involving reorientation of the self from complacency or error to a state of right religious knowledge and action."[41] Sanders applies an interpretative structure on the narratives, which she believes elicits from them some description of the concrete situation of the slaves, their loyalties, norms of moral reasoning, and their religious beliefs concerning God, humanity, and human destiny.[42] Her essay shows the divergent ways that ex-slaves remembered their situation: Their attitudes ranged from nostalgia to abomination. But according to Sanders, all of their moral estimations of slavery were based on the criterion of humane treatment.[43] Their loyalties—either to their ex-masters, whites, or to others—were grounded on their own judgments of whom they regarded to be "good Christians" or exhibited Christian virtues.[44] And the norms of their moral reflection were shaped by their reliance on the authority of their Christian faith in God's divine command, their good sense to apply rules and principles of sound moral reasoning, their capacities to define and pursue their own desires, and their sense of the fitting in the situation at hand.[45]

Sanders also shows theologically how divergently the ex-slaves interpreted their recollection of emancipation. What they all had in common, she says, was the presumption that freedom was central to their overall interpretation of religion. And the primary inference that she draws from her analysis of the ex-slave narratives is that "if there is any social ethic at all among the ex-slave converts, it is indeed an ethic of liberation and not

one of submission to the institution of slavery or to the bondage of oppressive religious beliefs and ideas.[46] In *Empowerment Ethics*, Sanders reiterates
the claims of her initial studies of ex-slave narratives.[47] However, her aim
is to press more strongly than she does in *CLST* the ways that the ex-slave
narratives function as testimony to the present generation of black Christians. For these ex-slaves, it was "Christian Religion" that was central to
their liberation ethics and played a determinant role in forming the moral
consciousness of African American slaves of previous generations. The moral
wisdom that she attempts to bring forward into the present from these testimonies is that "the religious testimony of the former slaves should be read
as a graphic illustration of the most critical hermeneutical challenge facing
Bible-believing Christians, namely, the struggle to be faithful to God's call to
freedom and justice in the midst of a society that offers attractive compro-
mises with the evils of oppression."[48]

To be sure, *CLST* collaborators acknowledge that there exists an inherent diversity of approaches and organization of the materials constituting
the slave narratives. Nevertheless, each author also sees a thematic unity in
the ex-slave's religious utterances. These utterances substantively express the
definitive, exceptional, and liberation faith of African slaves in the United
States. According to Hopkins, black slaves maintained faith in a "God [who]
ruled with unquestioned omnipotence and realized release from total cap-
tivity. And Jesus assumed an intimate and kingly relationship with the poor
black chattel."[49] Hopkins continues: "Slaves emphasized both the suffering
humanity of Jesus as well as Jesus's warrior ability to set the downtrodden
free. Moreover, the slaves distinguished their humanity from the white slave
master. For blacks, God and Jesus called them to use all means possible to
pursue religiously a human status of equality."[50] Throughout their essays in
CLST, each theologian rehearses a similar configuration of themes, including the black slaves' rejection of sacred and secular spaces, their rejecting oth-
erworldliness while affirming the intercession of spirits and Spirit possession,
and their privileging community over individualism.

I think it is fair to say that for the collaborators of *CLST*, the slave narratives
represent and express the African American cultural world that slave religion
created. In slave culture, the slaves' "dogged and creative strength fashioned
a new black collective self behind the closed doors in the slave quarters or
deep in the woods late at night. Here slaves developed a culture of survival
that included all the dimensions of a thriving but enchained community."[51]
Slave religion gave rise to and fulfillment of the new black consciousness
in black religious history. It formed "a collective African American being, a
new people in the hell of slavery, the most common bond among all who

suffered as chattel was slave religion," says Hopkins.[52] For the members of this theological program, the slave narratives are underexplored and undermined sources for a distinctive, common spring on which the nurturing of black and womanist theologies may depend for their vitality, their substantive unity with the historic black faith, and their moral wisdom. Slave narrative theology is an ideological approach to the use of black religious sources. In its hermeneutics of narrative return, the alienation of black theology from traditional black Christian faith is overcome by a "traditioning" of slave religion and its moral consciousness that admits the ex-slave narratives into an authoritative canon for constructive black and womanist theology.[53]

As a critic, I am not interested in engaging in an interminable debate over such matters as Africanisms and retentions in African American religion. On this issue, I find Coleman's account quite persuasive.[54] However, I am more interested philosophically in the kinds of inferences that black constructive theologians draw from such arguments than in establishing the facticity of such phenomena. Here I will confine myself to what I call "the problem of equivocation" that runs throughout the slave narrative theology program. Simply put, it is my perception that in their forced pairing of the religious utterances of the enslaved and free—that is, the ex-slave's talk of freedom, human dignity, justice, and redemption—with the typifying utterances of black liberation theology—black radicalism, struggle, protest, survival, resistance, and hope—these theologians are engaging in an act of ideological equivocation.

In other words, what I take to be the *lived theology*—that is, the everyday and ordinary piety—of these ex-slaves, expressed in mostly Christian, evangelical, and abolitionist categories in their narratives, these theologians transform into instances of black liberation motifs from slave religion to the present. Here, ex-slaves' talk of freedom is equivocated as identical with the ideology of black liberation theology. The effect is that it is not so much black theology of liberation that is in need of justifying itself to the black churches, which are typically evangelical in faith, liberal in politics, and reformist in social action. Rather, the black churches have to assess their social and theological practices in light of a prior yet contiguous history of radicalism and subversion, struggle and resistance, suffering and hope displayed in the liberational forces of slave religion.

The slave narrative theology movement seems not only to identify nineteenth-century black evangelicalism with black liberation theology, it also appears to collapse slave religion (antebellum) into the ex-slave narratives (postbellum) the *CLST* collaborators are mostly using. For these collaborators, the ex-slave narratives authentically "re-present" slave religion. It may be the case that the narratives represent the religious understandings of late nineteenth-century and early twentieth-century ex-slaves. But what these ex-slave narratives disclose theologically, morally, and culturally about slave religion is a point not of ideological but of historical contention.

The narratives with which these theologians are working were collected by Federal Writers' Project of the Works Progress Administration (WPA) in the 1930s. The utterances of these ex-slaves not only display the spirituality and piety of an evangelical, conversionist theology but also represent abolitionist redactions within the formation of institutional black churches in the post–Civil War period. The *CLST* case for black theological and moral exceptionalism (as displayed by the narratives) depends on whether the ex-slaves interviewed are reflecting the antebellum conditions of slave religion as it was practiced in the invisible institution in distinction from the post-bellum redactions that abound throughout the narratives. Therefore, the question is, What can the historically specific evangelical theology and piety among the ex-slaves interviewed tell us about the religious beliefs and worship practices of antebellum slave plantation communities?

John W. Blassingame gives a wide range of factors coloring the WPA materials, which should give theologians at least considerable pause in drawing almost exclusively on these materials for a slave narrative theology. At least three kinds of problems ought to be considered. The first concern is the collecting of the materials themselves, where Blassingame says the historian's tools were not applied to the method of interviews and recording of oral lore. This raises a major sociological issue, namely, "whether the interview situation was conducive to the accurate communication and recording of what the informants remembered about slavery." Here, Blassingame reminds us that with few exceptions (in Virginia, Louisiana, and Florida), the WPA staff was exclusively white. "Discrimination in employment led to a distortion of information, since during the 1930s caste etiquette generally impeded honest communication between southern blacks and whites."[55] This climate of distrust greatly affected the flow of undistorted information by both informants and interviewers so that "the contemporary state of race relations almost always affect[ed] what blacks [were] willing to tell whites."[56]

Moreover, readers of the slave narratives must be cognizant that many of the informants at that time still lived in areas in which their masters' descendants continued to reside and on whom many were still dependent for their livelihoods. Thus these interviewees were not likely to say anything that might undermine the already vulnerable relations they maintained with these descendants and other whites in their towns. Blassingame cites a former slave, Martin Jackson:

> Lots of old slaves closes the door before they tell the truth about their days of slavery. When the door is open, they tell how kind their masters was and how rosy it all was. You can't blame them for this, because they had plenty of early discipline, making them cautious about saying anything uncomplimentary about their masters. I myself was in a little different position than most slaves and, as a consequence, have no grudge or resentment. However, I can tell you the life of the average slave was not rosy. They were dealt out plenty of cruel suffering.[57]

Second, not only were there considerable questions surrounding the adequacy of the interviewers to perform ethnography under a climate of distrust and vulnerability; informants also could not trust how their stories would be used or reported. Blassingame notes that many of the interviews are not verbatim accounts so that "although there is no indication of the extent of the rewriting on the facts sheets, it is clear from other sources that it frequently went well beyond 'soft' copy editing, or the correction of typographical errors, inconsistencies, misspelled words, and punctuation. The informants' stories were often revised substantially before they were typed and listed as official records."[58]

Third, and perhaps most considerable for our purposes, concerns the long gap between the "actual slave experience and the interview." According to Blassingame, "Two-thirds of the informants were at least eighty years old. And, since only 45 percent of the informants had been fifteen years or older when the Civil War began, an overwhelming majority of them could describe only how slavery appeared to a black child."[59] He raises the critical question: Are the WPA narratives representative of antebellum slave populations? His answer:

> Apparently not. Since the average life expectancy of a slave born in 1850 was less than fifty years, those who lived until the 1930s might have survived because they had received better treatment than most slaves. Taken at face value, there seems to have been a bias in many states toward including the most obsequious former slaves. This is especially true when most of the informants had spent their lives in the same locale as their former master's plantation. Since the least satisfied and most adventuresome of freed slave might have migrated to northern states or to cities after the Civil War, the WPA informants may have been atypical of antebellum slaves.[60]

Blassingame offers a compelling set of weaknesses for drawing historical facts of slave culture and slave religion in the antebellum South from the WPA narratives. This should give caution to contemporary theologians who want to use them to derive a constructive black theology of liberation that pairs with antebellum slave religion and slave culture. However, such suspicions on my part of the value of these materials for a slave narrative theology are not in themselves sufficient to count against their value as a source of religious insight into African American religious experience.

My criticisms of the slave narrative theology are cautionary. From my genealogical approach, the theologians do not adequately take into account the historical thresholds that occurred from the earliest formations of the invisible institution on plantations to the formal conversion of slaves by evangelicals and the abolitionist debates on the meaning of Christianity prior to and after the Civil War but especially during Reconstruction. Therefore, they see a direct correlation between black theology of liberation, slave religion on the large plantations in the antebellum era, and the formal organization of the ex-slaves into Protestant churches prior to and after emancipation. For the *CLST* collaborators, such a correlation or pairing seems evident from the slave narratives. I have no doubt that the ex-slaves' evangelical beliefs and piety, their lived theologies, are faithfully expressed in their narratives. However, the *CLST* writers assume what I do not—namely, that there is a direct correlation between their own commitments to black liberation theology and the evangelical-biblical faith and piety of the ex-slaves and slave religion. Hopkins says: "Blacks felt the powerful living presence of divinity in the midst of their daily burdens and concentrated in the Invisible Institution. These radical religious experiences colored their biblical interpretation; and thus, they produced a theology of liberation."[61] Of such a claim, I am most suspicious.

Although ex-slaves and black liberation theologians may favor the idea of freedom in their theological understandings, the equating of black evangelical religion with black theology is an equivocation that distorts what freedom and religion mean in their historical moments, contexts, and traditions. At a 2006 meeting of the Society for the Study of Black Religion, James Cone told listeners that everywhere he heard the word *freedom*, he translated it into *liberation* because the word *freedom* had lost its critical radical force for social change.[62] Such slippage has unfortunately come to hold the slave narratives hostage to the ideological interests of black liberation theology. I want to discourage such cognitive reductions in our theological methods if what remains is a distorted understanding of the differences in religious experience and theological thinking that provide black history and black religion with multiple trajectories of interpretations of religious protest, spiritual formation, theological positions, and political engagements.

I do not object to black theologians' ideological interest in relating contemporary black religious thought historically to the religious beliefs, patterns of worship, and the moral consciousness developed by African slaves in the context of American slavery. However, there is a fundamental danger of hermeneutical violence that occurs when the equivocation strategy results in radical distortion of our sources of religious insight. As Franz Von Brentano said so eloquently in 1874 when discussing the equivocation of mental and physical phenomena, "experience shows that equivocation is one of the main obstacles to recognizing distinctions," and "it must necessarily be the largest obstacle here where there is an inherent danger of confusion."[63] While not an error per se, the conscious equivocation of black theology with black evangelicalism in the ex-slave narratives, and of ex-slave narratives with antebellum slave religion, put us in grave danger also of blurring the fields of difference that mark our peculiar historical contexts and hence our sources of religious insight. Moreover, this loss of historical distinction is unlikely to be effective in the *CLST* theologians' attempts to overcome the forms of alienation that characterize the black theological academy's relation to the black churches and to black contemporary culture. The problem of equivocation results in a hermeneutical tragedy.

THE OPACITY OF BLACK RELIGIOUS KNOWLEDGE

Like the collaborators of *CLST*, I also think that the test for the interpretative adequacy of African American theology and a pragmatic theology of African American religious experience is the way our religious insights allow us to take hold of the cognitive, spiritual, and moral richness of African American religious experience and history. Historical research into black cultural life and experience is not only a legitimate task of African American theological reflection on religious experience; it is a methodological requirement. However, I find the genealogical path more adequate for lifting into critical consciousness the worlds of difference displayed in the study of African American religious experience than the ideological approach that pervades much of black theology. Unlike the ideological approach, the genealogical path resists suspending the worlds of difference that African slaves and black Americans created for the sake of theological unity around solidarities of race, class, gender, and sexuality. As in the previous chapter, to explicate this genealogical path to the sources of religious insight, I am indebted to the hermeneutical phenomenology of Charles H. Long.

For Long, the significations of black religion constitute historical relationships between the signifier and the signified; however, he is always clear to admit that if the relationship between the signified and signifier is arbitrary, then the religious significations are open to change, transformation, and reconstitution as the relationships are altered through their various exchanges of power. Long suggests that "the languages and experiences of signification can be seen for what they are and were, and one might also be able to see a new and counter-creative signification and expressive deployment of new meanings expressed in styles and rhythms of dissimulation."[64] In black religion, religious experience is the center of such changes, adaptations, adjustments, novelties, and differences.

While Long does not employ the aesthetic category of the grotesque to describe these forms of creative exchange in black religious experience, he comes close to this language in several places. Referring to the sense of terror that Pascal experienced in his contemplation of the "eternal silence of infinite spaces" that marked his modern mathematical consciousness of nature—a consciousness to which he himself contributed—Long also suggests that Pascal "struggled simultaneously with the fundamental problems of human creativity and human nature."[65] Both terror and wonder are present together in the experience; they are mixed and unresolved. Here, creative possibilities and terrifying dread embrace in Pascal's meditations, as he faced "the creativity that has come into being through the new understanding of nature, [and] God as a structure of intimacy has disappeared and a new world latent with creative possibilities and terrifying dread appears."[66]

The grotesque signals the unresolved ambiguity of apparently opposing dispositions and affections entailed in Pascal's experience of the infinite. Before such a reality, any number of unresolved affective and cognitive responses might be elicited in the experience. On the affective level, appreciation and fear, love and loathing, and cries of ecstasy coupled with anguish are all possibilities. On the cognitive level, sometimes experience of the divine might be taken hold of in belief and bafflement or speech and silence. In his attempt to analyze the duplicity of these religious responses, Long appeals to the aesthetic category of irony.

For Long, such cognitive doublings such as those between belief and bafflement or speech and silence are radically ironic. They are ironic in the sense that silence presupposes words, yet the power of silence—its manifestations—remains undisclosed. Long admits that the mere absence of words is not equivalent to silence. Rather, "silence forces us to realize that our words presuppose a reality which is prior to our naming and doing."[67] However, it is not every instance of silence that captures Long's gaze. Rather, it is archaic silence that Long seeks to expose in speech. In this case, speech is a testimony to the silence. For as the archaic condition and possibility of speech, the silence radically transcends the speech act. In this recognition:

> We are given a philosophical orientation that sees all language as
> enveloped in silence. In other words, the interrelation of language and
> silence gives us a new understanding of the totality of the language
> and ranges of experience of the human being. The value of the new
> position is that it is possible to include within it that which goes by
> the name of rationality and that which is historical.[68]

Both the possibilities of speech and action and thought and life are constitutive qualities of human existence. Each is an ontic structure, for each is
copresent as a fundamental quality of the human being. The unity between
speech and action, thought and life, and rationality and historical existence
lies in the archaic silence—or what I called in the introduction "the unity of
experience"—that conditions their possibilities. It does not fundamentally
lie in the historical understandings, languages, or cultural experiences of any
one group or people. Therefore, while historical existence is the "taken for
granted" or the "ordinary position" for religious reflection, by virtue of its
particularity historical existence is not a totality. It is not to be degraded, but
it is also not to be equated with the infinite. "The religious being knows
that humanity participates in a reality which is more than historical and cultural," says Long.[69] The totalization of geography, history, and culture in the
European self-estimation remains the great cognitive, moral, and religious
fault of Western expansionist ideology. European genius disclosed itself in
the garb and power of infinite speech and action, naming and transcending
the "silent" Other against which European culture named and defined itself.
This double signification, between the signifier and the signified, enacts
power relations that, from Long's perspective, create intrinsic ironies for both
the signified and the signifier. Tracing the ironies requires attention to the
history of their effects.

The hermeneutical orientation suggested here is dialectical. On the one
hand, black historical consciousness of such ironic effects means that black
existence, being signified upon by colonial powers, turned the racial significations on the signified ones into a symbol system of meanings that ironically doubled back upon the signifier and resulted in a totalization of both
black and white self-consciousness. On the other, the totality that signified
black existence, at the same time, conditioned a history of recoiling effects.
The recoiling responses by the signified ones are displayed in their own creative powers of word and symbols to constitute themselves both against the
negations suggested by Other and within the emancipatory effects of Western racial significations. Long sees this double signification entailed within
W. E. B. Du Bois's famous double consciousness thesis:

Blacks, the colored races, caught up into this net of the imaginary and symbolic consciousness of the West, rendered mute through the words of military, economic, and intellectual power, assimilated as if by osmosis structures of this consciousness of oppression. This is the source of doubleness of consciousness made famous by W. E. B. Du Bois. But even in these symbolic structures there remained the inexhaustibility of the opaqueness of these symbols for those who constituted the "thing" upon which the significations of the West deployed its meanings. This doubleness of consciousness, this existence in half-lights and within the quasi fields of human infection, is the context for the communities of color, the opaque ones of the modern world.[70]

I find Long's opacity metaphor provocative for thinking about the double significations he sees in racial symbolism. I also think it equally effective in thinking about a pragmatic theology of African American religious experience. The metaphor is a signification of the grotesquery of African American experience. The metaphor should not be associated with any cognitive failure on the part of the theologian to understand race and religion. Therefore, the opacity of black religious thought is not an instance of epistemic obscurity. Rather, it is benign. The image is of a glass having become opaque as a result of being cast into a fire or of a stained-glass window so intensely colored that light is blocked from fully illuminating what is inside. In both cases, the opaque quality of the darkened-glass and stained-glass windows denies the quality of transparency to both objects. Opaqueness, therefore, becomes an identifying characteristic of both objects.

The metaphor strikes at the very root of modern epistemology. It balances scientific, philosophical, and theological goals of making transparent, clear, and distinct what in historical existence is the taken-for-granted, unexamined, and often distorted understandings of ordinary experience. To borrow Francis Bacon's language, sources of religious insight are "put to the rack" in order to force from them their truth-value. The intellectual task is to expunge from the murky, opaque, nontranslucent, and ambiguous historical conditions of human life the concealed universal and necessary values. The truth lies underneath or behind the historical; however, the "shady" language of opacity runs counter to the languages of epistemic certainty, clarity, and transparency in both Western theological method and philosophical thinking. As an aesthetic metaphor, opacity installs a limiting factor on such intellectual preoccupations toward synthesis.[71]

For many African American theologians, the principles of religious disclosure (clarity, transparency, and distinction or uniqueness) continue to remain regulative intellectual ideal ends in theological method. However, in our attempts to understand and render black existence and black religion cognitively, morally, and spiritually transparent, which is a legitimate aspect of theological method, we also bump against the opaqueness, the grotes-query, of black life and black religious experience. Unfortunately, too many African American theologians have not transcended the Western epistemic paradigm preoccupied with ocular clarity, transparency, and synthesis in theological method. The opacity of black religious life reminds academic theologians of something that many ordinary believers know all too well, namely, that in matters of African American faith and life, "we see through a glass darkly."

Black sources of religious insight testify to the opacity of black religious reflection. Wherever one turns in our autobiographies, spirituals, folktales, and folk music, in slave narratives and ex-slave narratives, and in our partici-pation with black popular culture and religion, opacity balances our inten-tions to make transparent their meanings, values, purposes, and uses. Such a preoccupation with distilling from black sources their clear, distinct, and exceptional countercultural intentions and values puts at risk what brings the black academic theologian to black sources in the first place. What is at risk are their particularlities, their historical, creative testimonies to dif-ferent worlds of black religious experience and creativity. Their ironies are suspended for clarity; their moral ambiguities for ethical transparency; their serendipity for the strategic; and their creative plurality for the unitary and exceptional. The risk is one of hermeneutical violence to the opaque ones whose opacity leads us "crawling backward" into the religious and historical experiences that gave rise to their worlds of religious difference, the stuff of the study of black religion.

Long says that methodological attention to these worlds, their pow-ers and manifestations, will enable African American religious thinkers "to make common cause with folklorists, novelists, poets, and many other non-theological types" whose intellectual goals are to understand and inter-pret black historical existence and its political, moral, religious, and cultural meanings.[72] Engaging black sources this way not only takes advantage of the familiar sources of religious insight; attending to the opacity of these black sources of religious insight is also a regulative aspect of a pragmatic theol-ogy. The adequacy of African American pragmatic theology depends on its ability to take into itself the widest ranges of sources from black history and culture. Story-telling, myth making, memory recovering, theologizing black culture, dancing, shouting in churches and fields, leaping on stage, engag-ing music that uplifts the spirit and evokes both black tragedies and general human ones as well, making and watching films that depict the struggles of blacks toward freedom as well as those that depict the often ironic and comedic realities of black life—all these are sources of religious insight.

In creative exchange, all sources of black religious insight open us to a plentitude of transformative ways of being in the world—indeed, ironic forms of freedom that are always framed by finitude and transcendence. Yet every source is also a thing most opaque and ambiguous. As Long says:

> But what expression would a freedom deriving from people who had indeed endured and overcome oppression make? If this freedom is not to be simply the sentimental imitation of the lordship-bondage structure with a new set of actors, it would have to be a new form of freedom. As stepchildren of Western culture, the oppressed have affirmed and opposed the ideal of the Enlightenment and post-Enlightenment worlds. But in the midst of this ambiguity, for better or for worse, their experiences were rooted in the absurd meaning of their bodies, and it was for these bodies that they were regarded not only as valuable works but also as the locus of the ideologies that justified their enslavement. These bodies of opacity, these loci of meaninglessness, in the words of Shils and Bastide, were paradoxically loci of a surplus of meaning, meanings incapable of universal expression during the period of oppression. These opaque ones were centers from which gods were made. They were the concrete embodiments of matter made significant in the modern world. They formed new rhythms in time and space; these bodies of opacity were facts of history and symbols of a new religious depth. The totalization of all the great ideals of Western universalization met with the factual symbol of these oppressed ones. Opaque theologies emerge because the strategies of obscuring these peoples and cultures within the taxonomies of the disciplines of anthropology as primitive or the classification of them as sociological pathologies is no longer possible.[73]

Black sources of religious insight are as wide as black culture is expansive and as open as black culture is expressive in its significations, creative possibilities, and ambiguities. From the perspective of a pragmatic theology of African American religious experience, being open to the unresolved ambiguities of black religious life, its powers and manifestations, its limits and forms of openness is basic for judging the adequacy of our theological judgments.[74] If our hermeneutical task is to disclose both the light and the dark features of our religious lives, then a pragmatic theology of African American religious experience warrants balancing ocularity—a balancing of the clear, transparent, and distinct or exceptional—with the opacity of black religious life and experience.

Here, Will Coleman's *Tribal Talk* is a welcome interlocutor in the creative exchange with my pragmatic theology. I remain suspicious of the theological inferences he draws from the forms of difference displayed in the variety of narratives he uses for constructing the cosmological, epistemological, and spiritual exceptionalism of black religious experience in contemporary black theology. Nevertheless, he accents a profound appreciation for a plentitude of openness displayed in the creative exchange of ritual and dance, drama and stories, sermons and singing, and scriptures and doctrines:

> [*Tribal Talk*] explores the relationship between black theology, herme-
> neutics, and the idiom of African American discourse. In doing so, it
> strives to demonstrate a "multivoiced" praxis of storytelling and inter-
> pretation. It also illustrates the multifaceted roles of imagination and
> language in presenting, re-presenting, preserving, and transmitting a
> cosmology (that is, a mythology of origins as well as mythic orienta-
> tion) and an epistemology (that is, a way of knowing) that make the
> religious experience of West Africans and of African Americans a part
> of the larger experience (of slaves and masters) in the Americas (the
> United States, the Caribbean, and Brazil) and unique to the religious
> orientation of slaves. The religious sensibilities of slaves receive the
> most emphasis, to make up for the heretofore neglected dimensions
> of the same in traditional scholarship in general and in theology in
> particular.[75]

As a cautionary note to the specter of reductivism hovering over slave narrative theology, a pragmatic theology of African American religious experience requires that what is taken up and refracted through our black sources of religious insight are never without their unresolved ambiguities of light and dark, hope and tragedy, limits and situated forms of transcendence in African American religious experience. In and through their ambiguity, black sources of religious insight may not only be in creative exchange with our contemporary concerns, they may also be sources of creative conflict.

CONCLUSION

To conclude, notwithstanding how legitimate and necessary the stereo-scopic position that I have proposed may be for a pragmatic theology of African American religious experience, as a moral stance, it is a difficult position to maintain with consistency. This is especially the case when we are met everywhere with the need for academic theologians—black theo-logians of liberation, womanist theologians, slave narrative theologians and pragmatic theologians—to raise morally prophetic judgments on both the deleterious effects of white supremacy on African American cultural practices and experience and on an increasing black culture that appears to be growing alienated from centers of care and nurture that black religious institution can provide but often do not (I shall have more to say about this in my final chapter). Thus I understand why some in the black theological academy might be irritated with the sort of view that I hold as an African American pragmatic theologian and find it to be a distraction from prophetic, liberating action.

Nevertheless, I think that the genealogical path I have taken methodologically is an important balance to the ideological path that governs the slave narrative theology. If by attending to the opacity of black religious life and sources we become more open to more religious knowledge not less, to more criticism not less, to more stories, poems, biographies and narratives, to more and even better myths that emerge in our creative exchange with these sources, then the genealogical path I have taken through the grotesque and the opaque will have been well worth it. From the perspective of a pragmatic theology of African American religious experience, this commitment requires a creative exchange that takes hold of the widest ranges of African American religious experiences and interprets these experiences in the largest contexts of historical existence and culture. Still, this hermeneutical activity is everywhere profoundly met with the ambiguities of African American existence and religious life. Thus, in the next chapter, I take up the topic of evil and suffering in African American religious experience. There I shall carry over in a more determinate manner a phenomenology of redemptive suffering as a symbol of creative exchange.

CHAPTER 3

Faith on Earth

A Defense of Redemptive Suffering in African American Religious Experience

> Will not God bring about justice for God's chosen one, who cry out day and night? Will God keep putting them off? I tell you, God will see that they get justice, and quickly. However, when the son of Man comes, will he find faith on the earth? (Luke 18:7-8)

IN *Tales of Good and Evil, Help and Harm*, the philosopher Phillip Hallie suggests that reflecting on human suffering and evil is an opportunity for thinkers to consider the widest ranges of the possibilities of human transcendence against apparently insurmountable limits. I agree, but I also think that this sentiment is not very pronounced in contemporary African American theological writings on black suffering and evil. To some, it appears too sentimental and optimistic. A formidable theologian such as Anthony B. Pinn is likely to say that such a view distorts and mitigates the real suffering that people experience. It softens the blows, weakens their pain, and finds something good in experiences of suffering and evil. Pinn thinks that the very idea of redemptive suffering is theologically absurd and bankrupt.[1]

Other theologians, such as Delores S. Williams, will surely say that my view is really another kind of evil. It makes persons who have themselves been sufferers surrogates and servants on behalf of others. Redemptive suffering thereby reinscribes roles of servanthood and surrogacy that have too long defined black women's experience. Notwithstanding the work of other womanist theologians who have taken up the critique of redemptive suffering in their accounts of evil and suffering, Williams's *Sisters in the Wilderness* account is my focus here, as it remains one of most sustained and succinct treatment of the problem.[2]

I must say immediately that while I share neither Pinn's nor Williams's views on "redemptive suffering," like them, I too take human suffering and the moral evils we inflict on each other seriously. Their realities are too real, present, and unmeasurable to trivialize. Nevertheless, I still regard the idea of redemptive suffering as a possibility of transcendence in the everyday, ordinary experience of human beings living in a world in which suffering and evil are pervasive. I affirm both Pinn and Williams that human suffering and the evils that arise from human intervention in the world, its processes, and moral actions are the responsibility of human agents themselves. However, I also argue that redemptive suffering is a human possibility that is copresent in the creative exchange of suffering and arises as an emergent potentiality of the world framed by finitude and transcendence.

My talk of human suffering and evil is general rather than race-specific. This is because I do not think that particular instances of human suffering and evil offer any basic distinctions in what it means for anyone to suffer and experience evil. Nor do I play the "comparative suffering and evil" game. While I was a graduate student and chair of the Black Graduate Caucus at Princeton, at a series of meetings black and Jewish students discussed what some call the black/Jewish question: Which of us, blacks or Jews, are entitled to bear the title of the historically most victimized group? We compared narratives of atrocities committed against us. Of course, black students appealed to the Middle Passage and transatlantic slave trade, to stories of the millions of African slaves who never survived the horrors of plantation life and of those who survived the humiliation of inbreeding, splitting of families, alienation, the historic effects of discrimination, lynching, and burning. Jewish students evoked the Holocaust story, Nazi terror and experimentation, anti-Semitism, and Jewish defamation. For both African American and Jewish students at the table, it did not matter whether any of us personally experienced the atrocities in our stories. The weight of each story was meant to trump stories evoked by the other. Those stories of suffering and evil judged to be most horrific in quality, duration, and numbers provided one with a privileged status of victimization. Such games trivialize human suffering and evil wherever they are found.

My talk of suffering and evil is concerned with their *human* character. One must never lose sight of the fact that we are talking about human suffering and evil wherever experienced. I hold that neither race nor ethnicity should have so great a power over our thinking that we come to regard suffering and evil as so particular that we fail to see their effects on the whole of humanity beyond particular experiences. We also should not be so overwhelmed by the experiences of human suffering and evil that we fail to see what William James regarded as "The More" in the way of human possibilities for change, transformation, and transcendence (this is what I describe in the introduction as the creative exchange).[3] I take creative exchange and the creative events that arise from it to be the substantive content of redemptive suffering, and here I will try to make good on this claim. But first, in order to situate my critiques of Pinn's and Williams' accounts of suffering and evil in black theology and womanist theology, I make a brief excursus into "the modern problem of evil."

THE MODERNIST PROBLEMATIC

By talking about the "modern problem of evil and suffering," I am not suggesting that philosophical and theological reflections on suffering and evil have not been taken up as enduring questions in Christian faith from the beginning. Yet with modernity, evil and suffering appear to have spawned a continuous philosophical industry among Christian thinkers.[4] Thinkers such as Alasdair MacIntyre and Kenneth Surin have discussed premodern dispositions toward the problem of evil and suffering at some length. In an interesting essay, MacIntyre clarifies the distinction between the religious rationality of the premodern believer and the modern disposition of the philosophical Christian skeptic. He writes:

> Up to the seventeenth century we should in our society all have been believers and indeed there would be no question of our being anything else. We should not merely have believed that God existed and was revealed in Christ but we should have found it obvious and unquestionable that this was so. Since the seventeenth century, even for those who believe, the truth and intelligibility of their beliefs is not obvious in the same sense. What accounts for the fact that what was once obvious is now not so? What accounts for the fact that nobody now believes in God in the way that mediaeval men did, simply because men are aware of alternatives? And more importantly still, what makes some of the alternatives appear as obvious to modern sceptics as belief in God did for pre-seventeenth-century Christians?
>
> I pose this question as a background to another. If we can understand why one group of men in the past found Christian beliefs obviously true and intelligible and another group now find them opaque, and we can locate the difference between these two groups, perhaps we shall also be able to locate the difference between contemporary believers and contemporary sceptics.[5]

Surin also is quite helpful here. He locates premodern Christian resolve with belief in the omnipotence and goodness of God and suffering and evil in the liturgy of conversion.

> The goal of the true Christian philosophy is its attainment of blessedness, and there is no way to blessedness except that which God has revealed in Jesus Christ. . . . The only realistic hope for the solution to the problem of evil therefore is the unfathomable will of the ultimately nameless God. . . . So it is conversion—which comes about when the human will co-operates with divine grace—that solves the problem of evil.[6]

Both MacIntyre and Surin offer historical notes that distinguish premodern Christian attitudes toward suffering and evil from the modernist disposition of philosophical religious skepticism. From their accounts, what relative resolve Christians might have had toward suffering and evil was clearly found in the life of faithful devotion to God, trust and faith in God, and hope of blessed union with God. This position of Christian faith, trust, and hope does not negate the harsh realities of human suffering and evil. For premodern Christian thinkers, however, experiences of evil and suffering did not call into question their warrants for holding faith and trust in God. Any resolution to their experiences of suffering and evil was inextricably bound up in the mystery of faith in God's providential care and ends.

When compared to Pinn's and Williams's points of view, it is exactly this premodern Christian point of view on evil and suffering that is radically called into question. Both theologians' positions appear to me to be deeply entrenched in the modernist formulation of the "problem of evil." Both thinkers push the question of evil and suffering in directions that require either jettisoning belief in the existence of God (Pinn) or radically mitigating belief in the moral character of God (Williams). Both strategies are quite alien to the faith and trust of Christian believers throughout history who have been victims of evil, and I argue that both strategies are radically out of sync with the everyday, ordinary faith, trust, and hopes of oppressed blacks whose sufferings are the provocation for these theologians' liberation theologies.

I see both thinkers as being deeply rooted in the legacy of seventeenth-century philosophical Christian skepticism. For brevity's sake, Richard H. Popkins's understanding of this tradition will have to suffice as explanation:

> Since the term "Scepticism" has been associated in the last two centuries with disbelief, especially disbelief of the central doctrines of the Judeo-Christian tradition, it may seem strange at first to read

that the sceptics of the sixteenth and seventeenth centuries asserted, almost unanimously, that they were sincere believers in the Christian religion. Whether they were or not will be considered later. But the acceptance of certain beliefs would not in itself contradict their alleged scepticism, scepticism meaning a philosophical view that raises doubts about the adequacy or reliability of the evidence that could be offered to justify any proposition. The sceptic in either the Pyrrhonian or Academic tradition, developed arguments to show that the evidence, reasons, or proofs employed as grounds for our various beliefs were not completely satisfactory. Then the sceptics recommended suspense of judgment on the question of whether these beliefs were true. One might still maintain the beliefs, since all sorts of persuasive factors should not be mistaken for adequate evidence that the belief was true. Hence, "sceptic" and "believer" are not opposing classifications.[7]

A major element in Christian philosophical skepticism is one that seeks to relate God's attributes (insofar as God is understood as having a nature that is simple [simplicity], undivided [noncomposite], absolutely independent of another [aseity], absolute in power [omnipotent], knowledge [omniscience], and will—the so-called incommunicable attributes) and God's moral perfections in goodness, justice, and truth (communicable attributes) with the reality of evil and suffering in the world. For these religious skeptics, the distinction between "nonmoral evil" and "moral evil" was essential to their resolutions.

Nonmoral evil is suffering that people experience as a consequence of some natural misfortune. On April 16, 1998, the day began beautifully—sun shining, winds calm—a perfect day to leave my office at Vanderbilt and go do some work on my newly purchased home in East Nashville's Historic Edgefield district. While painting, I noticed that the sky was beginning to turn dark and ominous. I decided that I had better head back to campus where I was then living in a dorm. As I drove over a highway overpass on my way back to my Vanderbilt apartment, I found myself in the throes of a tornado. I thought to myself that it was beautiful inside the winds yet I also experienced dread as the gusts picked up the front end of my vehicle from the surface, suspending it on the back rear end. I saw people all around me running for shelter, wind-carried signs floating past, shop windows breaking, and trees toppling. Within an hour of painting my new home, the neighborhoods of Historic Edgefield and East Nashville were devastated by fallen trees, destroyed homes, pulled-up walkways, torn-away roofs. A church building that had been standing only moments before when I passed it on my way to my apartment collapsed. At Vanderbilt, trees were down and we lost one of our undergraduate students to the tornado.

In Historic Edgefield, my neighbors seemed at a loss for words or adequate responses to the destruction. I was tempted to respond with anger because I was now broke, having exhausted my savings when closing on the house I had bought only a few weeks earlier. How was I going to pay for damages to the home, yard, and walk not covered by insurance? But with whom could I be angry? God? Nature? From my theological position, those terms were equivalent. But Nature could not intend to subject me to its powers. The tornado had no motive or intention to harm me, or anyone else for that matter. It did not know our names or where we lived. Nature was doing what nature does. To be sure, the experiences of my community and its families were tragic—tragic but not evil. To use the words of the seventeenth-century philosophical skeptic, Baruch de Spinoza, what suffering we experienced that day in April can only be judged to be "evil so called." To name such devastation "evil" is, on his account, to make a concession in speech to the inadequacies of our understanding and ideas about the natural conditions under which tornadoes occur.

By contrast to nonmoral evil, Christian philosophical skeptics define "moral evil" as the suffering and pain that people experience as the consequence of human interactions and interventions with each other. I regard moral evil as the "wickedness" (the control and malice, the cruelties and meanness, the destructive acts directed against groups and whole peoples) that we humans inflict on each other out of our human biological motives of aggression and our emotional desires and willful intentions to satisfy some idolatrous good. Edward Farley puts it succinctly, that "idolatry corrupts our capacity for aggression. To put it more strongly, when idolatry affects our biologically rooted strivings for satisfaction, it mobilizes our capacities for aggression and gives them a new agenda. And with this new agenda, we transgress the built-in limitations of animal aggression which curtail fight to death and serious injury."[8] Wickedness has its home in the embodied relations between aggression and idolatry that turns individuals into haters, people into murderers, and in some cases murderers into champions of a powerful group to control and subjugate others by sheer malice. Tales abound. But for clarity, consider one instance.

On February 23, 1999, James Byrd was walking home from his niece's bridal party in Jasper, Texas. Driving around that night were three men: John William King, Shawn Berry, and Lawrence Russell Brewer. One of the three recognized Byrd and persuaded the others to give Byrd what would turn out to be a ride through hell. King initially objected to giving Byrd a ride in the back of the truck. But after picking Byrd up, King informed the others that he wanted to scare the man. After beating him unconscious and stripping him, they chained Byrd to their pickup truck and dragged him along two-and-a-half miles of a Jasper County road. His ear and right arm were ripped off his body and skin from his knees and elbows was stripped down to the bone. The wickedness committed against Byrd was neither the effect of any natural disaster nor the consequence of an accident or human error. It was wickedness committed out of human agency and guided by human intentions beyond aggression but moved by the felt need for exacting control, malice, and an idolatrous need for power. The effects of these three men's wickedness extended not only to Byrd's family but also to Byrd's community, people, state, and country. Such wickedness is evil.

Drawing on Spinoza again, if the evils we ascribe to nature are only "evil so called," then ascribing evil to nature is really a concession to the inadequacy of our ideas about nature, its patterns, operations, and powers. Ascribing evil to nature is not only an inadequate idea about the order or the way of things; it is also an inadequate idea about God, whom for Spinoza is called "Substance" or "Nature" writ large.[9] To associate acts of evil, whether moral or nonmoral, to Nature or God, is a concession to an immature religious imagination. Here, the religious imagination seeks to reconcile human pain, sufferings, and the evils that we inflict on each other with a formal cause of all things—namely, God or Nature. For Spinoza, God is understood as the formal cause of all things and hence is not the efficient or material cause of evil. To ascribe evil or any action to Nature is to project purposive intentionality or agency onto a metaphysical subject. It is an act of anthropomorphizing. Rather, on Spinoza's account, evil or wickedness results from the exertion of our own human wills and freedom and not from a divine will or purpose.[10] Therefore, for an early modern philosophical skeptic like Spinoza, human suffering and wickedness are cognitive problems that are resolved by a critical point of view about human actions and thoughts. In the end, it is an ethical problem, not a theological one.

A century after Spinoza, British Christian philosopher David Hume carried forward the skeptical formulation of the problem of evil and suffering; his formulation of the problem has become standard.[11] His argument is derived from what he perceived to be a certain inconsistency between the Christian view of the nature of God on the one hand, and the reality of human misery in history and experience on the other. Hume's basic question is not, Why do bad things happen (and not only to good people), but, Why do they happen *at all* if God is wholly benevolent toward the wellbeing of humanity? He describes the human lot as filled with social woes and miseries, violence and treachery. It is replete with sufferings that result from natural disasters and pain and diseases of both the body and mind. "All the goods of life united would not make a very happy man, but all the ills united would make one wretched indeed; (and any one of them almost) and who can be free from every one?, nay, often the absence of one good (and who can possess all?) is sufficient to render life ineligible," says Hume.[12] From his depiction of human suffering and evil, Hume raises the skeptical question that crystallized the modern problem of evil and suffering: "Can you still persevere in your anthropomorphisms and assert that moral attributes of the Deity, his justice, benevolence, mercy and rectitude to be of the same nature with these virtues in human creatures? Is God willing to prevent evil, but unable? Then is he impotent. Is he able, but unwilling? Then is he malevolent. Is he both able and willing? Whence then evil?"[13]

I think that it is important not to read Hume's skepticism too strongly. For Hume, pervasive human suffering and evil call into question a certain picture of God's nature as a powerful moral agent; however, it does not call into question the existence of God per se. Another point of clarification is in order here. Like Spinoza, Hume's skepticism is not strictly speaking of a theological epistemic problem. It is ethical. Hume does not treat the problem of evil and suffering as a problem with the logical consistency of our propositions about God's existence. Therefore, he takes neither the atheist nor agnostic turn in philosophical skepticism with respect to God's existence. His question underscores the rational warrants for attributing moral agency—as a necessary category—to God. His point appears to be that even if evil is not a sufficient basis for undermining the probability of God's existence, the moral attributes of God are improbable theological inferences to be drawn from the facts of human moral experience. In other words, Hume thinks that there is little analogical correspondence between what the believer holds concerning God's character and agency and what people morally require and expect of oneself or others.

For instance, under normal conditions, a morally responsible person would be obliged to actualize a state of affairs in which evil is eliminated or, at least, repressed to the greatest degree possible within the powers of the moral agent.[14] Such reasoning at least is the basis for many states legislating "Good Samaritan" statutes. Given the pervasiveness of human suffering and wickedness in the world, God's morals appear quite at odds with the moral expectations we hold over human agents whom we judge virtuous by their motives and acts toward either eradicating evil and suffering or ameliorating their effects where possible. For Hume, the pervasiveness of evil is incompatible with the belief that God is absolutely free to execute God's divine intentions, benevolence, goodness, and mercy. Hume's problem is how to account for the probability of God's existence while maintaining the reasonable probability that God is absolutely free as a moral agent. Hume's response is to jettison the moral attributes of God while maintaining that people may postulate from general human experience belief in the existence of God with great probability. From moral experience, however, people are less warranted in postulating with absolute certainty or a great degree of probability that God is an absolutely good moral agent:

> Were all living creatures incapable of pain, or were the world admin-
> istered by particular volitions, evil never could have found access into
> the universe; and were animals endowed with a large stock of pow-
> ers and faculties, beyond what strict necessity requires; or were the
> several springs and principles of the universe so accurately framed
> as to preserve always the just temperament we feel at present. What
> then shall we pronounce on this occasion? Shall we say, that these
> circumstances are not necessary, and that they might easily have been
> altered in the contrivance of the universe? This decision seems too
> presumptuous for creatures, so blind and ignorant. Let us be more
> modest in our conclusions. Let us allow, that if the goodness of the
> Deity (I mean a goodness like the human) could be established on
> any tolerable reason a priori, these phenomena, however untoward,
> would not be sufficient to subvert that principle; but might eas-
> ily, in some unknown manner, be reconcilable to it. But let us still
> assert, that as this goodness is not antecedently established, but must
> be inferred from the phenomena, there can be no grounds for such
> an inference, while there are so many ills in the universe, and while
> these ills might so easily have been remedied, as far as human under-
> standing can be allowed to judge on such a subject. I am sceptic
> enough to allow, that the bad appearances, notwithstanding all my
> reasoning, may be compatible with such attributes as you suppose;
> but surely they can never prove these attributes. Such a conclusion
> cannot result from scepticism; but must arise from the phenomena,
> and from our confidence in the reasonings, which we deduce from
> these phenomena.[15]

On Hume's account, the experience of human suffering and evil may not warrant a believer in abandoning belief in God's existence. However, the realties of human sufferings derived from pervasive wickedness are over-whelmingly sufficient grounds for doubting the moral nature and character of God. Hume's doubt about the existence of God results in a mitigated skepticism that finds the moral attributes ascribed to God to be incom-mensurable with belief in the existence of God. His doubt about the moral nature of God is total.

The early modern skeptical perspectives of Spinoza and Hume on evil and suffering are in sharp contrast to premodern Christian thinkers as described by MacIntyre and Surin. For premodern Christian thinkers, questions about evil and suffering were raised and reflected upon without requiring the abandonment of faith and trust in the moral goodness and justice of God or abandoning belief in the existence of God as an agent of providence. The mystery of evil and suffering is resolved in Christian liturgy. Suffering and evil are taken hold of in ritual practices and devoted service to God through the spiritual disciplines of prayer, steadfast belief, and hope of blessed union with God. The problem of evil and suffering is resolved by faith in God. For thinkers such as Spinoza and Hume, faith requires the correction of human understanding and critical attention to the adequacy and inadequacy of our ideas about God's existence and human wickedness. In the arguments of Delores S. Williams and Anthony B. Pinn, I find contemporary currents of this modernist tradition embedded in their accounts of black suffering and divine racism.

SUFFERING AND EVIL IN BLACK AND WOMANIST THEOLOGY

As I read Pinn and Williams, each takes up the problem of black suffering and evil under the modernist paradigm in distinction from the premodern Christian attitude. While Williams is not prepared to call into question the existence of God per se, her account of suffering and evil is framed by the existential crisis of black women's historical experience with oppression: How is God present here and now in the suffering of African American women? On close reading, however, Williams's primary focus is not on God but on Jesus/Christ in the experience of African American women's suffering. When reflecting on God, she says it is God who keeps black women bound to surrogacy and servanthood, not liberation and self-determinacy. Yet Williams's view is greatly mitigated such that God is also the source that provides black women with the means of surviving and promoting their quality-of-life struggles. This point of view is clearly explicated by Williams in two fundamental biblical stories: the Hagar story and the Cross.

Hagar, whose story appears in Genesis 16:1-16, is the Egyptian servant of Abram's wife Sarai. Her story is framed by a promise given by God to Abram guaranteeing a great posterity to be borne of Sarai and Abram; however, Sarai is past child-bearing years and is childless. She encourages her husband to take Hagar to be a birthing surrogate for herself. Sarai delivers Hagar to Abram "to be his wife" on her behalf but only for the purpose of birthing a child. Hagar conceives, but the pregnancy creates spite in Sarai toward her surrogate and servant. After Sarai complains to her husband, Abram returns

Hagar to Sarai so that she may do as she will with her servant. Sarai's harsh treatment of Hagar sends the servant fleeing into the wilderness. When confronted by God in the wilderness, Hagar is ordered to return to Sarai and Abram, armed only with a promise of greatness for her posterity.

A few chapters later, in Genesis 21:1-21, Hagar and Sarah (her name changed) clash over an apparent rivalry between Ishmael (Hagar's child) and Isaac (Sarah's son). Sarah's unresolved spite for Hagar and Ishmael results in their being expelled into the wilderness with only minimal provisions provided by Abraham. Their water exhausted and her son near death from thirst, Hagar weeps. A messenger of God comes to Hagar and instructs her to pick up her son to take him to a place of fresh water. The angel does not intervene for Hagar's sake but for her son's. The Lord provides sustenance because the Lord heard Ishmael's cry. Hagar is no longer the surrogate and servant of Abraham and his wife; she is now the surrogate and servant of God. She is used by God to bring about God's plan for Ishmael's posterity.

For Williams, this story is paradigmatic of African American women's experience of oppression. She writes:

> Because she was a slave, Hagar had no control over her body or her labor. Her body, like her labor, could be exploited in any way her owners desired. Her reproduction capacities belonged to her slave holders, Abraham and Sarah. Thus surrogacy became a major theme in Hagar's story of exploitation. Surrogacy has also been a major theme in African American women's history. But whereas Hagar's experience with surrogacy was primarily biological, African American women's experience with surrogacy has been primarily associated with social-role exploitation.[16]

Williams takes from the story three identifying moments: (1) black women have no control of their bodies (physical oppression); (2) they have been economically oppressed insofar as their labor is exploited by surrogacy and servanthood; and (3) black women have been defined by social roles that their owners forced on them during slavery (coerced surrogacy) and they forced on themselves due to social pressures for their survival after slavery (voluntary surrogacy).

Williams sees this surrogacy pattern in God's action toward humanity in the crucifixion of Jesus. She surveys the history of atonement theories in Western theology, particularly the vicarious atonement—the idea that Christ stands as a substitute or surrogate for humanity in the execution of God's judgment on the sins of the world. In his death on the cross, Jesus acts both as a surrogate and a suffering servant. He suffers in order to fulfill God's will to redeem humanity. Williams summarizes the meaning of this event for African American women:

> . . . Jesus represents the ultimate surrogate figure; he stands in the place of someone else: sinful humankind. Surrogacy, attached to this divine personage, thus takes on an aura of the sacred. It is therefore fitting and proper for black women to ask whether the image of a surrogate-God has salvific power for black women or whether the image supports and reinforces the exploitation that has accompanied their experience with surrogacy. If black women accept this idea of redemption, can they not also passively accept the exploitation that surrogacy brings?[17]

The surrogacy of Jesus entails a life of suffering and servanthood that is determined and ordained by God (coerced surrogacy) and an act of Jesus' devotion to God (voluntary surrogacy). Williams asks: What salvific power can such an image of an innocent person dying for others have for African American women whose historical experience has been patterned on acts of surrogacy in the story of Hagar and the crucified Christ?

Williams's answer is that African American women's salvation does not require sacred surrogacy. Indeed, for Williams:

> Black women are more apt to see Jesus/Christ as spirit sustaining survival and liberation efforts of the black community. Thus black women's question about Jesus Christ is not about the relation of his humanity to his divinity or about the relation of the historical Jesus to the Christ of Faith. . . .Whether we talk about Jesus in relation to atonement theory or Christology, we womanists must be guided more by black Christian women's voices, faith and experience than by anything that was decided centuries ago at Chalcedon.[18]

Black women's salvation depends on Jesus' life of resistance and their own survival strategies that transform their identities from the social roles and multiple exploitations of surrogacy.[19] Their salvation is in a vision of ministry advanced by Jesus. She says: "The resurrection of Jesus and the kingdom of God theme in Jesus' *ministerial* vision provides Black women with the knowledge that God has, through Jesus, shown humankind how to live peacefully, productively, and abundantly in relationship."[20] The ministerial vision of Jesus entails words of judgment, healing, exorcizing evil, faith, prayer, compassion, and love. In other words, black women's salvation is ethical, not vicarious.

For Williams, the question of suffering and evil is not overcome by appealing to the cross, which is a symbol of sacred surrogacy and exploitation and which glorifies the "sin of defilement." African American women's hope is an ethical hope. It involves two elements: (1) survival, because, as Williams puts it, this is the condition of black women's experience that seems to have no end; and (2) sustenance for their quality-of-life struggles to provide for their lives and the lives of their families.[21] God provides the resources and conditions for their survival and struggles. God is present to black women as the God who cares, who meets them through their lives of prayer and struggles, and supports them in their lives of resistance. But God does not liberate them. Rather, liberation must be the work of black women themselves for themselves. Williams concludes:

> The greatest truth of black women's survival and quality of life struggle is that they have worked without hesitation and with all the energy they could muster. Many of them, like Hagar, have demonstrated great courage as they resisted oppression and as they went into the wide, wide world to make a living for themselves and their children. They depended upon their strength and upon each other. But in the final analysis the message is clear: they trusted the end to God. Every important event in the stories of Hagar and black women turns upon this trust.[22]

Williams's theology of evil and suffering is consistent with the modernist strategy that calls into question the moral character of God without abandoning belief in God. However, her position on the moral character of God ought best to be understood as ironic, if not paradoxical. Williams holds to the biblical faith that affirms the agential nature of God. God is for her an actor in history and makes claims on human subjects. Therefore, Williams is committed to a theistic construal of God. Moreover, her view of God is also the predominant faith of believing black women whose religious experience Williams takes seriously as the point of departure for womanist theology. When Williams evaluates God's actions, however, God is biblically revealed as the God of surrogacy and servanthood. This is a theological inference from her making paradigmatic the Hagar story and the vicarious atonement of Jesus in her interpretation of God's agential character. Having made these two biblical stories paradigmatic in her interpretation of black women's social experience, Williams risks reducing God's agency under the metaphors of servanthood and surrogacy.

I suggest that Williams's tendency toward reducing God's agential character under servanthood and surrogacy puts her ironically between a rock and a hard place. She has the difficulty of squaring her theological construal of God under surrogacy and servanthood on the one hand, with the lived theology of African American believing women on the other. From the perspective of lived theology, many African American believing women embrace as spiritually empowering the symbols of surrogacy and servant-hood as well as other symbols Williams's revisionist theology is likely to reject. The critical question is, How do these agential symbols of God's deal-ings with black women guide their religious understandings and apprecia-tion of God as loving and caring (which are symbols that Williams herself wants to commend)? Moreover, what are we to make of the many other ways that black women experience God? In African American women's reli-gious experience, God is more often than not spoken of and affirmed as their master, father, king, and lord. Therefore, how are critical theologians to understand and appreciate even those theological symbols that may cause them to cringe upon hearing them but which black women themselves take ownership of by appropriating them as symbols of their spiritual nurture and empowerment?

To put the issue more pointedly, I find persuasive Williams's social cri-tique of surrogacy and servanthood in her description of African American women's experience. However, theologically I see these symbols entailed to the lived theology of African American women's spirituality where they appear to undergo a transvaluation of the historic roles they have socially performed in black women's experience. Listening to the lived theology of many African American women, such symbols as servant, master, king, and lord that the critical academic theologian finds oppressive and malforma-tive appear to be enduring, empowering, and transforming symbols in black women's spirituality and Christian social witness. Indeed, attending to the testimonies of many believing black women, I find it difficult to imagine an account of African American women's Christian social witness that does not have the imprint of either surrogacy or servanthood inscribed upon it.

Williams's critique of redemptive suffering through her criticism of surrogacy and servanthood is ironic or paradoxical because she does not acknowledge the transvaluation of these social symbols in African Ameri-can women's spirituality. The paradox arises in Williams's constructive pro-posal to counter redemptive suffering. Her proposal is that black women's spirituality and religious commitments are to be normatively framed by the transformative power of the ministerial vision of Jesus; however, it is difficult to understand this vision in a way that does not also entail some account of servanthood and surrogacy as performative practices in the ministerial vision of Jesus. Therefore, Williams has the task of showing how this vision is not itself an instantiation of the symbols she wants to reject. Without such an argument, her position enters into a performative contradiction in which the symbols she wants to reject are regulative moral ideals in African American women's spirituality and Christian social witness.

In the end, Williams's critique of redemptive suffering is paradoxical regarding God's moral character. On the one hand, God does not liberate African American women from their perpetual social experience of surrogacy and servanthood but occasions it. On the other hand, God provides the resources for their survival, resistance, and quality-of-life struggles, but does not liberate them from the perpetual power of surrogacy and servanthood that God occasions in their experience. The paradox occurs in Williams's hermeneutical intention, as a womanist theologian, to be faithful to the complex character of African American women's spirituality and their biblical faith, while at the same time remaining faithful to her own criticism of redemptive suffering. These symbols are logically entailed in her account of redemptive suffering, which she interprets from the Hagar story and the vicarious atonement of Christ. Notwithstanding her radical criticism of surrogacy and servanthood in her critique of redemptive suffering, Williams remains a mitigated skeptic on the moral character of God.

By contrast to Williams, Pinn follows the atheist wing of philosophical skepticism in his account of black suffering and evil in black liberation theology. Although Pinn finds Williams's account of redemptive suffering nearly persuasive, in his estimation, she does not go far enough to call into question the existence of God. For Pinn, the major theological pothole to avoid in any critique of suffering and evil is "redemptive suffering." As Pinn defines it, redemptive suffering suggests that oppression is inherently evil but offers some secondary benefit.[23] Pinn thinks that Williams is right in her sustained criticism of suffering and evil in black women's experience of surrogacy and servanthood. He also understands her to be offering a critique of redemptive suffering. However, he criticizes her for minimizing something so essential to the Hagar story itself, namely, that it is God who puts Hagar into her experiences of suffering.[24] Rather, Williams's position is mitigated on God's moral character. God is the provider of resources for survival, sustenance, and resistance (not liberation) and insofar as African American women's strength of survival and resistance emerge from their experience, she has a minimalist view of redemptive suffering.

Pinn's book *Why Lord?* is a radical deconstruction of black liberation theology through the critique of the theodical problem in black theology. Pinn states the problem thus: "The theodical problem in Black Theology is that theological strategies, which have a theistic grounding and entail redemptive suffering in the meaning of Black liberation, are detrimental to an adequate account of blacks' liberation because such strategies undermine human

responsibilities for enacting liberation."[25] This statement presents three moves
that an adequate critique of suffering and evil in black theology must entail:
(1) it must offer a radical critique of God's existence (theism); and (2) a radical critique of redemptive suffering, if (3) blacks are to find within their own
human resources power toward liberation.

Before summarizing Pinn's argument, I think it is important to be as clear
as possible on the terms with which he works. In a succinct passage, Pinn
clarifies crucial terms:

> Suffering and unmerited suffering are used interchangeably (with ref-
> erence to African Americans) to denote moral evil. Moral evil denotes
> oppression, injustice, inequality, and the resulting psychological and
> physical damage. The problems of evil and "theodicy" interchangeably
> connote attempts at resolving the contradiction between traditional
> Christian understandings of God as powerful, just and good, and the
> presence of suffering (as defined above), without negating the essen-
> tial character of the Divine. Liberation because of my understanding
> of suffering and "theodicy" will mean a vision of life without the
> assumption of God-ordained and permitted moral evil (i.e., human
> responsibility for moral evil).[26]

From the quotation above, Pinn equivocates by equating the problem
of evil (Hume's formulation of it) with theodicy. He then logically connects these concepts with redemptive suffering. Redemptive suffering
entails belief in a "proactive" God or force who ordains in our experiences
of suffering some secondary benefit. Pinn proposes that suffering here is
"interchangeable" with unmerited suffering in African American experience. Hence, the terms are logical equivalents. From this move, suffering is
understood as moral evil, which denotes oppression, injustice, inequality, and
the physical and psychological effects resulting from human actions.

Pinn's notion of philosophical adequacy does not admit any account of
evil and suffering of the sort that I described as the modernist problem of
evil. From his point of view, such a language game—one that attempts to
justify rationally some aspect of God's being and moral character in light of
pervasive human misery—has framed the trajectory of Western European
Christian thought from Augustine and Irenaeus to Hume and Kant: It is
thoroughly Eurocentric. However, Pinn also sees this trajectory dominating
African American religious thinking on suffering and evil from the formation
of the spirituals to twentieth-century African American theology, including
black liberation theology and womanist theology. His basic contention is
that theodical strategies do not serve black liberation theologians very well

in their own accounts of black suffering and evil. This is because lying behind these strategies are the historical effects of the Western theodical game. When blacks take up this game, they find themselves with no distinctive alternative beyond the Western theological tradition. Even the two who come so close to his own point of view, William R. Jones and Delores Williams, fall short of an adequate alternative to black liberation theology's accounts of black suffering and evil. Remarking on Jones and Williams, Pinn writes:

> It turns out, then, that even the two thinkers—Jones and Williams— who question traditional theological assumptions in actuality maintain them: the activity and responsibilities of God are given new packaging. Things required of God are adjusted so as not to contradict an unchanging reality of Black oppression. That is, Jones resolves the problem of evil by limiting God and making humans responsible for evil. Williams manages the same effect by limiting God's responsibility to the area of survival. In both cases suffering persists while God's intentions remain good, and this allows for the continuing feasibility of redemptive suffering.[27]

Pinn's position is indeed radical. If theology requires a radical departure from the modes of theological inquiry on God and human suffering taking their point of departure from black suffering and evil, then any talk of redemptive suffering is incommensurable with liberation. For brevity's sake, I will outline Pinn's basic argument in six propositions:

> P1. If suffering is inherently evil, then any good that results from the experience of suffering must be extrinsic and secondary and not a basic good.

> P2. Any secondary good that follows from the unmerited suffering of blacks transfers the actualization of that good to another power, force, or agent but not to those who themselves suffer.

> P3. Since freedom from oppression is the result of another's action in the experience of suffering, freedom cannot be attributed to blacks themselves.

> P4. Black liberation entails blacks' unmerited suffering by another (God) and requires the one who oppresses (God) to be also their savior or liberator.

> P5. If it is to be consistent with its ultimate end, the liberation of blacks from oppression by blacks, black liberation theology requires the death of the God who oppresses and simultaneously liberates blacks from oppression.

P6. In the end, blacks must take full responsibility for their own liberation.

Pinn's radical critique of redemptive suffering is highly persuasive when one accepts his definition of redemptive suffering. It is clear that for Pinn redemptive suffering is fundamentally a theological construct. The concept logically entails belief in a personal God who carries out some sort of intention (pedagogical, moral, or coping) in the suffering and pain of black people (P1). Moreover, as Pinn sees it, these intentions in and through the suffering of African Americans are secondary to the experience of suffering itself (P2). Although Pinn himself does not make the following move, I think that his case for jettisoning belief in God in his critique of redemptive suffering would be strengthened by several addendums or glosses. My addendum to P1 reads: *As God occasions blacks' suffering (disproportionately to the suffering of others), God must also take special delight in their experience of suffering since God has absolute power to prevent anything God does not enjoy.* Therefore, the actualization of the disproportionate suffering of blacks delights God, or God would prevent it. My addendum to P2 would then follow: *Any secondary intention or benefits derived from black suffering might be seen as compensatory. They are compensation by God for God's sadistic delight in the suffering of blacks.*

With these addendums to his argument on redemptive suffering, God is both the cause of black people's suffering because God delights in their unmerited sufferings, and God makes good on their suffering as compensation for God's trafficking in black sufferings and miseries. Given the glosses on Pinn's theological construal of divine racism, black humanism's jettisoning belief in God is welcomed and warranted just as African Americans are warranted in purging from their communities those who benefit from the miseries of their communities suffering from the ravages of crime and death generated by drug trafficking. Pinn profoundly asks: "[W]hat are the true possibilities for transformation when God's intervention is not apparent, but is desperately appealed to? How strongly does one fight for change while seeking signs of God presence?" He concludes that "humanity is far better off fighting with the tools it has—a desire for transformation, human creativity, physical strength, and untapped collective potential."[28] Given the addendums to Pinn's account of redemptive suffering, his quotation of James H. Cone in the epigraph of *Why Lord?* is worth considering: "If God is not for us, if God is not against white racists, then God is a murderer, and we had better kill God. The task of black theology is to kill gods that do not belong to the black community, and by labeling black history as a source, we know that his is neither an easy nor a sentimental task but an awesome responsibility."

I am sympathetic to Pinn's overall intentions in criticizing the idea of redemptive suffering in African American religious experience, if indeed the doctrine does the sort of work he claims. What responsible critical theologian would want to promote a doctrine that is inherently detrimental to blacks' liberation from oppression? According to Pinn, redemptive suffering counteracts efforts at liberation by finding something of value in black suffering. Its essence goes against active social transformation. It is diametrically opposed to liberation in such a way that the two ideas denote radically incommensurable ways of being in the world and nullify each other: "One cannot embrace suffering as redemptive and effectively speak of liberation," says Pinn.[29]

If Pinn's claims on the detrimental effects of redemptive suffering are sustainable, one would be morally warranted in eliminating the doctrine from one's constructive account of evil and suffering in black theology; however, I am not persuaded by his negative claims regarding the doctrine. I think that he is right in insisting that the doctrine of redemptive suffering is predominant in the historical faith traditions of African Americans as they reflect on evil and suffering. In subsequent books, Pinn has documented well the predominance of redemptive suffering in African American religious experience of evil and suffering. I also think him fair in his substantive treatment of the many kinds of interpretations the doctrine opens up in African American religious experience.

The interpretations he explores include pedagogical, moral, and cooperative responses and effects of evil and suffering that are "secondarily" derived from black people's suffering. Therefore, Pinn is correct to hold that in African American religious experience, redemptive suffering is basically a theological construct that accents (1) God as the supreme omnipotent and all-knowing creator and king; (2) God's will and goodness are simple and undifferentiated so that God's moral character is by nature good; and (3) God must have some eternal good to be derived from blacks' suffering that bares testimony to God's providential care for sufferers and God's triumph over evil. No doubt such an interpretation of God's dealings with black sufferers is derived from their biblical faith in African American religious traditions. Although Pinn has documented well the above interpretations of redemptive suffering in African American religious traditions, I think it is a categorical error to define redemptive suffering as being a fundamentally theological doctrine. My position is that while the symbol *redemptive suffering* may be construed theocentrically, such an interpretation is not necessary for adequately understanding and appreciating the forms of transcendence signified by the symbol.

FAITH ON EARTH

Unlike Pinn and Williams, I do not think of redemptive suffering as being necessarily a theological symbol. Moreover, I do not think that the substantive elements signified by the symbol are derived benefits of suffering. They are not benefits, goods, ends, or virtues that are derivative or consequences of prior acts of suffering. Like Spinoza and Hume, I hold that suffering resulting from human moral actions renders redemptive suffering an ethical construct. Pinn's and Williams's accounts of redemptive suffering tend to treat any goods, ends, or benefits as derived from acts of suffering in a manner that is causal such that if one experiences some unmerited suffering, then some good will eventually follow. I agree with both thinkers that such a causal relation of suffering to good ends valorizes suffering itself; however, I cannot deny that through suffering basic capacities for faith, hope, love, endurance, courage, forgiveness, and other moral excellences or virtues are unleashed. These are manifestations or events that arise from creative exchange. These virtues are not sequential effects of suffering. Rather, they are copresent or emergent potentialities in the creative exchange of human beings themselves with suffering and evil.

I understand why redemptive suffering has all too often been conceived of as a kind of trade off between God, suffering, and sufferers. The logic lies not only in the Christian story but also in the duplicity of redemption itself as an economic symbol. Redemption is not inherently a theological symbol. At its root, it is an economic sign that is symbolically rendered theological. Among the meanings of redemption (*redimo*) are acts of buying back, recovering by payment as in a ransom, buy up as in property, or procuring as in great works of art for a price. It does not take much imagination to see how or why in the Christian imagination that what is redeemed in these economic senses is fallen humanity incapable of redeeming itself. We are redeemed by an economy of grace in which God procures in exact payment the human debt satisfied by the transaction of the cross. Hence, redemption has been foremost signified economically by the vicarious atonement of Jesus Christ. While humanity may be eternally redeemed, however, the world, dominated by principalities and destructive powers, is not yet under the sovereignty of God. Evil and suffering persist. Having been eternally redeemed in Christ, however, Christian believers have every "revelatory" warrant (based not only on their election in Christ and predestination but also in their confidence in prevenient grace) for believing that God is working some good in the world, or in them, or that God will make right their suffering. The redeemed says confidently:

Question 1: What is your only comfort in life and in death? That I belong—body and Soul, in life and in death—not to myself but to my faithful savior, Jesus Christ, who at the cost of his own blood has fully paid for all my sins and has completely freed me from the domination of the devil; that he protects me so well that without the will of my Father in heaven not a hair can fall from my head; indeed, that everything must fit his purpose for my salvation. Therefore, by the Holy Spirit, he also assures me of eternal life, and makes me wholeheartedly willing and ready from now on to live for him.[30]

In the economy of grace, the objective modality of redemption has been a matter of having been saved by the act of another, in this case by God. This belief is expressed not only in doctrine but also in songs of thanksgiving and adoration and in testimonies about the goodness of the delivering power of the blood of Jesus. In African American churches and homes, everyday, ordinary believers sing: "I know it was the blood / I know it was the blood / I know it was the blood for me / One day when I was lost / He died upon the cross / I know it was the blood for me."

Within the economy of grace, however, redemption displays not only an objective modality of being acted upon by another but also an agential or responsive modality, as in converting one's stock into a yield or an investment into a pay-off. This, too, is a signification of the economy of grace in which people reflexively draw on willpower, self-determination, self-assertion, self-worth, and even an unrecognized and unacknowledged surplus of power, capacity, or potentiality to stand, to reach beyond their perceived limitations, and to be at ease when all around is, as the hymn says, "sinking sand." This is the "responsibility" modality of the economy of grace that we call "redemptive suffering."[31] In the economy of grace, redemptive suffering ought not to be understood as a matter of efficient causality such that x causes y. Rather, under the responsibility understanding of agency, the relation is more like formal causality in which it is the nature of x to be at the same time y such that if x, then y, and that relation cannot be otherwise. But the responsibilist character of x to y is organic. Unless it is materially influenced by the relation of x to the world, environment, or circumstances of life, y cannot display itself. Now where x is suffering people, we must remember that it is they who, at the same time, display from within themselves a surplus of willpower, self-determination, self-worth, capacity, and potentiality to stand through, find meaning in, and even be empowered by a surplus of good. This is not because of the sufferings they endure or the evils that afflict them. Rather, within the economy of grace symbolized by redemptive suffering, these manifestations of transcendence are copresent in the creative exchange of sufferers in and through their suffering. They are not the derived benefit of suffering and evil. The following story will help bring home this rather abstract account of my responsibilist understanding of redemptive suffering.

Not in recent years has the death of a friend affected me so as that of my friend Miles. I have known loss and grief in my lifetime. I have witnessed the suffering and pain of friends and loved ones now gone because of cancer and AIDS. I am no novice to human misery. But Miles's death made me aware that there are persons who suffer well and experience a good death. Miles and I embraced the excellence of friendship in and through his suffering. He and I were about the same age; we liked the same music and we drank the same cocktail (gin martini). He liked to read novels. Even as he lay in his hospital bed at the VA hospital, he was reading *Harry Potter and the Sorcerer's Stone*. He could not read much toward the end, but he would not put the book down. He slept with it.

Miles was dying of prostate cancer and in great pain. As I lifted him in and out of his bed, he would cringe as his body touched the bedsheets. His body hurt. I could do nothing to ease his misery. Even as he slept—due to high doses of morphine—his eyes never seemed really to close. It was as if he felt he would miss something if he slept.

As a philosophical skeptic, I responded to Miles's suffering with anger and rage at his God and his Christ. I kept asking myself, Why isn't Miles bitter? Like Job's wife, I wondered why he would not just curse God and die. Still, he kept faith with both God and Harry Potter throughout his suffering. He even had me read the Bible to him and hold his hands to pray. When his body shivered as he lay in bed, he reached out to me in the chair that had become my second home. I would take his hand, climb into his bed, and hold him to keep him warm until he would fall into sleep. Miles would say to me at times, "Victor, we don't have much more time." Then he would grow silent and look out the window, smiling as if Jesus was outside his window calling to him, calling him home. Home—not Antioch, Tennessee, or Nashville, but *home* the way Stephanie Mills means it when she sings the song by that name from *The Wiz*. He maintained faith throughout his suffering and in me as his friend who was losing a friend. On Christmas eve, I made plans to stay with Miles until Christmas Day. It was about 8:00 P.M. He sat up and his spirit was light. He looked at me as I sat in my now-familiar chair by the door where he expected me to be. He said in a soft voice, "Do me a favor. Please go have a martini for me tonight," he said. I agreed and left his room, expecting to come back in the morning after toasting several martinis to Miles and several more for myself. Miles died before I could get back to his room to celebrate Christmas Day with him.

Neither Miles's story nor our friendship is unique. But his story is illustrative. How marvelously human that he could maintain faith on earth through so much suffering! Miles's faith was not a derivative of his suffering. Like millions throughout human history, he maintained faith, hope, love, and friendship throughout his suffering. Faith is copresent in the suffering. This means that we do not suffer in order to obtain faith. Such virtues as faith, courage, endurance, temperance, friendship, and magnanimity are not excellences peculiar to Christians, whether black or other. These human excellences, these human capacities and possibilities, are already present in human miseries, struggles, and sufferings. They are not derived from the miseries, struggles, or sufferings.

H. Richard Niebuhr says: "Questions of faith arise in every area of human existence though the word seems to be primarily religious, so that it is associated with such other terms as God, church and creed, we also use it with its synonym and antonyms, in many other connections."[32] Niebuhr is referring to the ways that we adjure one another to have faith in democracy, science, or technology. We adjure one another to keep faith with others—those living and deceased. We commend persons of good faith. And we have witnessed in more recent times the power of faith to destroy and devastate when faith in God is turned against an enemy. Niebuhr says:

> The experience of the twentieth century has brought into view that abyss of faithlessness into which men can fall. We see this possibility—that human history will come to its ends neither in a brotherhood of man nor in universal death under the blows of natural or man-made catastrophe, but in the gangrenous corruptions of a social life in which every promise, contract, treaty and word of honor is given and accepted in deception and distrust. If men can no longer have faith in each other, can they exist as men?[33]

As I argued in this book's introduction while discussing Gustafson's account of religious experience, whether racial or other, the meaning and value we assign to the experiences of suffering and evil are matters of interpretation.[34] As Niebuhr suggests in the above quotation, the meaning of faith is also derived from within a community of interpretation. Stanley Hauerwas succinctly makes the point in his discussion of suffering:

> We assume that suffering is a natural category—after all we all have had the experience of suffering. But our assumption that we have had a common experience of suffering is misleading. Our ability to recognize our suffering means that suffering takes place in an interpretative context. In a sense, therefore, we must be taught that and

how we suffer. That such is the case, however, does not prevent us from characterizing the general nature of suffering, as long as we remember that in fact we do not suffer in general, but from this or that in this or that way.[35]

Therefore, what is derivative in a pragmatic account of evil and suffering is meaning and our valuations of our experiences of suffering. What meaning and value Miles saw in his suffering was given as an effect of his participation in community with me and others, but especially his black church family. Such meaning and value are creative events in creative exchange. Suffering did not create his capacity for faith. Suffering and the limits of the world occasioned it. Through his participation in a religious community, his understanding and appreciation of his sufferings displayed in his faith was given interpretation in the languages of God's will, love, and providential care. I cannot say that he was wrong or misguided.

There is no clean distinction between inquiry into the meanings of both God and faith. In the responsibilist approach to theology; theology deals with the "God of faith" and at the same time "faith in God." This is the grotesquery of theological discourse. We cannot bracket faith in order to inquire into its substantive content, whether of God, Christ, evil, or suffering. We begin with faith and participate in it. As I read Niebuhr, faith is human before it is ever theological. It points to the universal in human experience. He says: "[Faith is a] fundamental personal attitude which, whether we call it faith or give it some other name, is apparently universal and general enough to be widely recognized."[36] It is "the attitude and action of confidence in, and fidelity to, certain realities as the sources of value and the object of loyalty."[37] Faith displays passive and active modalities. Passively, it is the confidence and trust that one has so that one trusts in what gives him or her value. Actively, faith signifies loyalty to that which conditions one's confidence and loyalty. Trust is the passive side of faith and loyalty is its active side.

When Niebuhr himself took up the active aspect of faith (loyalty), he agreed with Josiah Royce that loyalty is ordinary, universally expected, and socially necessary, although "the causes to which loyal men [sic] commit themselves are varied, but the spirit of fidelity, or its form, is always the same."[38] Niebuhr writes:

> Selfhood and loyalty go together; that however confused the loyalties of selves may be, however manifold their causes, and however frequent their betrayals, yet it is by fidelity that they live no less than by a confidence in centers of value which bestow worth on their existence. Centers of value and causes may, however, be only two names

for the same objective reality from which and for which selves live as valued and valuing beings.[39]

Faith is the general context in which our various interpretations of religious experiences, even the experiences of suffering and evil, obtain their meanings and significances. Faith entails two dynamic intentionalities, namely, trust and loyalty. It involves trust and loyalty to oneself, others, and, by enlargement, to a cause that transcends every other cause.

However, faith is neither a blind trust or confidence in another, others, or events, nor is it an unconditional loyalty or fidelity to a person, value, or cause. Such faith is not creative because the exchange does not entail the qualitative value of worth or worthiness beyond affective relations. Conditioning both the passive and active modalities of faith is the "assertional" modality. It is the modality of belief. Tyron Inbody is worth quoting at length on this point:

> Assent (believing that), trust (believing in), and loyalty to (faithfulness), though distinguishable, cannot be separated. . . . We cannot embrace saving faith without affirming certain claims; we cannot trust God without believing something about God—for example that God has come to us in a saving way in Jesus Christ, that Christ indeed can and does save us. "It's impossible to please God apart from faith. And why? Because anyone who wants to approach God must believe both that God is, that he exists and that he cares enough to respond to those who seek him" (Heb 1:6, *The Message*). Even if faith is primarily trust and confidence, beliefs are the way by which our recognition of God's graciousness to us is interpreted and nourished. Even though we may not be self-conscious about those beliefs, we are believing something. Faith as belief, trust, and loyalty converge as saving faith when we become conscious enough about our faith to say, "I believe," meaning "I believe most deeply that . . . I base my deepest confidence in . . . I am loyal to the conviction that. . . ."[40]

One does not have to hold belief in a personal God with human characteristics of thought, will, or agency in order to affirm this unity of trust, loyalty, and belief in faith. It is enough to keep in mind this unity as we seek in our various interpretations of religious experience to be attentive to the structures of trust and confidence, loyalty and fidelity, and the beliefs that inform these modalities in people's experiences of evil and suffering. In creative exchange, faith reaches beyond the immediacy of evil and suffering as a creative possibility copresent in suffering. This surplus of value, creatively exchanged in the event of suffering and evil, may be interpreted theistically by some, as humanity writ large by others, or it might be what Henry Nelson Wieman called his ultimate commitment to creative interchange. The surplus of value may even be interpreted in the sort of black humanism commended by both Williams and Pinn. Capacity for faith, hope, and love can be theologically interpreted, but these human capacities need not be. What is clear is that all suffering—its meaning and value—is understood, interpreted, and appreciated within communities of interpretation, trust, and loyalty. Niebuhr says: "Thus faith exists in the I-Thou community, in the reciprocity of trust and distrust which responds to fidelity and infidelity, shifting back and forth between selves who have this peculiar nature that they cannot live as selves save in covenant with others."[41]

Agreement on the meaning of one's suffering is achieved in the trust and loyalty derived from our particular communities of faith and interpretation. We African American religious thinkers may disagree over our various interpretations of "black suffering." What is not debatable, it seems to me, is that in the economy of grace signified by redemptive suffering, copresent in black suffering are emergent potentialities of creative exchange, deep human capacities that sustain the oppressed under horrendous human ill will. In *The Creative Encounter*, Howard Thurman makes a very similar account of redemptive suffering. Of the two spiritual disciplines that may prepare one for creative encounter with the divine, Thurman lifts up prayer and suffering. He says: "There is at least one other discipline aside from prayer that may contribute significantly to the meaning not only of religious experience but may throw light upon both principals in the religious experience. I refer to human suffering."[42]

Thurman identifies two "roadblocks" to religious experience as he considers the phenomena of suffering. The first is the sheer reality of pain and the other is the of hostility toward God in one's suffering that often accompanies that pain. Magnifying the problem of pain is its association with evil. That is, actual pain, discomfort, and frustration with pain makes the whole of life "feel" absurd. Here, pain meets the profound sense of evil. Thurman is not speaking philosophically of abstract evil but of evil as a felt quality of the one who undergoes unrelenting pain; pain that robs the individual of the "lift and renewal" that religious experience brings, pain that makes such an experience seem "remote and unreal."[43]

Thurman appears here to evoke the now-classical distinction between moral and nonmoral evil discussed earlier in this chapter. That suffering which comes by way of human wickedness is sin (moral evil), and that which is the effect of the limits of the world on our bodies and mental powers may be best understood as having the felt quality of evil. Thurman's response, however, is most consistent with the premodern description of the Christian attitude toward evil discussed by MacIntyre and Surin, for Thurman says that Christian faith brings the assurance that "God is the final answer to all that there is, which includes evil itself."[44] As we wait for the final deliverance, however, Thurman evokes suffering as a spiritual discipline. He says that "the suffering is real and must be dealt with. It is in dealing with personal suffering and pain that the discipline of spirit may—I emphasize the word may—guide one to the heart of religious experience. That it has this possibility is my only contention."[45]

Here, Thurman's position squares with the claims I have been trying to argue for, namely, that the symbol of redemptive suffering does not reference any secondary benefits, goods, or virtues derived from suffering. Rather, such powers, virtues, goods, or benefits are copresent in the experience of suffering as human possibilities, which Thurman describes as the effects of the human spirit. According to Thurman:

> Suffering calls up all the resources of the individual. It tends to dominate his total horizon pushing all else aside. It becomes a great rallying point for energy. The individual fights for survival either in body, in spirit, or in soul. In the primary demand that is made upon the resources of spirit, the individual comes to a point of focus. He becomes centered first as a defense against the complete conquest by the suffering itself. Often this seems hardly possible.[46]

The second spiritual problem of suffering, according to Thurman, is the hostility that suffering evokes in the individual toward God, whom the individual blames for his or her suffering. Here, we are met with Thurman's version of the classical problem of evil, expressed as "Why did God do this to me?" "Why am I punished?" or "I do not deserve it." The expressions are in the deepest sense theodical, a matter of injustice, but they are most reflective of the attack on the basic worth of the self, on human decency. "In my pain, there is a miscarriage not of justice merely but of human decency. Such acute hostility cannot be resolved or drained off until the individual faces God with his fact."[47]

> Here I do not mean accusing God in conversation with someone else about God and the why of the pain; I do not mean hiding one's hostility under the fevered words of someone else's outcry. No. None of these will do. What I am thinking of is this. At last the individual has to say directly to God in encounter how he feels completely and thoroughly. This is not easy because it is against the context of the

faith to "blow one's top" as it were to God about God. It is a form of arrogance, of bumptiousness, of blasphemy. Such behavior is to be irreverent. Thus we repress our true feelings about the evil with which we wrestle, and meanwhile our God becomes a sleeping ghost among the stark hills of our own barren wasteland.[48]

As MacIntyre and Surin point out, the problem of evil in premodern Christian attitude is one of devotion, confession, and the cultivation of the spiritual disciplines. For Thurman, the so-called problem of evil is resolved in the spiritual discipline of devoted Christian confidence in God's purposes and faithful surrender:

> What hostility may do is to serve as a guide through the wilderness of our suffering until we are brought to the door of the temple. When we face God with our hostility, a kind of ultimate suction takes place which empties us completely. This is achieved in our confession to Him about how we feel toward Him, toward life, and perhaps toward ourselves about our suffering. Out of our struggle, we may be given insight into the suffering itself; we may be given quiet assurance, or we may relax our intent into His Purpose, or we may turn it over to Him in quiet obedience. But this must be truly done.[49]

As I read Thurman, his position is not that suffering produces faith, trust, hope, or love, or any other possible good or virtue in the individual who suffers. Rather, it is in and through suffering that these qualities of human spirit are brought to bear on the immediacy of suffering. Suffering occasions possibilities in the experience of the one who suffers.

> Suffering requires an ultimate answer. It must be dealt with in a manner which seems to be at least provisionally conclusive. The logic of the tragic fact is to lead the individual to whatever are for him ultimate considerations. All of his powers are focused on the issue involved in trying to reduce his suffering to a manageable unit of control or to get rid of it. There is concentration of the self already, and this is one of the prime requisites for the religious experience. There is at the heart of this concentration a search for an ultimate fact capable of dealing with the rigors of suffering. Hence the sufferer stands in immediate candidacy for the very core of religious experience. It should be pointed out that the attitude that I have discussed calls attention to one of the live options of the human spirit in dealing with suffering, which option has the possibility of "readying" the spirit for religious experience.[50]

While Thurman's discourse is most focused on the sufferings of individual persons, I want to emphasize that the transformative powers exchanged in our experiences of suffering not only change us at the personal level but also at the societal level, where our sufferings may occasion our capacities to help. Within our communities of faith and interpretation, our experiences of suffering occasion human possibilities of transcendence over the immediacy of misery, despair, and closure. African Americans who have historically experienced the worst brutalities under white supremacy that human consciousness can imagine have also displayed such a faith in their cultural testimonies and monuments, songs and poetry, autobiographies and sermons, prayers and literature, art and dancing, and in scholarly critiques of white supremacy. Powers such as faith, hope, love, self-control, resistance, courage, resilience, and more are irreducible substantive creative events symbolized by redemptive suffering. From my interpretation of redemptive suffering, these capacities and their actualizations enrich and empower us all. They do not do so because of suffering itself. No. What virtues and excellences are disclosed in the suffering of a people are copresent as emergent potentialities of suffering. They are not derivative. This is how I understand the powerful symbol of redemptive suffering in my pragmatic theology of African American religious experience. Such a view does not require belief in the personhood of God, but believing in a personal God is neither incompatible nor incommensurable with my interpretation.

CONCLUSION

In the economy of grace, redemptive suffering is a grotesque symbol. To some like Pinn and Williams it is a debilitating symbol when construed as suggesting that suffering and evil are justified when they are deployed by God to cultivate certain virtues or produce certain moral goods, benefits, or outcomes for a people. The benefits then outweigh the means, namely blacks' unmerited suffering. I am sympathetic to both Pinn's and Williams's criticisms. They, however, foreground the objective modality of redemption within the economy of grace. When redemptive suffering is used to sustain the status quo of evil and suffering, it is a malicious symbol and we are warranted in radically exploding its significance in African American religious experience. However, my defense of the symbol accents the "responsibilist" modality of redemptive suffering in which in and through such suffering there is an exchange of powers, capacities of worth and value that issue in faith, hope, and love, not because of evil and suffering but as copresent in suffering.

The great stories of our heritage, as diverse as they are, display within our various religious traditions the capacities of African American people to maintain faith, hope, and love, not only for ourselves as a race, but even for humanity by enlargement. We turn to the stories of the past, not only to understand and appreciate the human possibilities of faith in and through suffering. These stories also provide witness to the present generation of another human possibility. Suffering occasions the possibility of help. Phillip Hallie says:

> After Cain killed Abel, Cain asked God, with some asperity, "Am I my brother's keeper?" And much of the rest of the Bible is an answer to that question. The prophet Isaiah reflected his answer in these words, "Correct oppression, defend the fatherless, plead for the widow," and many pages before and after the Book of Isaiah reflect the same reply. But not only ink reflects it. Living human experience reflects it, and reflects it as clearly as living human experience reflects a cold no to Cain's question. For instance, the experience I know best is my own, and my experience is like the puddle outside our kitchen window, a tiny, temporary mirror of long demands. In the curse of my life, I have seen and felt many demands for help, and have seen and felt many cold and hot refusals to meet that demand.... I have helped strangers, I have hurt strangers, and I have not given a damn about them. Strangers are different from beloved intimates: Helping is the nerve of intimacy, it is what intimacy is. Mutual love is mutual need satisfied.[51]

This human capacity toward transcendence over suffering sustains us from the false sense that we are fated by dehumanizing powers of white supremacy. The capacity to help is also not derivative—however limited it may be at times and however forgetful we may be of the need to help others. In discussing medicine as a moral art, Hauerwas makes a similar claim when he says:

> It is the burden of those who care for the suffering to know how to teach the suffering that they are not thereby excluded from the human community. In this sense medicine's primary role is to bind the suffering and the nonsuffering into the same community. Unfortunately, medicine is used too often to guard us from those who suffer.
>
> But this is hard to say these things without being misunderstood. I am not saying that we ought to welcome suffering. We certainly ought not to enjoy suffering and we rightly think that anyone who does must be pathological, for that is our attitude toward masochism. Suffering should not be sought, but it ought to be accepted, at least in certain forms.
>
> Nor do I want to claim that suffering ought to be accepted because by doing so we will be better people. Suffering is seldom a

school for character, but rather a test of character. It may reveal us as better or worse than we had thought ourselves to be. Suffering can just as easily destroy us as it can make us more resolute. Suffering cannot be justified, therefore, because it may provide us with an occasion to grow. Indeed, as Iris Murdoch is fond of pointing out through her novels, suffering is seldom ennobling, because it takes an extraordinary person to survive either great suffering or happiness. My point, however, is that even if suffering is destructive in particular instances, the destruction is still a sign of strength as our pledge as humankind that we continue to be willing to risk caring.[52]

The capacities to help and care, as well as of our other redemptive symbols, their meanings and values, may appropriately be interpreted and appreciated within our various communities of faith and helped through sermons and prayer, through giving not only to the maintenance of our religious structures but also for benevolence, outreach to the poor, and the volunteering of our time, gifts, talents, and energies to make a difference for those whose lives are defined by misery. In 2005, Hurricane Katrina showed us not only some of the worst aspects of human misery but also our government's capacity to care at its worst. At the same time, however, it also showed the better side of human capacity to care for the needs of others. Whatever acts of help emerged in the disaster are creative events. They are the fruit of creative exchange between human misery, suffering, and wickedness and human sympathy, faith, hope, and love. In the next chapter, I substantiate "religious experience" itself within the creative exchange between Howard Thurman, pragmatic naturalism, and the problem of prayer.

CHAPTER 4

The Smell of Life

A Pragmatic Theology of Religious Experience

I am convinced that neither death, nor life, nor angels, nor rulers, nor things present, nor things to come, nor powers, nor height, nor depth, nor anything else in all creation, will be able to separate us from the love of God. . . . (Rom 8:38-39a-b)

"Impossible . . . Nothing is impossible . . . Come on, Mouse, dig! Dig, Mouse . . ." Phillipe Gaston, *Ladyhawke*[1]

THIS CHAPTER IS MOST CENTRAL to this book because it articulates why this is a constructive theology of African American religious experience. I take experience to be no mere happening of serendipitous events and exchanges, but the occasion of creative events and exchanges between human beings and nonhuman others. Rather, it is interpretation that gives meaning and value to our experiences. In this chapter, I use the concept of creative exchange to "construct" my understanding of and appreciation for African American religious experience.

Before proceeding to the more explicit discussion of this construction by way of Howard Thurman, Josiah Royce, Henry Nelson Wieman, and James Gustafson, I situate my discussion within a contemporary parable that moves experientially through the form of exchange that theologian Gordon Kaufman calls "serendipitous creativity." Kaufman says:

History unfolds in quite surprising ways and quite unexpected directions—both good and evil—as it gradually produces the vast network of folkways, institutions, languages, ideologies, values, practices. The historical order of being we call "culture" is created, with its goods and values—but also its enormous tensions and its momentums toward destructiveness, including oppression, corruption, war, even human self-annihilation. The great literary symbol of this outwork-ing of human creativity is Frankenstein's monster; the great factual symbol is the discovery of ways to harness the energy of the atom. The creation of the human imagination with the greatest potential for good, it seems always to threaten to get out of control and to bring about enormous destructiveness and evil. This capacity or fea-ture of history, to produce vastly more than we human inventors and creators and purposers expected or intended is what I call the "seren-dipity of history." Most of what we men and women count as goods peculiar to human existence have resulted from this serendipity; our complex institutional structures and divisions of labor; our intricate languages, making possible highly nuanced modalities of experience, consciousness, and self-consciousness; our very historicity, and hence our capacities for creativity and for taking responsibility for ourselves and our future; in short, all that is truly distinctive about our human-ity—our humanness itself, the distinctly "spiritual" dimensions of our existence, or capacities for humaneness.[2]

For Kaufman, serendipitous creativity is a way of taking hold of the ambi-guities, the grotesquery of the natural and human conditions that feed the religious imagination and give rise to our symbolic constructions of God in human experience. The parable of *Ladyhawke*, I think, illuminates Kauf-man's description of serendipitous creativity. Serendipitous creativity sug-gests that our experiences are open to meaning and significance when they are reflected upon as a unity of memory and feelings, senses and affections, events and spaces, and enchantment and disenchantment, even while under-going them, and that these experiences can be meaningfully interpreted through the symbol of God.

LADYHAWKE: *A PARABLE*

As I begin this chapter on religious experience, *Ladyhawke*, one of my favor-ite movies, comes to mind. This movie impresses me for its power to enchant my world, which has for me become disenchanted by the routines of every-day, late capitalist social experience. *Ladyhawke* begins with a boy's voice, that of Phillipe Gaston, a thief also known as the Mouse, making his escape through the sewers of Aquila, his prison home. He is talking to God. Bearing the stench of the sewers on his every breath, Phillipe bargains with God. His prayers are ordinary and reflexive. He and God are together in the sewers. In his everyday, ordinary conversation between himself and God, Phillipe crawls his way to freedom, saying: "It's not unlike escaping Mother's womb. God, what a memory!"

For Phillipe, praying is ordinary and so is bargaining with God: "Lord, I'll never pick another pocket as long as I live, I swear. But here's the problem—if you won't let me live, how can I prove my good faith to you?" Crawling and talking to God in the sewers, he finds a ledge to fix his steps. "If you've heard me, this ledge will remain steady as a rock, and that thing coming at me won't be what I think it is. If it is, there'll be no hard feelings, of course . . . but I'll be disappointed." Needless to say, Phillipe finds a way to an opening where he exclaims, "I don't believe it. . . . I believe it. I'm coming. It's Phillipe, Lord, Phillipe. You won't regret this, Lord. I'm a wonderful person." This is Phillipe's first encounter with serendipitous creativity.

Phillipe emerges from the sewers and his conversation with God with the smell of life upon him. Once freed, however, he steals clothing for himself. And remembering his bargain, he says: "I know I promised, Lord, never again. But I also know that you know, what a weak-willed person I am." He washes away the stench of the sewers, enters an inn, and orders the finest drink available not only for himself but for all who would join him in a toast. He boasts: "We drink to a special man, my friends, someone who has seen the dungeons of Aquila, and lived to tell the tale." Yet, for all his cunning and pride, he has no idea that the inn is filled with guards from Aquila who are there to retake him. With the guards pursuing him, a stranger intervenes at the very moment when Phillipe can only say, "God have mercy on my soul." The stranger is Navarre, the former captain of the guards at Aquila. Phillipe thus meets his second serendipitous encounter with creativity. Having saved the Mouse from the trap laid out for him, Navarre presses Phillipe into his service as a squire. Now, the Mouse *feels* trapped into a service that is anything but enchanting. Under the felt weight of his service, he complains:

> Comrade-in-arms! Slave is more like. See to the fire, feed the animals, gather the wood. . . . Look at me, Lord! I was better off at the dungeons of Aquila! My cellmate was insane, and a murderer, but he respected me! He's a strange one, Navarre. Why did he save my life? He wants something from me, I can see it in his eyes. Well whatever it is, I'm not going to do it! I'm still a young man, you know! I've got prospects!"

Indeed, Navarre does want something of the Mouse, but it will require his absolute devotion to a cause that he did not choose for himself and a loyalty that he did not forge out of his own experience. Rather, it is a loyalty forged out of his serendipitous encounter with the tragedy that surrounds Navarre and his hawk companion.

While in his post as captain of the guards, Navarre encountered the beautiful Isabeau. She had come to live with her cousin at Aquila after the death of her father, the count D'Anjou. Navarre and Isabeau fell in love but kept their love was a secret because the Bishop of Aquila had his own sensuous intentions for Isabeau. But their love was betrayed to the bishop by their confessor, the drunken friar, Imperious. Furious with envy, the bishop swore that the two lovers would never celebrate their love for each other. Imperious describes the bishop's passion as a "sort of madness. He was possessed! He swore that if he could not have Isabeau, no one would." He called upon the powers of the Evil One, sold his soul to the dark powers, and released a curse upon the two lovers. Isabeau would become a hawk by day and transform into her human form at night; Navarre by day would be human in form but by night be transformed into a wolf. Imperious mourns their tragic fate: "Poor dumb creatures, with no memory of the half-life of their human existence, never touching in the flesh. Only the anguish of a split second at sunrise and sunset, when they can almost touch . . . but not." Within the tragic sense of life, Phillipe is not the only one to have regular conversations with God. Imperious, Navarre, and Isabeau all talk to God out of their own distinct sense of fatedness.

God listens and makes a way for these unfortunates' redemption and fulfillment. Imperious is shown in a vision how the curse may be broken. Navarre and Isabeau must confront the bishop together in their human forms. Only then will they be free to enjoy the smell of life on each others' human bodies once again. In the serendipity of their tragic existence, the possibility of their redemption also involves the thieving Mouse and the drunken priest. In the enchanted yet tragic condition of their serendipitous encounters, redemption is not in the power of their own hands. They are constrained by the limits of being human and animals, bound by the world and its limits. Redemption will depend upon the world, its processes, and possibilities. For as long as there is night and day, redemption is not possible for the four companions. Yet, in a vision, Imperious sees an impossible possibility. He is given an insight that "three days hence, in Aquila, there will be a day without a night, and a night without a day."

With a mild hope but strong resolve to bring their tragic existence to an end, the four companions enter Aquila as the bishop celebrates Mass. Navarre is bent on killing him. Isabeau is present as the hawk. Imperious enters Mass as a priest. And the Mouse finds himself once again making his way through the drainage system of Aquila, hoping to find a path that will allow him to open the doors of Aquila for his compatriots. And still morning and night were as they have always been. Except this day, in one moment, a moment that transcends the ordinary expectations of day and night, the sky darkens. The sun is eclipsed by the moon. At that serendipitous moment, there exists a day without sun and a night without day. The curse that defines their existence is broken. Isabeau and Navarre are restored to embrace each other in all of their humanness. Imperious finds forgiveness. The Mouse is redeemed. And the bishop is brought to ultimate justice for his evils.

> Imperious: "I fully intend to meet you at the pearly gates, little thief. Don't you dare disappoint me!"
> The Mouse: "I'll meet you there, Father. Even if I'd have to pick the lock."

THE INNER WITNESS IN THURMAN'S PHENOMENOLOGY OF RELIGIOUS EXPERIENCE

My account of religious experience is drawn from my reading of American pragmatism and empirical theology and takes a pragmatic naturalist point of view. On the question of religious experience, I usually find myself in conversation with Howard Thurman, who, to my mind, has given the fullest philosophical attention to the idea of religious experience, at least in African American religious thought. While I share much with Thurman on the social and ethical demands of personalism, I do not share his epistemological foundationalism or, better, his personalistic idealism for grasping in consciousness the reality of God. Nevertheless, the social and moral consequences of his personalism I think are quite compatible with the pragmatic theology I propose. Thurman allows me to gain clarity on my own position. Hence, he is for me a profound interlocutor on the question of religious experience. His account is based on the *creative encounter* between the individual as subject and self, as private and personal, and the divine personality in whom we have our being and on whom our lives are held in a comprehensive coherence with our experience of the world. My account of religious experience is constructed on the concept of *creative exchange*. The difference in our positions will hang on the logic of radical subjectivity and the a priori of personality on the one hand, and radical empiricism on the other. In the remainder of this section, I give a close reading of Thurman's phenomenology of religious experience from the point of view of radical subjectivity or what he calls the "inner witness" before taking up my own position in the following section.

For Thurman, the creative encounter is a reflexive experience within an "inner process" or, to be more exact, an inner event or series of events that are typified as religious experience. At its core, the experience is personal and, hence, private. By *private*, Thurman has in mind a concept of radical subjectivity in which the world of the self is "my world." It is the inner world "within where for us the great issues of our lives are determined. It is here that at long last the 'yea' and 'nay' of our living is defined, declared. It is private. It is cut off from immediate involvement in what surrounds us. It is my world."[3] Although that's a radical view of subjectivity, Thurman insists that the self, as personal and private, is not a projection of the mind. It is not epiphenomenal but actual; it is the *real*.[4] Consider Boston personalist Edgar S. Brightman on this point:

> Any system of metaphysics rests in one or more first principles. First principles obtain in numerous fields. For example, there are first principles of logic (we have just assumed coherence), of method, of epistemology, of quantity (is the universe a unity or a plurality?), and of quality (what kind of reality is ultimate—mental, material, or neutral?). In answer to the question of quality, men have consists of atoms and the void, of unconscious energy, or of Space-Time, of process, of monads, of neutral entities, or of spirits and ideas. A personalist is one who holds that what seems not to be a self is a part or aspect or experience of a self or selves. Nothing exists except in, of, and for a self. For personalism, personality or selfhood is a first principle.[5]

Here, the self is the condition for the possibility of mind itself with all its powers and activities such as thinking, reasoning, judging, and valuing. The real is personal. It is an inversion of Descartes's dictum: "I think, therefore, I am." Rather, "I exist, therefore, I think." The individual experiences his or her existence even before having a theory of either experience or the self. It is a reflexivity of subjectivity itself that feels itself personal and private while, at the same time, such a feeling is itself made possible by an inner consciousness of the "not self." Thurman explains it this way: "True, I am not only a child of my nature, of parents, but also I am a child of my nation, which in turn makes me a child of my civilization and the cultures and civilizations long since passed into history. But there remains a private, personal world which I claim as uniquely my own."[6]

It is important to Thurman's account of religious experience that the inner awareness is a priori. It is an immediate perception, a direct and unmediated form of consciousness so that knowledge of the self is a direct perception of "my self." Thurman's position lies deeply in the personalist legacy of Albert Cornelius Knudson. Gary Dorrien says of Knudson:

> Though he blasted the Barthians unmercifully for basing their theological affirmations on a self-authenticating revelation, he had his own version of a self-authenticating religious basis, the theory of the religious a priori that he borrowed from Schleiermacher and Otto. Knudson believed that the appropriation of this theory rescued religion from skepticism and dogmatism in the same way that Kant saved reason; just as Kant theorized that there are principles immanent in the mind that make experience possible, the doctrine of the religious a priori posited that religion is woven into the structure of the human mind. Like the Kantian categories, the religious a priori explained the possibility of experience (in this case, religious experience), but like the Kantian categories, it resisted all attempts to explain the explanation. The religious a priori made religion underivable and therefore self-authenticating.[7]

For Thurman, the religious a priori is the condition for the possibility of religious experience, and religious experience is a corollary of personality. Religious experience is conditioned by an inner, immediate, and direct perception of the self's "exposure to God." Here, Thurman deploys William James's idea of "knowledge by acquaintance" to fill out the claim. He writes:

> Such an experience seems to the individual to be inclusive of all the meaning of his life—there is nothing that is not involved. There is present here what William James refers to as "acquaintance-knowledge" as contrasted with "knowledge about." It is immediate experience and yet experience that is purely immediate is not quite possible. The individual is never an isolated, independent unit. He brings to his religious experience certain structural and ideological equipment or tools. This equipment is apt to be very determinative in how he interprets the significance not only of his religious experience but also the significance of experience itself.[8]

Thurman's account of the a priority of religious experience, as an immediate and direct inner intuition, runs into an apparent paradox. The paradox is this: while the percept is immediate, it nevertheless is substantiated by mediating structures of the life-world of the individual. That is, the social life-world substantiates the individual as personal and private. If we grant the apriority of acquaintance-knowledge, then the individual stands in the subject-position of an "experiencer."[9] Brightman is helpful here:

> A man cannot know himself thoroughly without searching into all
> the knowledge from within and from without that he can discover in
> order to shed light on his own purposes and character. . . . It is neces-
> sary to add that individuals do not experience themselves as alone in
> the world; everyone is aware of a social environment. However one
> construes its possibility, the fact of communication with others is a
> fundamental fact about every self, and social communication is a most
> important way of knowing about personality.[10]

For Thurman, the individual and what is experienced are nonequivocal,
and cannot be equivocated, if Thurman is not to fall into solipsistic absur-
dity. But how can he evade this readily anticipated criticism? He has to turn
to a more substantial account of the individual, and this, it seems, weakens
his claims for the a priority of the self. He finds himself needing a "total
self."

> "In authentic religious experience the individual is himself totally
> involved. This involvement includes the context of meanings, experi-
> ences, and values by which the *persona* is defined. He does not come
> into the experience *de novo*, but rather does the individual come into
> the Presence of God with the smell of life upon him."[11]

As a phenomenological reduction, the *total self* is a substantial self with all
the sociocultural tools, equipment, or, as Thurman says, "raw materials of his
experience." These materials are progressively integrated into the appercep-
tions of radical subjectivity (what Brightman calls "from within and from
without") that signify the individual. The raw materials then "become parts
of what he [the individual] defines as his own person, his own personality, or
his own self. But the individual is never completely one with his experience.
He remains always observer and participant."[12]

Like the direct and immediate perception or a priority of personality, religious experience is also a priori, that is, an immediate and direct intuition
within the radical subjectivity of the individual. It is perceived as intrinsic,
sui generis, and qualitatively "supremely worthy." The religious a priori is
not a modality of the individual's subjectivity. Rather, it is the individual's
prehension of the "extraordinary in religious experience." In the experience of the individual, the religious a priori is the conscious awareness "of
meeting God" as another personality in experience.[13] Thurman's language
is one of "encounter," "confrontation," and a "sense of Presence." As such,
the religious a priori is apperceived as the "not self." Here, the experience
might be best understood in terms of the German concept of *Erfahrung*. It
is a knowledge that is acquired by direct observation, participation, or by

acquaintance with the "facts" of experience. Thurman himself describes this mode of apperception as an event in which:

> The individual is seen as being exposed to direct knowledge of ulti-mate meaning, *ne plus ultra* being, in which all that the individual is, becomes clear as immediate and often distinct revelation. He is face to face with something which is so much more, and so much more inclusive than all of his awareness of himself that for him, *in the moment*, there are no questions. Without asking, somehow he knows.[14]

The religious a priori is grasped as a form of "synoptic" intuition:

> The mind apprehends the whole—the experience is beyond or inclu-sive of the discursive. It is not other than the discursive, but somehow it is inclusive of the discursive. As [Lerone?] Bennett puts it, "It is the knowledge of the subject of all predicates." It is precisely because of this synoptic apprehension that the individual in the experience seems to come into possession of what he has known as being true all along. The thing that is new is the realization. And this is of profound importance.[15]

What is the form of this realization or what I would call this instantiation? It is the instantiation of a relation, of an encounter between two parties, two persons, the individual and God. This instantiation is an acknowledgment by *the inner witness* of the individual as a "total person." Thurman calls the intu-ition within the subjectivity of the individual *the residue of God-meaning*. "In religious experience God meets the individual at the level not only of the individual's needs, but also, in my judgment more incisively, at the level of his residue of God-meaning and goes forward from there."[16] This is an elusive concept in Thurman's phenomenology and deserves a more thorough treat-ment than I can supply here; however, it is perhaps best to grasp the meaning of this concept from the perspective of its temporal modality. It is "prelimi-nary," "a starting point of communication," and "a conscious toe hold for God." I understand the "residue of God-meaning" to be the condition for the possibility of encounter between God and the individual. It effectively makes possible the recognition of what is or what is not the divine in expe-rience. In this way, it is preliminary to the encounter itself.

Moreover, the residue of God-meaning has a typifying function in the subjectivity of the individual. That is, it allows the individual to discriminate in experience those forms of encounter, confrontation, engagement that substantially and qualitatively have the value of what we mean by God. The residue is not representational in function. That is, it does not represent, by way of the idea of God, a prior event or experience of God, such that when the idea is evoked, then God is present by proxy in the subjectivity of the individual by the idea.[17] Rather, the residue of God-meaning substantiates or "realizes" communion with God. Most simply put, the residue of God-meaning says in the subjectivity of the individual: "Yes, this is God."

For example, I imagine losing my puppy, my "little big boy," Sebastian, after raising him for six months. I look for him and do everything I can to find him—from posting fliers, contacting the Humane Society and animal clinics with his description, driving through neighborhoods, going through yards, calling his name—all to no avail. I just can't find him. One day while walking through the park, I spot a now fully grown black lab that reminds me of Sebastian. On a whim, I call his name, "Sebastian! Sebastian!" His ears perk up; his head turns; his tail wags. He runs to me and by every family resemblance with human emotions that he displays, at that moment of encounter, I know that he "realizes" who I am. There is in his consciousness a residue of paternal-meaning that connects him to me. He "knows" me as his father and he knows himself as "little big boy." The relation is actual, not representational. It is not the idea of Sebastian that makes this particular dog my dog. Rather, the name *Sebastian* functions in his consciousness as a condition for the possibility of actual and mutual recognition.

On Thurman's account, there are two dimensions in religious experience that signify the God-meaning residue. The one is *metaphysical* and, hence, universal, and the other is *personal* and, hence, relational. At the metaphysical level, the God-meaning in experience signifies God as

> . . . all-inclusive, all-comprehending, and in a profound sense universal. This means that God is not merely the creator of creatures, of all objects animate and inanimate, but also and more importantly, that God is the Creator of life itself. Existence is the creation of God; life is the creation of God. This is of more than passing significance. The effort is to provide some kind of crucial rationale for the aliveness of life. We are, all of us, impressed with the fact that there is what is defined as a live quality present in all living things.[18]

Above, I described the residue of God-meaning as the condition for the possibility of divine recognition in experience. As Thurman takes up this first dimension of God-meaning, the mode of recognition here is a boundary condition in which recognition of God satisfies the condition for the Absolute in experience. As with Schleiermacher, it is a profound intuition of the radical sense of dependency of all things on God, the Creator. God is the absolutely inclusive whole in and through which all particulars are related.

However, most crucial for Thurman is that the metaphysical dimension of God-meaning conditions the "living quality present in all living things." As God is the Creator of life; life intrinsically has the quality of being alive. Thurman says: "Life itself is alive. It is the quality of aliveness that bottoms and sustains all of the welter and variety of particular manifestations."[19] As a metaphysical principle, this dimension of God-meaning acknowledges "a subject of which all living things themselves are predicates." In God, we move and have our being. God predicates all living things intrinsically as living and, hence, existing. This metaphysical principle may be summed up best thus: *I, an existing thing, intuit this particular living-existing thing as my life.* This awareness of being a living thing is Thurman's first dimension of God-meaning. It is the dimension in religious experience that assures the individual that all of life has an intrinsic integrity or comprehensive coherence—a really real beyond the apparent—that is metaphysically assured. Thurman summarizes thus:

> In sum, the encounter with God, if it is to be satisfying, must be with One who is seen as holding within His context all that there is, including existence itself. This provides an ultimate point of reference for the final fact of experience of whatever character altogether. The significance of the assurance cannot possibly be overestimated. It suggests that here the human spirit is exposed to an ultimate clue to all levels of reality, to all the dimensions of time, and to all aspects of faith and the manifestations therein. If there is to be found anywhere an ultimate dependence on the fact of integrity, this is it. The individual, if he is assured in such an encounter, has the confidence of ultimate security. Such is the first demand that is made upon religious experience as defined.[20]

The form of assurance that Thurman ascribes to the first dimension is only a formal assurance grounded on the intuition of God as an intrinsically integrated whole. The second dimension of God-meaning Thurman calls personal. However, it might be better to understand it as a relational dimension of religious experience. Here, we are met with "someone who is capable of dealing personally and privately with the individual."[21] In this relational realm, the individual is more than a clog in the vastness of the universe. Rather, there is a qualitative dimension in the God-meaning residue that relates the individual to God, who is to the individual more than the condition for the possibility of existence and life.

> Deep within there is the need for recognition, for being personally regarded that persists and permits of no substitute. . . . Suffice it to

say here that one demand that is made upon religious experience is that it be private, personal, individual, and therefore unique. It is never sufficient for the individual to have a clue merely to ultimate significance in general, but there must be provided in the religious experience a *sense of the ultimate worth* of the individual himself as a private person.[22]

In religious experience, the God-meaning intuits a relational moment in experience that acknowledges the value and worth of the parties involved, namely, God and the individual. The experience is creative. It is not casual, random, or taken for granted. Rather, it has the characteristic of being serendipitous in the individual's experience. That is, although the context may be mundane—a Sunday drive or a walk or even listening to one's favorite song or watching a favorite movie—the context is nondeterminative. Even in such mundane moments, however, the individual may become "completely irradiated with the presence of God."[23] Thurman suggests that such an encounter ought not to be thought of as if the individual were a totally passive receptor for the event. Rather, the will of the individual is always cooperative and permissive in the experience. The individual is a ready and willing participant to the encounter. This openness or permissive will of the individual and God's openness to the individual, grasped as an intuition, together signify the creative encounter.

> When one has been thus prepared, a strange thing happens. It is very difficult to put into words. The initiative slips out of one's hands and into the hands of God, the other principal in the religious experience. The self moves toward God. Such a movement seems to have the quality of innate and fundamental stirring. The self does not see itself as being violated, though it may be challenged, stimulated, inspired, conditioned, but all of this takes place in a frame of reference that is completely permissive. There is another movement which is at once merged with the movement of the self. God touches the spirit and the will and a wholly new character in terms of dimension enters the experience.[24]

Religious experience, then, is profoundly relational. As I read Thurman, this recognition of God-meaning conditions the possibility of those elements that most outwardly connote religious experience, namely, worship, devoted service, praise, thanksgiving, and the assurance that all is well, despite human misery, pain, and suffering.[25] This is what is meant by comprehensive coherence. All is well because God is the all-inclusive guarantor of existence and life (metaphysical dimension) and assures that the individual's life is of supreme worth to God (relational dimension). In a summary note, Thurman says:

> Religious experience in its profoundest dimension is the finding of man by God and the finding of God by man. This is the inner witness. The moral quality is mandatory because the individual must be genuine in his preparation and in his motivation and in his response. His faith must be active and dynamic. It was pointed out earlier that the individual enters the experience and/or the preparation for it with the smell of life heavy upon him. He has in him all his errors and blindness, his raw conscience and his scar tissues, all his loves and hates. In fact all that he is as he lives life is with him in this experience. It is in his religious experience that he sees himself from another point of view. In a very real sense he is stripped of everything and he stands with no possible protection from the countenance of the Other. The things of which he is stripped are not thrown away. They are merely laid aside and with infinite patience they are seen for what they are. It is here that the great decision is made as to what will be kept and what will be discarded. A man may take a whole life-time to put away a particular garment forever. The new center is found, and it is often like giving birth to a new self. It is small wonder that so much is made in the Christian religion of the necessity of rebirth. There need not be only one single rebirth, but again and again a man may be reborn until at last there is nothing that remains between him and God.[26]

To conclude this section, there is much more to Thurman's account of religious experience that deserves serious philosophical attention. I have only isolated what I take to be those elements that have a preliminary role in his theory of experience, namely, the a priority of the self or personality grasped as a phenomenological reduction of radical subjectivity. As the large passage quoted above proposes, the test of religious adequacy in religious experience is the pragmatic test; it is practical. In religious experience, the qualitative relations and patterns of intersubjectivity between the individual to himself and to others best testify to the veracity and quality of the creative encounter. However, the ultimate assurance of the creative encounter is subjectively given in *the inner witness* of God-meaning in the individual's religious experience.

I am a great fan of Thurman and have the profoundest respect for his intellectual genius, so I am trepidatious that I have only touched on only one movement in his treatise on religious experience in *The Creative Encounter*— the one area in which he and I are in disagreement. I am not at odds with his social and ethical personalism, which is the extension of his strategy of grounding religious experience on the a priority of radical subjectivity. Rather, it is this very starting point of radical subjectivity that I find deeply problematic. I must agree with John Cobb's position that, as a metaphysical theology, personalistic idealism, predicated in the a priority of radical subjectivity, is simply unlikely to win a hearing among contemporaries who have abandoned any prospect for a critical epistemology based on speculative rather than descriptive categories:

> As long as one is secure in his conviction that reason provides an adequate basis for faith in a personal God, this situation must appear strange and to Christian theologians, by and large, eccentric. If, however, we recognize not only intellectually but also personally or existentially that reason supports faith only when it begins with a self-understanding or vision of reality that is not shared by the intellectual leadership of our time, then we can understand the fear of acknowledging dependence upon natural theology that characterizes modern theology and a whole.[27]

I take Cobb's point to be that any attempt to ground a naturalistic theology, such as personalism, on epistemic foundations of modernity's speculative reason, intuitions of psychical introspection, or a priori conditions of the mind or consciousness has little prospect of winning the ears of contemporary theologians and philosophers whose philosophical tastes are cultivated by post-Heideggarian and post-Wittgensteinian footings. For such religious thinkers, our biosocial, historical, and linguistic existence is the only condition we have for assessing meaning and value at all levels, but especially the meaning and value of individuals as persons. Thurman's epistemic foundations are simply out of sync with those of us who embrace the saturated and situated self as the given of meaning and value without the postulation of an unencumbered self or a "My-self" that is preliminary to the disclosures of the world. Notwithstanding Thurman's overture toward a "Total Self," the individual is rendered (literally a reduction as in making a sauce from scratch) the center of meaning and value in religious experience.

While Thurman's account of religious experience makes clear a relationship between mystical experience on personalistic terms, it also makes personalistic epistemology eccentric. Personal and, hence, private religion becomes the critical referee of what not only counts for God in experience but also for what is of social and moral worth. Through the radical subjectivization of aesthetic, religious, and moral judgment-intuition, intersubjective understanding and agreement are internal to the "Inner Witness."

Accordingly, the real may be personal, but what makes the person real? This is a question begged from the beginning.

My criticisms ought not to be understood as signaling anything like a total rejection of Thurman's overall discussion of religious experience. I think that his account of the spiritual disciplines as preparatory for the cultivation of religious devotion as well as the social and ethical demands of the creative encounter remain compelling. Rather, my disagreement is at the epistemic level. It concerns his assurance that God guarantees the comprehensive coherence of all our experience because God is personal. Given the grotesqueries of the world, the arbitrariness of good and evil, the serendipitous character of life, Thurman's postulate strikes me as being most doubtful. It was with these reservations in mind that I have sought a religious pragmatism in which the serendipitous, duplicitous, arbitrary, and grotesque characteristics of life are the beginning of religious reflection. As with Charles Sanders Peirce, the irritation of doubt is the starting point of inquiry. I have sought to construct a pragmatic theology of African American religious experience on such a ground.

TOWARD A PRAGMATIC THEOLOGY OF AFRICAN AMERICAN RELIGIOUS EXPERIENCE

The film *Ladyhawke* foregrounds the character of experience that Gordon Kaufman described as "creative serendipity." The serendipitous conditions of four lives are connected by surprising and arbitrary encounters in which the senses of fatedness, tragedy, and desperation are changed into possibility of faith, hope and love. A night without day and a day without night make possible horizons of meaning and value that the cohorts could not imagine for themselves except that nature found a way. When such creative serendipity happens, however, more often than not, there is a surplus of qualitative value in the experience itself, which Wieman identifies as creative interchange. I think that this same quality of life is immanent in Thurman's account of religious experience; however, for Thurman, this serendipitous creativity is taken up and resolved within the a priority of the inner witness of personality. Its ambiguity or grotesquery is resolved in creative union or communication. On my account, the senses of duplicity, ambiguity, or grotesquery that mark the serendipitous character of life are expressive of what Wieman and William James refer to as certain "felt qualities" of experiencing the world. By experience, I neither mean a pure unmediated sensation arising out of psycho-physiological neurons, nor do I mean it in a manner described by Wittgenstein as a private language game carried out in the subjective consciousness of the individual subject. Such states may be real enough, but such a construal of experience remains isolated by a totalized subjectivity of the individual subject.

Rather, I am speaking of experience in a more substantial, dynamic, and intersubjective manner with the world. "Whosoever feels his experience to be something substantial even while he has it, may be said to have an experience that reaches beyond itself. From inside of its own entity it says 'more,' and postulates reality existing elsewhere," says William James.[28] In talking about experience as a unity that reaches beyond the immediacy of a feeling or a subjective state of mind, John Dewey explicates the reflexive integration of aspects of human experience, which all too often remain unconnected— namely, art, aesthetic perception, and human experience:

> It is mere ignorance that leads then to the supposition that connection of art and esthetic perception with experience signifies a lowering of their significance and dignity. Experience in the degree in which it *is* experience is heightened vitality. Instead of being shut up within one's own private feelings and sensations, it signifies active and alert commerce with the world; at its height it signifies complete interpenetration of self and the world of objects and events. Instead of signifying surrender to caprice and disorder, it affords our sole demonstration of a stability that is not stagnation but is rhythmic and developing. Because experience is the fulfillment of an organism in its struggles and achievements in a world of things, it is art in germ. Even in its rudimentary forms, it contains the promise of that delightful perception which is esthetic experience.[29]

The senses of enchantment and disenchantment are aesthetic categories. They are felt qualities of experience. They name serendipitous or duplicitous qualities of rooms and spaces, people and sorrows, anxieties, play, and laughter. They signify in memory past events and places that although the events are no longer actual—except as memory—their felt qualities remain in the present and provide the conditions by which we take hold of the anticipated promises and losses of the future. It is in this way that we can speak of human experience as a unity of experience. The following story brings home this rather abstract understanding of experience and its ambiguity in an autobiographical manner.

I was a sickly child, suffering from rheumatic fever, a disease that can be fatal if left untreated. My days were filled with the anxiety of not knowing when or where I was going to pass out. It could be at the street corner waiting to cross to school, or in the line at Hamilton Park waiting to enter the swimming pool, or, most often, at church. By the time I was admitted to Chicago's Larabida Children's Hospital, the disease had nearly crippled me. I had never been away from my family for any great length of time. The hospital was a new space of the unfamiliar, yet in a very short time I got the hang of the routine. My temperature and vitals were taken three times a day. There was quiet time, of course. Bathing, eating, watching TV, tutoring, and arts and crafts all became routine, expected, and ordinary. I had a roommate, Roy, with whom I played games such as "A Barrel of Monkeys." Those games occasioned laughter in a space that was otherwise lonely and disenchanting.

In the days before being admitted in the hospital, I had been isolated within our home away from my brothers and sisters—a not-unusual occurrence in those days when one was sickly. The dining room in which I was housed felt like a funeral parlor, with its dark wood-paneled walls and stained-glass windows. When my siblings went off to school, I was left home alone in that room with nothing but my imagination and my favorite book, *The Sword in the Stone,* to keep me entertained. This book filled my waking and napping thoughts with visions of knights, dragons, King Arthur, and, above all, Excalibur, Merlin, and magic. Although I was ill and alone, that funereal room at those times felt enchanted in a way the hospital was not.

I knew that Michael, the boy in the next room, had an Etch-a-Sketch, and one day I decided that I wanted to play it, so I went next door and borrowed it from him. I delighted myself with creating crystal-like drawings by turning its two knobs to direct the flow of the lines and shaking the toy to erase those lines in order to draw new ones. Suddenly, a nurse came into my room and asked where I had gotten the toy. When I told her it came from Michael's room, she and the other staff members went into a frenzy. For the first time in my young life, I experienced a qualitatively different kind of fear. I knew what it was like to be scared by my brothers' antics, but this sense of dread was new to me.

Along with that sense of dread, for the first time, I also felt a sense of transgression. I had transgressed a boundary to get the toy. Michael was in an isolation room. I did not know what his sickness was or whether I would get what he had now that I had transgressed the space between our rooms. The sense of dread coupled with the sense of transgression was real and disenchanting. I was scolded, prodded, poked, and assigned to bed rest. After a week, I was allowed again into the routine world that my usual activities made enchanting. One night, I was wakened by the sounds of crying from the room next door. I did not need to know what was going on; I had heard those sounds before. In the morning, I was told that Michael had died that night, and that a new boy would be placed in the room next door. With

Michael's death, my enchanted world became dark, ominous, and disenchanted. These senses or felt qualities of the world have shaped how I understand and appreciate religious experience.

Although the events of my childhood are no longer available to me from an objective point of view, the experiences are present enough even in my adulthood as creative events that continue in religious experience to evoke the senses of enchantment and disenchantment. When I remember and imagine these events and experiences, these senses return to me as felt qualities of the world, of rooms and spaces, games played and toys played with, feelings of loneliness, fear, and dread evoked by youthful transgression and Michael's death. I do not think of my experiences and the senses they evoke as being anything like a purely subjective activity or a "private language game." Rather, they are "felt qualities" of religious experience. Moreover, these felt qualities of the world are not polarized or dichotomous so that the one is positive, empowering, and creative and the other negative, nontransformative, and disempowering. They are held together, unresolved in the creative actualities and possibilities of the world.

In *Pragmatic Theology*, I offered a conceptual account of several theological languages from which I find rich possibilities for interpreting religious experience. Among the categories are *finitude*, *transcendence*, *world*, and *grace*. With finitude and transcendence, I suggest that these categories ought not to be regarded as if they are inherently "theological." However, they can be given theological interpretations. For in agreement with James M. Gustafson, theology is a particular construal of the world so that finitude and transcendence can be rendered theological insofar as they circumscribe fundamental modes of the world and our human experiencing of the world. Theological languages are linguistic ways of taking hold of distinctive features of human life in the world. Again, as James puts it, they disclose distinctive felt qualities of the world.

Given the serendipitous character of experience, our world is so bound by limiting conditions that human beings will necessarily be thwarted by the push and pull of physical nature, environmental and ecological conditions, our bodies, disease, and mortality, despite all the imaginative powers we might muster to overcome these limits. We are not omnipotent. At every moment, our lives are met with limits. Indeed, finitude limits us in every action. As a consequence, in politics and public policy-making, in our moral commitments to advance human happiness, in our interventions into the ecological ordering of life, and in our social endeavors to create healthy, prosperous societies where peace and justice are the norms of all interhuman encounters, as Thurman himself says, the smell of life meets us at every step

with its limits. This recognition does not constitute a human fault. It is simply the recognition of the way things are. Finitude marks a basic quality of
all human experiencing of the world, even religious experience. We simply
must deal with it.

This recognition does not morally or spiritually fate us, however.
Copresent in the recognition of finitude and limits is that quality of experience named *transcendence*. Like finitude, transcendence is also a basic quality of human experience of the world. Even in the awareness of limits, we
move about and act in the world, *adapting* circumstances so that they cooperate toward satisfying some of our deepest goals. We *adjust* ourselves to the
limits so that we are not overcome by unwarranted feelings of futility, cyni-
cism, and/or the sense of fatedness. For the increase of life, we foster human
resources to create safe, healthy spaces where our children may be given the
best chances we can provide them to advance their lives. Yet, we know all
too well that not all will survive, that despite the hopes and dreams of parents
and the best of chances, some will die in birth, others from disease, still others will die from neglect and accidents and violence that surround them at
every turn. For the increase of knowledge, we find ways to provide generations with ideas, skills, languages, and practices that have proven successful in
sustaining human communities through ages of cultivation, years of distress
and war, and decades of famine and disease. We pass on to others lessons
learned in the hope that they will never undergo the negative experiences
from which our ancestors mined life-sustaining wisdom. This is what John
Dewey called *creative intelligence*.

Limits meet us at every turn with the smell of life, but we are not fated.
Notwithstanding the weight of social and cultural critics who see our present generation of black youth teetering on the edge of nihilism, our present
generation of African Americans is no more fated by the world than the
generations that survived the transatlantic slave trade to be transplanted in
the hostile social world which chattel slavery created. It was a social world
that sought to destroy in them that human capacity by which all are most
free—namely, their wills. In and through this human power, African people
in America hoped against the limits and brought forth a new community,
a new people, a new family, and new possibilities in religious experience
from the ruinous-destructive qualities of American Christianity. Thurman
eloquently takes up this point of view in *The Negro Spiritual Speaks of Life
and Death*:

> What, then, is the fundamental significance of all these interpretations
> of life and death? What are these songs trying to say? They express the
> profound conviction that God was not done with them, that God was

not done with life. The consciousness that God had not exhausted His resources did not ever leave them. This is the secret of their ascendancy over circumstances and the basis of their assurances concerning life and death. The awareness of the presence of a God who was personal, intimate, and active was the central fact of life and around it all the details of life and destiny were integrated.[30]

As finitude meets us at every step, so does transcendence. It conditions the possibility of freedom, openness, and creativity. It conspires with the human will to adapt our circumstances and adjust us to the ways of the world for the sake of human flourishing.

Finitude and transcendence are not empty concepts. They are copresent in our experiencing of the world. If religion takes up religious experience and life as an integral relation to the whole of the world, then finitude and transcendence can be grasped theologically through a conception of God. For God simply is the name for the totality or unity of the World. Religious experience entails a fullness of being, a plenitude of being that is irreducible to human actions, or to the particularities of human suffering, surviving, resisting, and liberation. Rather, when religious experience is construed as a plenitude of being, human life and practices are enlarged and interpreted within expanding intersections of physical, environmental, ecological, social, cultural, and moral worlds within a creative exchange.

This is exactly what Wieman meant by God. For him, it is a theological error to identify God with a human person or personality. He says that "God is not a personality. Personality can only exist in a society. Personality is generated by interaction between individuals. We do not mean that we first had this interaction, and out of it personalities arose. We mean, rather, that this kind of interaction develops concomitantly with personality. This kind of interaction is communication. It is the sharing of experience."[31] He then places this critique of divine personalism within the unity of experience when he says: "Personalities are developed just in so far as individuals develop a common body of experience which each can share with other."[32] For him, personality is fundamentally intersubjective. Wieman goes on to describe God as the creative event or creative interchange or interaction:

> Thus we see that under no circumstances can God be thought to be a personality. The idea is self-contradictory. Therefore, we conclude that, whatever else God is, he is not a personality. So much for the negative side. Positively, we would say that God is that kind of interaction between things which generates and magnifies personality and all its highest values. God, thus, is more than personality. Personality simply

could not function in the way that actuality must function which carries highest possibilities of value and which is, therefore, the rightful object of supreme and passionate devotion for all human kind.

But this interaction which sustains and magnifies personality and all its highest values, cannot be limited merely to the interaction between human individuals. Rather it must be identified with the process of progressive integration. Progressive integration means that interaction between things by which they come to share in common an increasing measure of structure. At the level of human personality this structure in common takes on the form of shared experience. Progressive integration at this level is the interaction which develops a richer body of shared experience, accessible to all men who will meet the requirements of participating in it. Such shared experience assumes the form of beauty, truth and love. Art, and that rationality called truth, constitute the form which all experience must assume if it is to be shared in common by all interacting individuals. When it is thus shared it constitutes these individuals into a community wherein the good of each is the good of all and the good of all the good of each. This is love in the religious sense. Maximum mutuality is the highest expression of God in the lives of men.[33]

Wieman understands God as the creative interaction within the wholeness of our experiencing the world, maximizing the conditions for the concrete actualization and ideal possibilities of love and community, that is, Beloved Community. In a significant passage, Josiah Royce eloquently makes the same point:

The real world is not something independent of us. It is a world whose stuff, so to speak—whose content—is of the nature of experience, whose structure meets, validates, and gives warrant to our active deeds, and whose whole nature is such that it can be interpreted in terms of ideas, propositions, and conscious meanings, while in turn it gives to our fragmentary ideas and to our conscious life whatever connected meaning they possesses. Whenever I have purposes and fail, so far, to carry them out, that is because I have not yet found the true way of expressing my relation to reality. On the other hand, precisely in so far as I have understood some whole of reality, I have carried out successfully some purpose of mine.[34]

When compared to Thurman and other personalists who insist on the comprehensive coherence of the world order guaranteed by God, on my account based on Wieman and Royce and in our experiencing of the world, the world does not always support the plan of the subject. Yet in that recognition, Royce says that some human purpose has been satisfied as the subject engages the creative exchange between finitude and transcendence.

Where finitude and transcendence are regarded as correlative categories of being, the world—its processes, patterns, and powers—does not only present limiting conditions but also possibilities for transcendence. The world is open to novelty. It discloses itself in the interaction and interdependence of all things to each other. It shows itself as processive, open, and relational. Transcendence remains not only a constitutive aspect of the world shared by all, it discloses a felt quality of religious experience when the self and community transcend isolated self-interests and seek human fulfillment and flourishing in relation to larger wholes. This happens in a creative exchange that entails the self with other selves and the community with other communities, even nonhuman others and communities. Thurman puts it this way:

> It is possible for the individual to move out beyond the particular context by which his life is defined and relate to other forms of life from inside their context. This means that there is a boundless realm of which all particular life is but a manifestation. This center is the living thing in human beings and animal. If a person or animal can function out of that center, then the boundaries that limit and define can be transcended.[35]

Like Thurman, Wieman, and Royce, I also think that this unification of the self and others in religious experience can be interpreted in a theologically meaningful (although not necessary) way in the idea of God. However, God is inferentially grasped by reflection on the world, its processes, patterns, and powers. God gives meaning and value to the whole of human experience in the world, because God transcends every particular experience in a unity of experience. The name *God* conceptually signifies the unification of every reality, where reality is understood as the undifferentiated totality of experience. God signifies the union of all life in its concrete actuality and ideal potentiality. Therefore, God designates the infinite in meaning and value. As Royce once proposed, God simply is the World:

> There is, then, no merely theoretical truth, and there is no reality foreign, in its nature, to experience. Whoever actually lives the whole conscious life such as can be lived out with a definitely reasonable meaning—such a being, obviously superhuman in his grade of consciousness, not only knows the real world, but is the real world. Whoever is conscious of the whole content of experience possesses all reality. And our search for reality is simply an effort to discover what

the whole fabric of experience is into which our human experience is woven. . . .[36]

On a pragmatic naturalist interpretation of religious experience, God names "an unrestricted field of value whose harmony involves an ever-enlarging process synthesis of the widest range and deepest contrast of relational data," says Nancy Frankenberry.[37] She further says that the Name—that is, God—"[enables] individuals (and cultures) to move from narrower, constricted patterns of perception and feeling to wider and deeper modes of sympathetic inclusiveness."[38] In a social world, where acts of racial and sexual violence appear to be normative in our interhuman associations, the Name elicits felt qualities of World experience that are signified by our sympathetic seeing, perceiving, and attending to others beyond the immediacy of our own narrow self-interest, families, race, cultures, ethnicities, and neighborhoods. By the Name, we expand and enlarge our capacities for moral sympathy that enters into creative exchange with all who suffer from malicious forms of prejudice and violence.

Gustafson gives a compelling interpretation of the significance of this conception of God/World when he argues that theology is a way of construing the World. For him, God is disclosed as the power(s) bearing down on us, sustaining us, and ordering human life within the nexus of natural and social processes and patterns.[39] God can be so understood symbolically to designate the powerful other that establishes the possibilities for human capacities to interact creatively with the processes and patterns of the world. However, Gustafson also reminds us that God also establishes limits to human well-being and human endeavors toward sustaining themselves against the world.[40] In an important passage, he raises a powerful consideration:

> I have opened the way to some uncomfortable conclusions. If God is "for man," He may not be for man as the chief end of creation. The chief end of God may not be the salvation of man. . . . Human purposes and human conduct have to be evaluated not simply on the basis of considerations derived from reflection about what is good for man. Rather, reflection is needed on how human life is to be related to a moral ordering objective to our species. It may be that the task of ethics is to discern the will of God—a will larger and more comprehensive than an intention for the salvation and well being of our species, and certainly of individual members of our species.[41]

Gustafson's conception of God attempts to hold together the unity of human relations to time and chance (finitude) and human capacities to render life humanly satisfactory and fulfilling (transcendence).

I suggest that God names the totality of the World itself, which is the union of life in all of its concrete actualities (finitude) and ideal potentialities (transcendence). The Name discloses the World in both its light and dark dimensions and human experience in both its tragic and comedic manifestations. Recognizing that the World—its processes, patterns, and powers—and human experience of the World are at every interchange met with limits to and possibilities for human flourishing, admits the language of *grace* as a powerful interpretation of religious experience. The involvement of Christian communities in politics, human misery, suffering, and mass alienation of people from goods that all require for a life that reaches beyond subsistence, struggle, survival, and resistance is related to a gracious estimation of the creative possibilities that God displays in the ordering of all things to each other and the integration of all our particular interests into larger wholes.

God/World is the condition for not only human limits in politics, social action, and moral endeavors but also conditions the possibility and potentiality for goodness, faith, trust, loyalty, and fulfillment in human experience. To recognize this potentiality is at the same time to recognize the signs of grace in the world. As philosopher of religion Robert Corrington notes:

> The dialectical movement between finitude and transcendence marks the human process during all stages of growth and decline. Neither dimension can assume priority in all respects, so that finitude is never bereft of those fitful moments of transcendence that move the self beyond the opacity of origins. Hope assures us that the destructive powers of origin will never completely overwhelm the human process, and that our radical expectations are secured against the forces of closure and death.[42]

The point here is that notwithstanding the ways our lives have been structured by choices, actions, and policies that we ourselves did not choose for ourselves, where there is great expectation for increasing social freedom, moral capacity, and constructing just policies, we are met with signs of grace. Through grace, great expectations are exchanged and copresent in situations where justice is denied, dreams deferred, and lives unfulfilled. Grace meets us in the creative exchange where malicious and vengeance-driven public policies foreclose the cultural fulfillment of democratic participation to a society of incarcerated young black males and people of color seeking freedom from poverty and terror as they stand outside America's immigration gates or because of the racism of the American criminal justice system, fueled by the war on drugs.

That grace meets us in the creative exchange of our moral and spiritual aspirations, actions, and religious experience can hardly be an invitation to quietism. The gracious potentialities of the world must be seized, taken up, and grasped with urgency if hope of a morally just political community is to be an end realizable in the present. We greet grace with a sense of urgency, if better housing, better health care, better educational policies, better living conditions for the poor, and better democratic participation is to be increased in our present moment. The urgency is great, for sin lies at the door of our moral endeavors and every potentiality of grace and transcendence is also met with the threat of closure. Limits to the signs of grace may not be seen as a concession to the ways of the world, but may also be limited or thwarted by our own human negligence to care for each other, by our own intentional desires toward selfishness and closure. Our own propensities toward totalizing private interests may also foreclose our capacities to discern the signs of grace. This possibility is taken up in classical Christian language of sin.

Notwithstanding how our moral lives are framed by finitude, limits, and sin, in a powerful poem in which Thurman ponders the mystery of human finitude (structured, as he says, by "the ebb and flow of oceans"), he nevertheless gives priority to the potentiality of transcendence and grace in his account of religious experience:

> There is some wholeness at the core of man,
> That must abound in all he does,
> That marks with reverence his ev'ry step,
> That has its sway when all else fails;
> That wearies the depth of frozen fears,
> Making friend of foe,
> Making love of hate,
> And lasts beyond the living and the dead,
> Beyond the goals of peace, the ends of war!
> This man seeks through all his years;
> To be complete and of one piece, within, without.[43]

PRAGMATIC THEOLOGY AND THE PROBLEM OF PRAYER

In this chapter, I have set forth a reading of religious experience in conversation with Howard Thurman in particular but one that draws on the tradition of American empirical theology. To be sure, my reading of Thurman is based on a more rigorous pragmatism than Thurman himself maintained. Still, I find great commensuration between him and my pragmatism. Here, I might

be charged with hermeneutical violence for making Thurman into the kind
of pragmatist that I wish him to be. However, I think that Thurman himself
was large enough and gracious enough in personality and intellect to allow
for such a reading or misreading. He certainly would regard my effort as
friendly. More serious, however, is that my reading also poses serious questions crucial for interpreting African American religious experience. It is not
so much questions about the nature of God as I have developed from my
pragmatic perspective that concern me as do questions regarding the nature
of religious devotion, piety, worship, and particularly the problem of prayer.
To put the question sharply: "What do adoration, praise, and prayer have to
do with Anderson's pragmatic God?"

Certainly my wrestling with the problem of religious devotion stands in
good company with thinkers such as Royce, Wieman, and Gustafson. The
turn I have made to a pragmatic naturalist understanding of God as World
leaves open questions about those forms of religious experience that are best
understood in terms of religious devotion. What is religiously significant
about devotion to a construal of God as a plenitude of being that is itself
disclosed by the dynamic interplay of finitude and transcendence, concrete
actuality and ideal potentiality? At the most basic level of religious experience, such a construal seems to confound most traditional understandings
of worship of God. When confronted by this problem, Royce himself was
led to define worship through a quasi-theistic or "personalist" understanding of God as that suprahuman reality that maximizes human possibility and
capacity for an ultimate devotion, which he called "loyalty to loyalty." God
is understood as that suprahuman "Cause" that transcends every mediate
cause to which persons give their loyalty and that is supremely worthy of
religious devotion (loyalty to loyalty). In the end, for Royce, religious devotion is an ethical orientation of persons' wills to the *Cause* that maximizes in
itself the concrete actuality and ideal possibility for trust and loyalty to the
Great Hope and Great Community. For Wieman, such a commitment is to
creative interchange.

However, Gustafson comes to terms with the problem of religious devotion by defining it in terms of Augustinian and Edwardsian piety, namely,
the "ordering of the heart."[44] To speak of the ordering of the heart is to see
religious devotion as a center of personal gravity. He says:

> There is a center of personal gravity or, to change the metaphor, to be
> oriented in life by a basic internationality that is grounded in a pattern
> of coherent loyalties or affections, does not simply imply that a fitting
> reordering of the heart ought not only to occur in relation to particu-
> lar circumstances: those interior to the person, those events in which a
> person acts, and those objects to which persons are attracted.[45]

Gustafson understands that what individuals may take to be their center of value and gravitate their hearts toward may vary among persons so much that, for him, "integrity" is not to be identified with the disposition of religious devotion. From his theocentric perspective, "the claim of theocentric piety and view of life is that the center of gravity, of affections and of our construing of the world is the Deity."[46] He evokes Augustine's understanding of religious devotion:

> In Augustine's terms, to love God as the supreme good is to reorder our other affections so that we can love God as the supreme good is to have the wrong center of gravity; it is to be basically disoriented in the proper valuations of other things. What is claimed about God, of course, makes a great deal of difference to a life that is ordered by supreme loyalty and supreme love. It is my position that God in relation to man and the world is an appropriate center of gravity; orientation to God will govern and order the heart in a way nearer to what human life is meant to be. . . . A reordering of the heart can be enabled not only by a theocentric vision, but also by theocentric love, loyalty, fidelity, and devotion. . . . Theocentric piety enables an enlargement of affections and loyalties, and an ordering of them under the divine governance.[47]

For Gustafson, the basic act of devotion is defined by his theory of consent. Like Royce and Wieman, he also sees religious devotion as consent to the divine governance as an ordering of "human agency based on our distinctive capacities [which] expands our casual accountability beyond the well-being of the human life to the well-being of various 'wholes' of which we are parts."[48] For him, theocentric piety and vision are expressed and evoked in those aspects of affectivity that arise in adoration, confession, supplication, thanksgiving, and intercession.[49] He says: "All of these forms can both express and evoke an expansion of the human spirit in the presence of the Powerful Other. Indeed, well-composed prayers, like great poetry, both affectively and intellectually become antidotes to the poison of the contractions of individuals and communities."[50] In religious devotion, through prayer, human life and "all things are reoriented in the presence of One before whose brightness the angels veil their faces."[51] In the end, acts of religious devotion express, enliven, sustain, and discipline our hearts toward genuine appreciation of the World—its powers, patterns, and processes.

From my pragmatic theology, I understand religious devotion to be an ethical alignment of persons to the givens of the world with both its limits to human experience and endeavors and its openness to the More in the way of human experience. I do not understand religious devotion as being directed in adoration, praise, and joy toward a divine personality. Following

Spinoza, such a confession is a concession to the inadequacy of our ideas about nature and the world. Rather, religious devotion is directed toward the World whose power to limit and transcend is disclosed in human experience personally, socially, morally and communally.

Religious devotion arises as a human possibility from our being in the world. It expresses in us the feeling of appreciation for life in the face of death, decay, and destruction and joy in a world full of sorrow and grief. The world gives rise to praise, which is expressive of our feelings of thankfulness and gratitude in a world that is not only full of heartaches, loss, grief, and misery, but that also exhibits in human experience novelty, openness, and a profound sense of peace when all seems chaotic, in disarray, and oppressive. Religious devotion requires attention to the ambiguities of the world; its light and darkness, its limits and possibilities. Religious devotion arises in our need to take hold of the world as friendly and unfriendly. In one of his prayers, Thurman himself expresses this pragmatic understanding of religious devotion:

> Our Father, Fresh from the world, with the smell of life upon us, we make an act of prayer in the silence of this place. Our minds are troubled because the anxieties of our hearts are deep and searching. We are stifled by the odor of death which envelops our earth, where in so many places brother fights against brother. The panic of fear, the torture of insecurity, the aches of hunger, all have fed and rekindled ancient hatreds and long-forgotten memories of old struggles, when the world was young and Thy children were but dimly aware of Thy Presence in the midst. For all this, we seek forgiveness. . . . Teach us to put at the disposal of Thy Purposes of Peace, the fruits of our industry, the products of our minds, the vast wealth of our land and the resources of our spirit. Grant unto us the courage to follow the illumination of this hour to the end that we shall not lead death to any man's door; but rather may we strengthen the hands of all in high places, and in common tasks seek to build a friendly world, of friendly men, beneath a friendly sky. This is the simple desire of our hearts, which we share with Thee in thanksgiving and confidence.[52]

From my perspective, religious devotion connects us to the ambiguities of the world and enables in us the fulfillment of the very basic human need for equilibrium or what Dewey called "satisfaction." It enables suffering and oppressed people to move beyond a life defined by struggle, survival, and resistance. It substantiates our genuine appreciation for the concrete, actual moments of authentic happiness, joy, satisfaction, and rest from our endeavors without regret for what we have left undone as we have tried to live well with the world and its limits.

Renita Weems captures something of these aspects of religious devotion when she describes an incident she experienced during a pastoral visit to a woman named Leah who was dying from cancer. I resonate with this story because it is the kind of experience that has historically shaped my own philosophical reflections on religious experience as a former pastor of two congregations and in my visits to people sick and dying with AIDS. Weems certainly brings a great deal of her own experience in pastoral care under such circumstances. Yet each visit has its own effects; there is nothing routine about them. Weems reports that "I've seen death enough to know that the woman is getting ready to 'travel'—a term used by Southerners to describe the final stage of transitioning, when the dying, drifting somewhere between life and the hereafter, begin slipping deeper and deeper into a coma. Her breathing is hard and erratic, her eyes slightly opened."[53] This time, Weems is in a situation where she is without the usual resources that she and her partner together bring to such pastoral moments, but she does her best. She sings a familiar song while searching her internal pastoral resources for how to speak to this dying woman's situation. Taking Leah's hand, her mind travels to other spaces where work has been left undone: things piled on the desk needing to be cleared, laundry unwashed, phone calls to return, notes to review for class the next day, and a manuscript to complete. Then, a soft voice asking "Is today tomorrow?" breaks the silence.

Responding more out of uncertainty of what the woman is asking than from intention, Weems responds: "No ma'am. Today is Thursday." The woman shakes her head, indicating that Weems has missed the mark. As Weems describes it, she is "shaking her head as if to let me know that I didn't get it, and perhaps annoyed a bit at my ignorance, the woman rolls her eyes to the back of her head and closes the lids over her eyes." Perplexed, Weems ponders the woman's questions. Unsettled, she makes a move to escape the ambiguities of that space. For Weems, the space opens up a new horizon for centering on the presence of God.

One question! How marvelous that this woman's dying question should disclose the limits of our own preoccupations with questions, especially for those of us who spend our careers answering and raising questions, but also clarifying the questions of others. Leah's question—"Is today tomorrow?"— cuts through the immediacy of our lived experiences with the routines of life and our regrets for work we've left undone. Yet, at the same time, Leah's experience of the world refreshes and enlivens our ordinary experiencing of the world. Weems's reflections are illustrative:

God speaks to us through the stuff of our lives and through the stuff of other people's lives also. We hardly recognize it as God when it takes place, and rarely are able to decipher what, if anything, it all means. Days, weeks, often years go by before we figure it out, if we ever do. Part of the reason we completely miss both God and the message is that we expect God in lofty places. We expect God to appear in those places where holy men usually conduct their affairs. If God speaks, it will be on mountains, in caves, in sanctuaries, in temples, in the cloister of one's study, in classrooms, in the library, where we're surrounded by books—anywhere but in a nursery, on a playground, in a kitchen, in a parking lot, at the checkout counter, or at the bedside of a decaying old woman. God shows up only where silence is cultivated, solitude is appreciated, and abstinence is the rule—we're told—not while we hold a frail body steady as it stoops over the toilet, or amid noisy children, or as we're driving down a busy freeway. . . .

But in the life of a loveless, lactating woman named Leah, a mirror is held up so that we might see ourselves—our failures, our lovelessness, and our opportunity for grace. In her story, we discover how the interruptions of life, nurturing and caring, can bring us into deeper encounters with God. The story reclaims the ordinary, routine, mundane, unspectacular work of being faithful to love. It's what in some circles is referred to as "the grace of daily obligations," glimpsing something you've never glimpsed before about yourself, a loved one, the past, an old wound, the present, while performing the routine, unspectacular acts of trying to serve faithfully those you care about.[54]

Weems speaks to an interpretation of African American religious experience in which the unexpected, unspectacular aspects of living become rich, powerful spaces for the creative exchange that I have been describing throughout this chapter. Adoration, praise, and prayer are our ways of expressing our valuation and appreciation for the World that meets us all with its limits and possibilities, its actualities and potentialities, its capacity to enchant and disenchant. Such a recognition evokes in experience serendipitous encounters with the stories of other people's lives, whether it is Phillipe's encounter with Navarre and Isabeau, or mine with Michael, the kid next door, whose shared toy opened me to a richness of experiencing the World that in memory continues to delight my world and whose dying keeps me appreciative of living.

CONCLUSION

To conclude, a pragmatic theology of African American religious experience connects us by memory and lived experience to the pains, sorrows, sufferings, and closures of the World, yet it looks beyond these realities to see the reality of Leah's "tomorrow," the surprising joys of life that find expressions in our adoration, praise, prayers of thanksgiving and gratitude. Such a sense of piety empowered the prayer tradition of the "old folks" whose oppression did not overcome their sense of transcendence. Consider this traditional prayer:

> Almighty and all-wise God, our heavenly Father! 'Tis once more and again that a few of your beloved children are gathered together to call upon your holy name. We bow at your footstool, Master, to thank you for our spared lives. We thank you that we were able to get up this morning clothed in our right mind. For, Master, since we met here, many have been snatched out of the land of living and hurled into eternity. But through your goodness and mercy we have been spared to assemble ourselves here once more to call upon a Captain who has never lost a battle. Oh, throw round us your strong arms of protection. Bind us together in love and union. Build us up where we are torn down, and strengthen us where we are weak. O Lord! O Lord! Take the lead of our minds, place them on heaven and heavenly divine things. O God, our Captain and King, search our hearts, and if you find anything there contrary to your divine will just move it from us, Master, as far as the east is from the west. Now, Lord, you know our hearts, you know our hearts' desire. You know our downsitting and you know our uprising. Lord, you know all about us 'cause you made us. Lord! One more kind favor I ask of you. Remember the man that is to stand in the gateway and proclaim your Holy Word. Oh, stand by him. Strengthen him where he is weak and build him up where he is torn down. Oh, let him down into the deep treasures of your word.
>
> And now, O Lord, when this your humble servant is done down here in this low land of sorrow; done sitting down and getting up; done being called everything but a child of God; oh, when I am done, done, done, and this old world can afford me a home no longer, right soon in the morning, Lord, right soon in the morning, meet me down at the river Jordan, bid the waters to be still, tuck my little soul away in that snow-white chariot, and bear it away over yonder in the third heaven where every day will be Sunday and my sorrows of this old world will have an end, is my prayer for Christ my Redeemer's sake and amen and thank God.[55]

The prayer expresses senses of piety that I am sure many African American revisionist theologians will find difficult to affirm. Yet the symbols of sovereignty, servanthood, rescue, and deliverance are undeniably deeply sedimented in the prayer tradition of the "old folks" and remain as well deep symbols of contemporary African American religious experience. The symbols are not likely to pass away anytime soon as long as they continue to inform and connect those who use them to the senses of piety that evoke them. In the address to "Almighty and all-wise God, our heavenly Father!" is the sense of dependence and care. In recognition of the precariousness of daily life and circumstances, the phrase "clothed in one's right mind" evokes the senses of thankfulness, goodness, mercy, and graciousness. Reliance on "a Captain who has never lost a battle" and the congregation's yearnings to be "built up where torn down, and strengthen where weak" evoke the senses of direction and responsibility.

The sense of obligation comes to expression as the petitioner cries out: "O Lord! O Lord! Take the lead of our minds, place them on heaven and heavenly divine things. O God, our Captain and King, search our hearts, and if you find anything there contrary to your divine will just move it from us." The senses of satisfaction and finality are expressed in consent: "when I am done, done, done, and this old world can afford me a home no longer, right soon in the morning, Lord, right soon in the morning, meet me down at the river Jordan, bid the waters to be still, tuck my little soul away in that snow-white chariot, and bear it away over yonder in the third heaven where every day will be Sunday and my sorrows of this old world will have an end."

I am certain that the devotion and senses of piety that come to expression in this model prayer in African American religious experience reflect a vision of God and piety toward God as a personality that hears and aids those who suffer and exalts those who are humbled. Although I think differently, I respect this vision of God. The task of a pragmatic theology of African American religious experience is not to explain away the power of this theistic piety. Moreover, the task is not to discount the power of the symbols of sovereignty, servanthood, rescue, and deliverance that have informed and empowered the spiritual, social, and moral lives of African American believers and continue to do so. However, I think that there is room for different ways of understanding and appreciating God in African American religious experience or in what Anthony Pinn foregrounds, namely, a *variety* of African American religious experience. I maintain that the task of every generation is to give the most faithful articulation of religious experience that we can, one that takes into account the widest ranges of human experience, of lived experience and our experience of the World.

"Impossible . . . Nothing is impossible . . .
Come on, Mouse, dig! Dig, Mouse . . ."

CHAPTER 5

Home and the Black Church

Centers of Value in a Pragmatic Theology of African American Religious Experience

For Flora Helen Anderson, "Mama" (1912–2007)

If anyone come after me, he must deny himself and take up his cross and follow me. For whosoever wants to save his life will lose it, but whoever loses their lives for me will find it. What good will it be for a man if he gains the whole world, yet forfeits his soul? Or what can a man give in exchange for his soul? (Matt 16:24-26, NIV)

When I'm through with all the day,
And I kneel at night to pray—God sees.
After I am gone to bed,
If I cover up my head—God sees.
Even when I'm sound asleep,
While the angels 'round me creep—God sees.
So you see I never fear,
God's protection's ever near—God sees.[1]

One group will not be able to see any value in the qualitative meaning unless it satisfies human want. To him we reply without equivocation: Qualitative meaning is good, is positive, intrinsic value, because it satisfies human want. That is to say, it is one ingredient in every instance of satisfaction.[2]

THIS LAST CHAPTER FOCUSES ON two sites of concrete actuality into which creative exchange transforms the unresolved ambiguities of our religious experience, substantiating them as signs of that creative exchange which Wieman calls God. Distinguishing his construct from the conception of God as a transcendent subject or personality, he says:

> We ignore the transcendental affirmation in the Jewish Christian tradition of a creative God who not only works in history but resides beyond history. The only creative God we recognize is the creative event itself. So also we ignore the transcendental affirmation in the Greek Christian tradition of the reality of Forms of value, uncreated and eternal, having causal efficacy to constrain the shape of things without themselves being events at all. The only forms of value we recognize are produced by the creative event. Even possibilities, so far as relevant to actual events are created. The form of the creative event itself at our higher levels of existence is determined by the creative process at more elementary levels. In our view the higher levels of existence spring from, rest upon, and are undergirded by the lower.[3]

The home and family and the black church are two key creative centers of value in African American religious experience. As both enter into exchanges with other centers of value, such exchange limits the internal and instrumental goods of both centers in ways that diminish their values, brings them into violence and corruption, and sometimes makes them centers of abuse. Internal to both sites are great contestations, conflicts, and unresolved ambiguities. As each site enters into creative exchange with other centers of value as well as with each other, however, the unresolved ambiguities of each center are transcended but not negated by the creative exchange of values. Rather, the value of each center is increased or enlarged as the home and family and the black church concretely actualize and contribute possibilities for the human fulfillment and flourishing of their members. Such moments of concrete actualization of possibilities that enlarge the value of each center make both centers creative events and concrete signs of Beloved Community. Wieman says:

> The active God derived from the Jewish tradition and the Forms derived from the Greek tradition are brought down into the world of time, space, and matter and are there identified as events display-ing a definite structure with possibilities. When we insist that nothing has causal efficacy except material events, by material we mean not

merely pellets of inanimate matter but also events that include bio-logical, social, and historical forms of existence. These, however, never cease to be material. Nothing has value except material events, thus understood, and their possibilities.

These claims rest upon an analysis of experience, revealing that no transcendental reality could ever *do* anything. It could not make the slightest difference in our lives except in the form of some hap-pening, some event. In other words, nothing could happen if it does not happen. But when the transcendental becomes an event, it is no longer transcendental. We cannot know anything, and nothing can make the slightest difference in our lives unless it be an event or some possibility carried by an event. Transcendental realities literally have nothing to do after we have discovered that all value, all meaning, and all causal efficacy are to be found in the world of events and their possibilities.[4]

Of all this book's chapters, this is the most autobiographical. Home and family and the black church have contributed to creative exchanges and events that have formed my understanding of religious experience. Through these centers I have come to understand and appreciate their unresolved ambiguities. I have also come to understand and appreciate their transfor-mative powers to contribute to the concrete actualization, signs, or events of Beloved Community. In my pragmatic theology of African American reli-gious experience, there is an explicit narrative quality that is always entailed in the unresolved ambiguities of home and family and the black church. There is always a narrative quality entailed in creative exchange in which we have our being. I proceed by discussing first the home and family and then the black church as centers of value. In each case, I track their unresolved ambiguities, their grotesqueries. In the final section, I relate both centers of value to the creative exchange that concretely substantiate these centers as possibilities, signs, or events of the Beloved Community.

HOME AND FAMILY AS A CENTER OF VALUE

Home: What a power symbol. It is the stuff of music, drama, art, and perhaps every modality of aesthetic experience. It evokes human affections from longing, trust, and comfort to distrust, hate, and sometimes killing rage. Even as it evokes senses of safety and protection, the same home may also evoke the senses of dread, helplessness, and even death. Steven Mitchell says:

> In intellectual circles in these (post)modern days, it is hazardous to speculate about cross-cultural, universal features of human nature;

everything is local, culturally specific, we are told. However, if I were forced to select an essential, wired-in aspect of human psychology, the sense of "home" would be high on my list. It is difficult for me to imagine a person—or human culture, for that matter—who doesn't orient itself around some sense of home; my place, where I am from, where I belong, where I long to return.[5]

As a deep symbol, home is powerful and sedimented deeply in African American religious experience. The symbol finds its way into spirituals, hymns, gospel music, sermons, prayers, and funerals. For better or worse, everyone's understanding of religion, matters of religious significance, and sense of spirituality is inextricably but not exclusively formed by home.

Reared in a home by religiously devout grandparents, my home was not always a place of safety, protection, peaceful coexistence, or a haven of rest. It always had the specter of death hovering over it. I was born in New York City, the youngest boy among ten siblings. My mother, Evelyn, died of cancer when I was three years old and my father, Frederick, died a year later from a heart attack, both at the young age of thirty-two. My father was the only son born to the grandparents who would rear me. As I noted in an earlier chapter in this book, my family was a mosaic of differences in skin color, hair texture, and even languages. This was because my mother had children by two partners prior to marrying my father. After my father's death, my siblings and I became wards of New York state until my father's parents adopted the five younger children who were generated by their only son. The adoption split my family in still-irreconcilable ways. The older children born to my mother and her two previous partners remained in the Bronx where they struggled to deal as best they could with a home broken by death and adoption. Even today, for some of them, resentment and estrangement are determinant features of their lives and their sense of home.

Life in Chicago with my grandparents was often difficult to negotiate. At the time of their adopting us, my grandparents were well into middle age and enjoying the fruits of their long labors. My grandfather always called his birthplace, Thomaston, Georgia, home. Being racially mixed and light-skinned—in those days, he was called a mulatto—his life was bitter and dangerous. The dangers came from both the white and black communities. At times in his youth he would play the tricky game of "passing," which put him at risk of being lynched. To the black community, especially his own family, his white body was observably different from the blackness of his brother, sister, and his mother. He was a constant reminder to them of the rape that defiled his family's sense of home. He did not stay there for long under such a shadow.

My grandmother (Mama), by contrast, was well educated by the standards of the small town of Barnesville, Georgia, in the early 1900s. After completing elementary school, one of her older sisters took her to Connecticut where she experienced life outside the South. There she did what many girls in the black community of her little town had no opportunity to do: she completed high school. Eventually she even attended teacher's college, although she had married in her early teens and had one son, my father, whom she named Frederick Douglass Anderson. She was a mama's girl and her sense of home was with her mother, her son, and her beloved Barnesville. She remained in Georgia well into the late 1940s, teaching school and cooking and cleaning for the woman she has always called "Madam," whom she credits with having taught her every trick of etiquette and finishing.

Mama reared my father alone because, shortly after marrying her, my grandfather was forced to flee Georgia when the local sheriff warned him that he had better leave in twenty-four hours or else he would be found hanging from a tree. The whiteness of his blackness was offensive to the white community and their perennial interest in keeping their young daughters uncontaminated by that mulatto vermin. So while my grandmother's sense of home was with her mother and Madam, the rails provided my grandfather a home for a while until the Army made him into a man. The Army, its regiment, orders, and unambiguous duties provided him with a sense of home. As I recall, he lived his life as if he had never left the Army. Most of the stories he would tell me were almost all episodes of what appeared to be his best years before my siblings and I entered his life. The Army, his stories, and adventures constituted his sense of home even until he died in a VA hospital in Chicago in 1984.

After the end of World War II, he sent for my grandmother from Georgia, removing her from her home with her mother. She left for Chicago under the coercion of her mother's sense of respectability and wifely duty, but she never quite left behind her nostalgia for the little town of Barnesville. Together there, my grandparents lived, worked, and managed to forge a new sense of home for themselves. They were married but not a family. My grandfather and his son, my father, never reconciled their feelings and the reality of abandonment that forever hovered over their sense of home. The lives of these two men were characterized by resentment and irreconcilable rage. My father eventually settled in New York, where he married my mother. But he had left behind in Georgia a son for whom my grandmother wanted a better life and through whom my grandfather sought forgiveness and redemption from the shadow of abandonment that he placed over the lives of both his wife and his own son. They adopted the child, Pat, and the three of them became a family, with Pat enjoying every luxury that two spoiling grandparents could bestow upon him. But in a single year, that was all turned upside down by five kids from the Bronx coming into their home.

My grandparents did their best to make two families into one, with my grandmother being the glue to a home that was defined by death. She never quite recovered from the death of her only son, and she would transfer that loss onto my brother, Barry, always telling him that he looked just like Fred, an association he resented for most of his childhood. I, on the other hand, looked like no one in particular. I resented my older siblings for their memories of my mother and father, since I was too young to remember anything about them. Sometimes they would gather into a bedroom and rehearse tales of New York and the Bronx, of older siblings left behind, of my mother and my father whose personalities in Chicago became bigger than life. I was daily surrounded by family, but home was still a place of shadows. Birthdays, holiday meals—which were usually the occasion for a family fight—and the routines of daily living were for me the arena of both happy times and dread, of joy and laughter as well as sorrows. The sense of dread was most pronounced in my experience.

As I noted earlier, I was a sickly child, and, although there were plenty of family members surrounding me, I was also lonely. The sense of loneliness is a powerful motive for the play of the imagination. Books filled my lonely hours with worlds unseen, and the Three Stooges funded my understanding of the comedic character of life. Being the youngest boy, I was privy to plenty of stories that made me aware of other presences in the house. There was Georgi, the ghost that resided in the attic. I could hear his footsteps late at night. There was the green man whose tales were told at night on radio station WVON in Chicago. He lived under the bed and sometimes in the closet. Then there was the story of Johnny and the boogie man who came into Johnny's house step by step, floor by floor, letting little Johnny know every time he reached a new floor, coming closer and closer until he reaches the fourth floor and got poor little Johnny. Pat enjoyed that story most as we three boys climbed into the one bed in which we slept and I, in the middle, curled up under Barry, shaking as I thought about little Johnny.

Night: Night was exceptionally dark. We boys slept in the basement. It was there that I became aware of both the power and limits of prayer. I prayed silently throughout the night like little Jenny in *Forrest Gump* who prayed in a cornfield that God would make her into a bird so she could fly far, far away. I prayed that this time someone would hear my silent cries when Pat snatched me from my sleep as I clung to my brother Barry, begging him to hold me. Many nights went by where I lived in dread and fear, living with the awful anxiety of not knowing at what hour of the night I would be snatched and carried from my bed, shoved into the blackness of the boiler room where I sat by the locked door, crying and praying in the pitch dark of night as our dog's red eyes glared through the darkness at me. When I was released, I prayed again, thanking God that my ordeal was over. Sometimes prayer kept me safe but other times it failed me, despite the rigor of my prayers. My older brother would lift the covers from my feet as I slept, then take a book of matches and burn the bottoms of my feet while threatening me into silence by promising something worse than his little tortures if I told. Other times he would knock me to the floor to piss on me.

In those times, home was a place of terror. I had no other protection than prayer and the occasional angel it conjured up to keep me company. I often wondered why God would not let Mama hear me when my brother would snatch me in the night and demand that I "be his pillow"—his euphemism for his frequent molestations of my young, sickly, little body. God seemed then most silent and most absent. That one's religious experience should be born out of the senses of the night, its nightmares, its secrets, and its shadows is not so unusual. Dr. Robert Coles tells of parallel moments in the experiences of children who in the mid-1950s were struck by a polio epidemic in Boston and whose arms, legs, or even the breathing centers of their brain were affected so that they could not breathe without the "iron lungs." He writes:

> Here were all these people, many of them children, who were paralyzed and facing the possibility, even the likelihood, of death. And I went about my medical work with them doing whatever could be done to sustain them and edge them toward rehabilitative work with people who would teach them how to compensate for their loss due to the polio virus. And yet in the midst of that work, I could not help but hear from these children all kinds of questions that were not directed to me as a physician, Maybe they weren't directed to me at all. They were directed ultimately, to what? They were directed to God, to nature, to fate, to circumstance, to chance, to luck. They were asking themselves Job's questions: Why did this happen to me? What did I do to deserve this? And what does this life mean anyway? If this is the outcome, I haven't even started and I'm through.[6]

Although I raised similar questions in the loneliness of my home, I never experienced the same sense of fatedness, despite years of torture and molestation. Just as ordinary as Phillipe's conversations with God were in *Ladyhawke*, so were my talks with God. I do not know whether God talked back with me, but I "sensed" that God had heard me and was speaking to me, edging me toward escape through the solitude of painting and drawing, playing church and preacher, and reading the children's Bible that Deacon Hamlin gave me when I was admitted into the children's hospital. I turned inward to find another me who was not the sum-total of everything that was happening to me in and through my body. Home was sometimes a place of joy and at other times a place of sorrow. Sometimes it was a place of dread and at other times a place of laughter. But it was never a place of fatedness. I learned at home that, in the end, God will make a way out of no way.

Years passed and well into my adulthood, long after leaving the home of my youth, long after the deaths of my grandfather and my brothers Pat and Barry, the shadows of home hovered over me like ghosts that would not let me escape. Neither my years in church nor in ministry could erase the nightmares of my youth, even as I found comfort and relief in them. I transferred my pain into service to God and others. It was a kind of bargain with God against the recurring nightmares of torture and molestation with which I learned to live. Unfortunately, several of my lovers at times could not.

One night when I was helping my grandmother prepare her house to sell, I slept in the room that she had preserved for me. In the night, I sensed a familiar presence hovering over me, pressing down on me and holding me down. I knew who it was. I knew its name. And in my nightmare, I prayed just as I prayed in my youth for God to help me, for someone to hear me. While under the oppression of the nightmare, I yelled, turning and fighting with every bit of strength I could muster to rid myself of the presence holding me down, but to no avail. Suddenly, I heard what I had prayed to hear during my entire youth. It was Mama's voice, now well aged and without all the distractions of our family life. It was me, her, and the nightmare. She yelled from her room, "Are you alright? Are you okay?" Then she opened the door to the room. At the very moment that she turned on the light and looked into the room, the nightmare and its molesting presence left me. It was finished. To this day, it has never returned. The years of praying came to fulfillment. The old folks have their religious ways for expressing such experiences of fulfillment when they say, "he may not come when you want him, but he's always on time."

My pragmatic theology of African American religious experience starts with experience of home and family. Mine is not a romantic, nostalgic, or idealized sense of home. I proceed from the deep ambiguities of home and family. Joys and sorrows, unresolved grief, memories of family members now departed, family meals, saying Bible verses before eating, being forced to go to Sunday School, playing church at home and imitating church shouters, learning and reciting Easter speeches—all these and more fund my religious sense of life. It was at home among family that I learned that if nobody else loved me, Jesus did. Notwithstanding how formidable home and family are in African American religious experience, neither are absolute centers of value. Their values are relative, vulnerable to distortions, and corruptible. Inasmuch as they can be centers of nurture, they can also be centers of violence, rape, molestation, torture, and silence. A pragmatic theology of African American religious experience requires an enlargement of our understanding and appreciation for the ambiguities of home and family. An adequate account of African American religious experience also requires a creative exchange between the immediacy of family and home and a social center of religious value. For many African Americans, the black church is that social home of religious experience.

THE BLACK CHURCH AS A CENTER OF VALUE

My faith was nurtured at Canaan Baptist Church in Chicago. Going to church was both a pleasure and refuge. It was refuge from much that went on at home, especially with my grandfather's severity. As a youth and teen, I devoted myself to playing gospel piano and organ and directing the young people's choir until I was too old to be in the choir. Mine was the era of James Cleveland and the great Chicago choirs like Father Charles G. Hayes and the Cosmopolitan Church Choir, the Reverend Clay Evans and the Fellowship Baptist Church Choir, Maceo Woods and the Christian Tabernacle Choir, and, of course, Reverend Milton Brunson and the "Thomies." Mine was also the era of the great Sunday evening radio broadcasts. I went to the broadcast services as if I were going to the movies, for entertainment, inspiration, new songs for the choir to sing, and cruising. During my early twenties, I was the minister of music at several black churches. Gospel music kept me sane in an insane home environment.

As a teen, I began to explore my latent homosexuality. I had no idea then that these explorations would occasion both my love and mistrust of the black church. It was the early 1970s, when the sexual revolution of the '60s had now traveled into a community of young black church boys who were discovering the unresolved experiences of anxiety and pleasure that accompanied our same-sex activities within the church. We were African American, gay, and Christian. All three factors drove us to practice sex in the secrecy of closets, on choir trips sleeping four (or more) to a room, behind buildings and trees, in the forest preserve, the backseats of cars parked in alleys, and even in the church cloakroom after choir rehearsals. We were church organists, pianists, and singers. For some of us, our choir robes were our first stab at doing drag, swaying our hips as we swished down the church aisles during the choir procession. For many of us, the black churches of our youth were a grotesque surrogate world of anxiety and pleasure, love and loathing, because of the unspeakable things we were doing in and through our bodies. The church was a place where many of us found refuge from the dirty secrets of home. But the church of my youth also had its secrets. It was also the site of predatory older men—musicians, deacons, ushers, and even preachers—feeding on our unexplored sexual imaginations and ambiguities.

One particular incident has been formative in my experience of the black church. Over twenty years ago, when I was a young minister in Chicago, I befriended Raymond, one of my Sunday school students.[7] He was a bright, creative, and popular teen, achieving excellent grades and active in our church as the youth choir director. He was also African American and gay. In the early seventies, not many of us knew anything about the word *gay*. In the idiom of that time and community, Raymond was a "sissy." Only a few of us knew Raymond's secret. His popularity and active participation in the church led him to conceal his sexual identity from his family, friends, and church. But I knew his secret. He and I talked about his feelings and fears, which he expressed more as anxieties and worries than as confessions or declarations. One had to read between the lines. If one were "in the life," one was expected to recognize who was gay either by some magical sexual intuition ("gaydar") or by an a priori understanding of the codes and signs uttered in quiet conversations or overt actions such as how one talked (a lisp, perhaps), walked (swishing), or a "waterfall" (or "fairy") wrist.

I first approached Raymond when I saw our church organist, a much older man, constantly pursuing and playing around with young boys like him in our church. When they would not yield to his seductions, he would ruin their reputations and their relationships with their girlfriends and friends with his vicious gossip. He was indiscriminate; he simply liked boys. It did not matter to him whether they were straight or gay. Raymond had become the target of his seductions, just as I had seen other boys become his victims, and just as I had been one of his victims as a teen. I had not talked to Raymond for a while. As a youth minister, I was busy with Bible study, prayer meetings and fellowship, and other church activities. I began hearing from Raymond's friends and parents that he was becoming withdrawn and his grades were declining. His parents wanted me to talk to him. He had only to complete the spring quarter to graduate from high school.

I tried to reach Raymond, but because I was too busy doing the Lord's work, I missed the opportunity. He tried to find me to talk one evening, calling several times, but I was nowhere to be found. The next day, I received a phone call that Raymond was found dead from a self-inflicted bullet to the head in the basement of his home. He was seventeen. At his funeral, I looked around at the church of my and Raymond's youth but especially at the organist who played for Raymond's funeral. I asked myself, How many would have to encounter him? How many would not healthily survive his seductions? I survived, Raymond did not, and others I now recall followed a downward spiral into unhealthy sexualities. Such stories are not unusual for many in black churches. In my experience, the unspeakable things that brought about Raymond's death and my long estrangement from the black church remain, for the most part, still unspeakable in black churches.

Peter J. Paris describes the black church as a surrogate world where the survival of African Americans out of slavery through segregation, their dignity as human beings, and their creativity as artists, scholars, religionists, reformers, and their prophetic witness to social justice were celebrated and empowered. Paris says:

> The multifarious functions of the black church justify the claim that they have been the institutional centers of the black community; the basic source of religious and moral values; diligent in protecting the community from the many varied abuses of racism by comforting the wounded, restoring dignity to the demoralized, hope to the despairing and redirection to those bent on harboring attitudes of bitterness and hatred as well as those oriented to acts of violence, prudent in devising and implementing forms of protests against racial injustices. Black churches have advocated the support of black business, established and maintained educational institutions, strengthened family life and provided a perspective for assessing the moral quality of the nation, and been closely allied with countless civil rights organizations and all other activities aimed at racial improvement. In short, they gave a long and impressive history of institutional primacy in a racially segregated situation.[8]

Paris's high estimation of the black church is echoed by C. Eric Lincoln, who practically equates the black church with black culture, most explicitly when he says: "The Church is still in an important sense 'The people.'"[9] He is worth quoting at length:

> To understand the Black Church, it must first be understood that there is no disjunction between the Black Church and the Black Community. The Church is the spiritual face of the Black Community, and whether one is a "church member" or not is beside the

point in any assessment of the importance and meaning of the Black Church. Because of the peculiar nature of the Black experience and the centrality of the institutionalization of religion in the development of that experience, the time was when the personal dignity of the Black individual was communicated entirely through his church affiliation. To be able to say that "I belong to Mt. Nebo Baptist" or "We go to Mason's Chapel Methodist" was the accepted way of establishing identity and status when there were few other criteria by means of which a sense of self or a communication of place could be projected. While this has been modified to some degree in recent times as educational diversification, and new opportunities for non-religious associations have increased, the social identity of the Black American as well as his self-perception are still to an important degree refracted through the prism of his religious identity. His pastor, his church, his office in the church, or merely his denomination are important indices of who *he* is. The Black Church then is in some sense a "universal Church," claiming and representing all Blacks out of a long tradition that looks back to the time when there was only the Black Church to bear witness to "who" of "what" a man was as he stood at the bar of his community. The Church still accepts a broad-gauge responsibility for the Black Community inside and outside its formal communion. No one can die "outside the Black Church" if he is Black. No matter how notorious one's life on earth, the Church claims its own at death—and with appropriate ceremony. The most colorful and protracted funerals in the Black community are often those of "nonchurch" figures who, by the standards of some other communion, might be questionable candidates for the unrestricted attention of the Church.[10]

Both Paris's and Lincoln's estimation of the black church make it an ubiquitous force to be reckoned with in any critical reflection on African American religious experience. For both scholars, it is the home of African American spiritual, social, economic, political, and cultural celebrations and empowerment. It is a comprehensive association of the interests of African American people. However, I am suspicious of these sorts of readings and find them deeply committed to what I have described elsewhere as an "Apollonian rhetoric of heroic genius."[11] That is, the black church is understood to be a symbol of the heroic, moral guiding virtues of black manhood and womanhood: strong, surviving, resistant, and self-determined. Such a rhetoric structures the meaning and significance of the black church within the cultural logics of masculinity, moral manliness, heroic discontent, and racial pride. This rhetoric crystallizes the black church's prophetic character, which is resistant to those elements of difference or differentiation that structure

black life today. African American religious thinkers and theologians tend
to rally their intellectual gifts in support of a recovery of African American
religious experience in the black church where the qualities of survival,
resistance, and the creation of a revolutionary institution are expressed in
mythical proportions. For instance, for Lincoln and Lawrence Mamiya, the
signifier *black* in black churches signals a collectivity that is identifiable with
the major independent black churches in which "The Black Church has no
challenger as the cultural womb of the Black community."[12]

I am not interested in setting my pragmatic theology of African American religious experience in radical opposition to such heroic depictions.
Rather, for all the work they do, I find historical interpretations of the black
churches such as Paris's and Lincoln's effective sources in the interpretation
of African American religious experience. Nevertheless, both depictions beg
a basic question that is crucial to an adequate pragmatic account of the
black church in African American religious experience. Heroic depictions
of the black church are adequate "historical" interpretations of the social
and cultural meaning of the black churches. But the pragmatic question is,
Are these heroic depictions viable interpretations for mediating meaning
and value in African American life, which is today widely differentiated?
Have the processes of social and cultural differentiation been so successful
as to render ineffective the ontological matrices that support these heroic
depictions such as "The Black Experience," "The Black Sacred Cosmos,"
and "The Black Church"? To put the question most crudely: "What has the
black church done for me lately?"

In a much-neglected chapter, Adolph L. Reed Jr. offers a countercritique
on black church ideology.

> The domain of the black church has been the spiritual and institu-
> tional adaptation of Afro-Americans to an apparently inexorable con-
> text of subordination and dispossession. It has been at various points
> in this century a central conduit for the reproduction of community
> life under severely restricted conditions. Whether the church's acqui-
> escence to the unpalatable secular order has been equally central in
> legitimizing those conditions or whether another course was even
> possible are issues open to debate. However, it is clear that the church's
> functionality as an integrative institution, as well as its vaunted success
> as a source of hope in a temporal situation apparently hopeless, has
> been predicated on acceptance of the essential structure of the world
> of material, social, and political relations as given. To that extent, the
> black church has developed as an inherently noninterventionist, and
> thus conservative quasi-secular institution.[13]

Reed's argument is an instructive instance of the critique of ideology applied to the "mythology" of the black churches. He tries to correct what he sees as "exaggerated," "heroic," and "histrionic" accounts of the church's claims to moral primacy and civic leadership in black protest politics.[14] He accents the less than avant-garde ways that the black churches and religious leaders interacted with the protest politics of the civil rights era. He also highlights the place of the churches as conduits for organizational sites and their role in the mobilization of black interests in politics. But the interests themselves, he argues, were not raised to public consciousness by the black churches, nor did the dominant leadership for the effective politics of civil rights come from the elite clerical wing of the protest politics.[15]

Rather, the black churches and their religious leaders tended to provide a structure of legitimization for black politics, but they themselves tended not to be strategic interventionists in protest activism. "A more accurate representation," Reed argues, "locates the church's role in protest politics mainly in provision of institutional support for activities initiated and led under other auspices."[16] Such auspices have been student movements, the NAACP, and other nonreligious-based grassroots protest organizations and coalitions, many of which were directed by the activity of professionals (teachers, lawyers, and the business class) and their respective interests. Reed's argument demonstrates the ways that social and political differentiation, particularly between the clerical elite class and the electoral elite class, has called into question any uncritical acceptance of the Apollonian myth of the black church. Whether black churches and their clerical elites are viable contenders for the moral and political loyalties of African Americans whose political activities are conducted under great social and cultural differentiations remains a question open for discussion. A pragmatic theology of African American religious experience cannot insist on answering this question affirmatively from the start, especially where the status of women in ordained ministries of the church and the moral standing of same-sex-loving members are at stake.

SEXUAL AND GENDER ROLES IN THE BLACK CHURCH

Lincoln and Mamiya point out that in all seven major black denominations membership is predominantly female and the leadership is largely male. They correctly assert that "traditionally in the black church, the pulpit has been viewed as "men's space and the pew as women's place."[17] This is not to say that in the black church women have been marginal to its cultural success in forming African American religious experience. The visibility of women is shown in their roles ranging from evangelists, missionaries, deaconesses, and lay leaders, to Sunday school teachers, vacation Bible school teachers, caterers, mothers of the church, and countless other "controlled places" for women for whom the black church is a center of value. It is true that, both historically and contemporaneously, "black churches could scarcely have survived without the active support of black women."[18] Still, the offices of preaching and pastor remain closed to too many African American women who have the sense of God's call to these ministries.

One of the striking elements in Lincoln and Mamiya's discussion of "The Black Church and Women" is the qualitative section on the pros and cons of women in the pastoral office. I offer a few excerpts from that section to suggest that opposition to women to pastoral ordination has little to do with genuine critical debate on the nature of the church and ministry, as the attitudes shown here are reactionary, unreflective, and display male hubris. On both sides, attitudes are measured by nondiscursive reactions. Here are a few examples:

> Negative No. 0358: "They do not have any business preaching. She has no voice. If she has any questions, let her ask her husband at home."
>
> Positive No. 0125: "A woman minister shows more concern to her flock."
>
> Negative No. 1865: Okay to preach but not as pastor. The doctrine of COGIC doesn't approve of the term preachers [for women]. [Call them] Evangelists."
>
> Positive No. 1189: "If the Lord can cause rocks to cry out, surely he can call women."
>
> Negative No. 1419: "She can be a 'pastor's helper'—but God didn't make her job to be a pastor; they may have the educational ability, but they're not God-approved."
>
> Positive No. 1748: "I am a woman, I understand women to be more thorough and genuine in caring and nurturing."
>
> Negative No. 1725: "In order to pastor, one must be blameless and the husband of one wife, that's what the Bible says, and there is no way a woman can be the husband of one wife. I don't care what kind of operation she has."
>
> Positive No. 1506: "They are my fellow yokemen. I strongly approve. I would be happy to serve under a woman pastor."[19]

While only a sampling of the attitudinal research done regarding women as pastors in the black church, these statements suggest that much of the discussion on the ordination of African American women remains at a highly nondiscursive level that is all too often trifling, dismissive, unreflective, and simply a volley of merely "semantic strategies" of renaming the office for the sake of accommodation and concession. The cost to the integrity and self-esteem of the black churches' most gifted members lies at the mercy of male pastoral hubris and chauvinism masked under the guise of "the Bible says."

Theologian Marcia Riggs says: "The Black Church since [E. Franklin] Frazier has functioned as a 'surrogate world' wherein African American men as clergy have perceived themselves as securing the rights of patriarchal privilege denied them elsewhere." She further comments that "as the 'father' of the household of God, African American men are able to garner the respect of and dominance over women that some maintain that they have not been granted in the larger society, and consequently cannot achieve even in their own homes."[20] Riggs provides an illustrative scenario:

> *Scenario A*: They don't think that I can do anything but cook. I have a MBA from Atlanta University, and what do I do at this church every weekend? Cook! We had our annual meeting last night; did any of them hear me? No! Those same self-righteous deacons (all men, of course) don't want to do anything that is different; therefore, anything that will serve women's needs was not even allowed on the floor for discussion. The only time that they think of us is when they want to raise some money by selling food. I keep telling myself that this is the last weekend that I will cook at this church, but then Sister Frances comes and asks me with that sad face of hers and here I am. I have some friends who are financial planners and investment counselors that I wanted to invite to the church to do some workshops with us to help us think of other ways to raise funds other than the sisters frying chicken every weekend, but no one wanted to hear my suggestions. Sister Frances may be right; the only way to get something done in this church is to put the idea into a man's mind and let him present it as if it were his idea.[21]

For many women, the black church is a home and center of value that dishonors their callings. It tears down rather than builds up their esteem. It exploits their bodies by subscribing them to auxiliary church leadership positions as teachers, directors of Christian education, deans of evangelism, and presidents of women's state conventions. This is not to say that such places of leadership are to be disvalued, especially if service to these auxiliary offices is a matter of a woman's own *sense* of calling. But when these places in the black church are controlled by the irrationality of pastors and church officials with hubris, African American women in the black church who are called to the pastoral office, feel estranged and have few options but to join other denominations, churches, and fellowships where their ordinations are celebrated, their gifts cultivated, and their self-esteem enlarged. For many, the sign *black church* is a "border marker" that says, "No Entry."

For many African American gays and lesbians, the black church is also experienced as a border marker saying: "Whosoever—Except You." Horace Griffin addresses the plight of these members whose place in the black church is one of pain, loathing, and abomination. Griffin suggests that even as many churches in the Western world have had significant discussion, debates, proposals and declarations on homosexuality over the past two decades, absent from these discussions are significant voices in the black church. He finds that when and where such discussion happens, it is too often reactionary, as seen in black church leaders' collusion with the Religious Right to oppose same-sex marriage.[22] A number of factors may account for the lack of any sustained discourse on homosexuality and the black church, including the churches' deeply rooted puritanical pietism surrounding sexuality altogether, deep commitments to biblical holiness, and racial apologetics. Of these three factors, Griffin says: "Two primary reasons account for African Americans' negative view of homosexuality: 1) Slaves were mainly converted to Christianity by conservative white Christians who were sex-negative and opposed to homosexuality; 2) African Americans have recognized that conspiring with mainstream society in targeting homosexuals as the 'despised other' frees them from the deviant label of being sexually immoral and provides a degree of social acceptance."[23]

Perhaps no issue has motivated many black church leaders toward activism more than the same-sex marriage debate. Amazingly, neither the pervasive poverty of black America, nor the devastation of HIV/AIDS in African American communities, nor the mass incarceration of African American young males, or even how African American men and women have been committed to fight an unjust war in Iraq has moved black church leaders to national activism more than the debate on same-sex marriage. The debate has forged new coalitions between black church leaders, white conservative evangelicals, and other constituencies of the Religious Right. About one hundred black church leaders joined in solidarity with the Bush administration in Washington, D.C., on May 16, 2004, to denounce legalized same-sex marriages. "Not on My Watch," a Texas-based coalition organized to mobilize the black churches against same-sex marriage, expressed offense that the gay marriage issue was being compared to blacks' struggle for civil rights in the 1950s and '60s. Bishop Frank Stewart, a spokesman for the California-based Zoe Christian Fellowship of twenty-one churches, says, "Gays have never gone though slavery nor been put down and abused like blacks. . . .

It's an insult to use that parallel."[24] A spokesman for the San Francisco Tabernacle Clergy has said that such comparisons "are offensive and belittle the cause of freedom and racial justice."[25] "As African American pastors, teachers, counselors and leaders, we see and live with the horrors of a declining society. . . . Same sex marriage would serve to advance the decline of marriage and . . . family values in the African American community," said Bishop Green of the Traditional Values Coalition.[26] On December 11, 2004, Bishop Eddie Long and Reverend Bernice King, the daughter the slain civil rights leader, led thousands of marchers in Atlanta from her father's tomb in the "Reigniting the Legacy" march. Among the main objectives of the march was the denunciation of same-sex marriages and its negative impact on the moral development of the black community.[27]

Within the "Black Sacred Cosmos," constructed by the black church, it is clear that on Paris's and Lincoln's assessment, black clergy have tended toward liberal progressivism in civil rights and other areas of social justice. However, in their sexual-gender attitudes toward women in the pastoral office and on the moral status of its same-sex-loving members, their social constructs of marriage, the black family, and sex do not differ in any significant ways from those of the conservative, white Religious Right. When black church leaders fail to recognize the everyday, ordinary existence of African American gays and lesbians in the church and the community, at work and play, in family life and in the pews, they vitiate the forms of generative care and creativity that same-sex-loving members cultivate in black cultural life and in the black church.

Yet, the presence of same-sex-loving members ironically keeps the churches themselves open to the "newness" of life and the creativity it fosters and nourishes. African American same-sex-loving members keep the black church itself sexually honest and open the church to wider worlds of sexual difference because these people are also fellow believers. This is why many do not leave the churches of their youth. For the very black churches that tacitly "accept" their presence without advocating for their sexual loves and practices are also the churches that nurtured their faith. This is its grotesquery. For many, the black church is not only a center of value; it is also their spiritual home.

While many black church leaders combat same-sex marriage and homosexuality, thankfully others are advocates and their churches are refuges for same-sex-loving members. Two examples are worth noting. First, "Operation: Rebirth is the first Web site dedicated to ending the religious and spiritual abuse against black gays and lesbians inflicted by black churches. The Web site provides resources that assist black gays and lesbians on reclaiming their religion and spirituality."[28] The site lists thirty-one churches throughout the United States that are places of empowerment for same-sex-loving African Americans. To be listed the churches give express permission to be included as Affirming Churches. "By being a part of this list, the churches are known to be radically inclusive, affirming churches who accept all people, who preach God's love to and for all people and who are active in their communities in supporting the overall welfare of all people regardless of race, creed, color, gender, socioeconomic background, or sexual orientation."[29] Prevalent among the list is the Unity Fellowship Church Movement (UFCM), founded in 1982 by the Reverend Carl Bean for primarily openly same-sex-loving African Americans. The mission of the UFCM states:

> The primary work of the Unity Fellowship Church Movement is to Proclaim the "Sacredness of ALL life," thus focusing on empowering those who have been oppressed and made to feel shame. Through an emerging international network, UFCM works to facilitate social change and improve the life chances for those who have been rejected by society's institutions and systems. Although its pivotal work focuses on the urban weak and powerless, the scope of its work is inclusive and has significance for all people.[30]

My second example of voices in the black church that stand for the advocacy of African American same-sex-loving members originally appeared in the *New York Times* on January 20, 2005, as an "Open Letter to MLK Jr." Fifty-six scholars, church leaders, students, and activists signed the letter. At its deepest level, the letter is a call to waken the black church to its true spiritual and moral genius, to waken the churches to an activism that is not motivated by conservative backlash, legalistic moralism, or fear of moral decay. Moreover, it calls the churches to an activism that is not motivated by black church entrenchment in the market-driven, capitalist opportunism of the black megachurch phenomenon which legitimizes a cheap faith-and-wealth gospel that abandons the poor for the monies of the middle class and wealthy. As the black church confronts itself with its own grotesque sexual-gender politics, there are voices calling the churches back to the basics, back to its authentic self, back to being a "Whosoever Church" that is driven by nothing less than an all-encompassing love. I quote an excerpt from the letter:

> Dear Martin:
> Every third Monday in January history compels us to remember and reactivate your legacy. How shall we honor you? And how shall we honor our deepest and truest selves? . . . Yours was the vision of a transformed nation, a society that dared to practice the very brotherhood—

and sisterhood—that it preached. In a time of tremendous social upheaval you joined the freedom-loving and justice-seeking tradition of your people, black people, and you did so at great personal cost. . . .

Today, in the imperfectly desegregated post-civil rights era, religiously inspired leadership continues to perpetuate a cruel sexual ethic, and in stark violation of their own best sacred inheritance. That black women continue to be relegated to secondary status and lesbians and gays are made to feel unwelcome, unworthy, and uncomfortable in what should be the most caring, compassionate and empowering of communions is a searing indictment against all the black faithful. . . .

The dominant views on sex, sexuality and gender in the Black Church are undermining community, diminishing the faith and leading many to abandon churches out of sheer moral frustration and exhaustion. Our churches have been slow to embrace gender equality. They have largely spoken only opposition and condemnation to same gender loving people and have been unable to proclaim a sexually liberating and redemptive word. Some black churches have concluded it is in their best institutional interest to participate in "special rights" polemics against this so-called "immoral humanity." As black clergy we offer here a more hope-filled perspective.

In the spirit of Jesus of Nazareth, we the undersigned clergy extend the divine invitation of human wholeness, healing and affirmation to "whosoever" (John 3:16). In the best of the Black Church tradition we say, "Whosoever will, let her or him come.". . .

Martin, on your day we vow to take a stand to love all black people. . . . The power is in our hands. This is where we must go from here.[31]

Unlike any other mediating institution of civil society and the African American community, as a comprehensive institution, the black church is a center of value where the public and private commitments of all its members meet. Faithfulness to the best of the black church tradition means that all members seek faithfully to promote in the public realm the civil and human rights of all without regard for race, gender, religion, or sexual orientation. All members seek to be faithful sustainers of norms and values that enrich the private realm of marriage, family, and sex, even if we have disagreement on what those norms and values should be.

Although I was reared in the black Baptist church, ordained in the church, and served the church as a pastor, for much of my adult life I have also been radically estranged from the black church. I have not forgotten Raymond or other youths whose lives have been destroyed by silence and denial within the church. Moreover, at Vanderbilt Divinity School, I have taught many

African American women in their preparation for ordained ministry and found myself spiritually enlarged by such creative exchange. These factors have prompted me to return to the church in recent years. It was not enough for me criticize the shortcomings of the church; I wanted to be a part of its moral and social renewal. With all of its unresolved ambiguities displayed in its sexual-gender politics, I am compelled to agree with Paris's and Lincoln's depictions of the social standing of the black church. It is indeed one of the greatest social and moral resources for the empowerment of the African American community. And as a religious center of value of the African American community, it will be judged by how it empowers and nurtures the love of all its members.

This is its pragmatic test of adequacy. The ongoing relevance of the black church as an advocate and refuge for all its members will require great faith, understanding, and appreciation of the gifts and loves of all its members. Great humility will also be required if it is to remain a home for the empowerment of all in the African American community. It is a center of value, but not an ultimate center. Like the home, its value is relative, vulnerable, and corruptible. This is its grotesquery, its unresolved ambiguity. It intersects with other centers of value competing for the trust and loyalties of African American people. It will not nor should not be understood as a totalizing center of value. Rather, the black church can only be enlarged in its creative exchange with the human center.

CENTERS OF VALUE AND HUMAN FULFILLMENT IN CREATIVE EXCHANGE

The home and family and the black church are centers of value. Each is a social site of nurture and love. Each contributes to the formation of faith and piety. Each is a site of generative care. Each is also a site of unresolved ambiguity because each is a human community. As human communities, each shares ontological structures that define any human community. In describing the church as a human community, James Gustafson elicits key significations that are not peculiar to the church, but constitutive of all human communities. He says:

> The Church can be defined as a human community with an historical continuity identifiable by certain beliefs, ways of work, rites, loyalties, outlooks, and feelings. Whatever else the Church is to systematic theologians and Biblical exegetes, it is a people with a history. It is a social entity with temporal and social dimensions. It is human and shares many characteristics of other human communities such as

nations, trade unions, and professions. As a human community, it is subject to various modes of study and interpretation.[32]

The understanding of the church as a human community goes a long ways toward understanding its capacity to enliven downtrodden spirits while fostering sexual abuse and exploitation of women. It is a refuge for the weary, hungry, homeless, sick, and seekers; but not for those whose sexuality keeps them outside the doors of reconciliation, whose same-sex-loving dreams are perpetually unfulfilled, and whose presence is an offense to the church's perennial concern for the moral development of the black family and community. How is it possible that the black church can be a center of value with such patterns of unresolved ambiguity? That it is a human community goes a long ways toward understanding its divine grotesquery, its internally unresolved ambiguities. Again Gustafson is quite insightful in describing the church in general as a human community: "There may be an irreducible uniqueness, a differentium that distinguished the Church from all other historical communities, but this does not make it absolutely different in kind. It is subject to the same social and historical processes as other communities, and thus to the same types of investigation. Many of the concepts that illume the nature of secular communities also illumine the nature of the Church."[33]

For instance, when Gustafson describes the church as a natural community that mediates the emotional and psychological needs of its members, he says:

> In any or all its emotional and psychological functions the Church resembles other groups. It bears the marks of a natural community, providing fulfillment of desires and needs that are common to all men. In it men receive recognition; they have a sense of belonging; they may be assured of the ultimate rightness and goodness of things. Even the suppressed drives of life may find socially acceptable outlets and religious sanction. One cannot conceive of a single form of Church life that has no emotional and psychological functions.[34]

The church is internally sustained by its peculiar politics, but like other political communities, power and interests define its politics as Lincoln, Mamiya, and Riggs show on women and ordination. As a social community, the emotional, familiar, educational, political, and social needs of the African American community meet. But these needs are brought into the church as members participate in other social communities that make claims upon their faith, loyalty, and trust. Because the black church is a human community, it necessarily competes with other social communities for the loyalty and trust of its members. The church cannot take the faith of African American members for granted because of an overestimation of itself as a center of value in the African American community. As a mediating institution, its power lies in its capacity to transcend its limits, its finitude, through a creative exchange not only with other communities but in a community beyond black and white and beyond sexual and gender politics. Transcendence lies in the creative exchange of the human need for human fulfillment.

Creative exchange is that structure of experience that maximizes the enlargement of human good, says Henry Nelson Wieman. It is a process that elicits in experience the creative potency of conflict. For every exchange entails limits to every particular good. Both the home and family and the black church are centers of human value that together contribute to creative exchange. As human communities, however, their values are relative, vulnerable, duplicitous, and corruptible when the instrumental goods that define each are rendered insular or parochial in meaning and value. It is simply the case that our homes and families, the black church, and by enlargement the African America community compete in the exchange with other centers of value that meet us as a plentitude of goods and values. This plentitude is also constituted by a plurality of instrumental goods that enter into conflict with one another, for every exchange limits the value of every home and family. It limits the value of the black church as well, and it limits the estimation of our racial/ethnic communities as members bump up against members of other racial/ethnic communities. In such interchanges, the internal meanings we assign to these centers, their value, their good, enter into conflict with the internalized meanings and values of other communities seeking to maximize their particular and instrumental goods.

What a less hazardous feat parenting would be today if parents and care providers could insulate the experiences of their children within the moral universe of their particular homes and families. But the necessities of living and thriving in a social life-world of school, work and labor, and civic life place our homes and families in conflict with the claims of these social institutions competing for their loyalties and trusts and constantly limiting the power of home and family to shape the values of their members, whether adults, teens, or children. No arena has been more contested in American society than the culture wars over family values and the place of religion in public education. Not even the protective strategy of home schooling can, in the long run, escape the inevitable exchange of value that meets our children as they engage others at play or at church. As much as we may try, the social exchange that occurs in the everyday and ordinary activities of daily life will test the norms and loyalties formed within the home and family. If we are not to diminish the intrinsic value of children as social beings or deny them the increase of their being as they seek the maximization of their personal and social equilibrium within the social life-world, conflict is essential, not consequential, in the inevitable exchange of values that occurs in the interhuman encounter which makes claims upon their creative exchanges in education, play, labor, markets, associations, friendships, sexuality, as well as on their religious convictions. Such an enlargement of value involves creative conflict with other centers of values.

As a human community, the black church is also a natural community. It is a community where the basic and natural needs of its members enter. It is in this sense that one can speak meaningfully of the black church as a comprehensive community. The centers of the home and family and other centers of civil society intersect with the church as concentric circles of value, for no one center can mediate the great constellation of human needs that beg for fulfillment and flourishing. In an essay I wrote some years ago, I spoke about these needs in relation to homosexuality and the black church. There I argued that

> Black religious leaders and church members participate in many communities of moral discourse, where they come in contact with, know, and associate with black gays and lesbians. They are their teachers, lawyers, ministers, musicians, bus-drivers, bankers, funeral home directors, siblings, uncles, and aunts. Some are also parents. My point is that black gays and lesbians are not a degenerative presence in the black community, they contribute to the flourishing of the black community. Moreover the basic human needs, desires, and goods that they seek to fulfill do not differ from those of the black heterosexual mainstream. Therefore advocating their needs, desires, and goods does not require theological justification any more than one requires theological justification to support the basic needs and goods of black heterosexuals. In African American contestations over homosexuality, I think that it is more morally relevant that black religious leaders and churches support the goods that gays and lesbians seek to fulfill, not because God requires it or requires that they love them but because what is at stake is nothing other than respecting the needs and natural rights of black human beings (gay, lesbian, straight or bisexual).[35]

As a natural community, the black church is a purposive community that participates in the fulfillment of its members' human and natural needs that transcend racial and sexual identities by the necessities of life. African American members have basic desires that they consciously elect to satisfy, if they think about what makes for a satisfying sense of personal wholeness. Such a constellation of goods might be fellowship and peace with others, peace of mind, and spiritual peace that unify their lives and world. As a mediating institution, the black church participates in a civil society in which the goods common to all are liberty and justice. The liberty of each to pursue what is necessary for sustaining physical life means that the black church has an intrinsic interest in promoting the health and safety of all its members, regardless of their sexuality or genders. Freedom to satisfy the need for knowledge—without which one is neither able to keep one's life from danger nor know what is publicly required of one in our democratic society—gives rise to the black church's interest in the fulfillment of its members' education. Fair employment and access to work are intrinsic interests of the church not because God requires it but because without work and labor members cannot maintain the material goods required for sustaining their lives, families, communities, or churches.

If people have a basic freedom to pursue every peaceful means of forming a common life with others, justice requires that they be free to move or locate to neighborhoods of their choosing without any threat to their well-being. They are at liberty to pursue those goods that will support their mental health or peace of mind. For some that means freeing themselves from sexual closets that protect them from the world of retaliatory abuses marshaled on them by the heterosexual mainstream of the African American community, including the black church. Justice requires that people be free to pursue the harmony of their choices and convictions in relation to their consciences—that is, to live truthfully, without fear of harm, undue incarceration, or intimidation. Justice leaves people free to pursue worship and believe as they will about the ultimate unity of life and the world without violating the religious liberty of others.

African American gays and lesbians are human beings with rightful claims to the fulfillment and flourishing of their bodily, mental, and spiritual integrity. This recognition is a sufficient basis for the black church to advocate for their protection from bodily harm, threat to life, gay bashing, sexual harassment, and sexual double standards, one for straight members and one for them. As human beings, possessing a natural right to associate, establish friendships, companionships, and families, I see same-sex marriage as entailed in the constellation of natural goods and desires that need no theological justification for their rightness. For too many members of the black church and the African American community, however, these very goods and desires, these liberties, remain unfulfilled and constrained only because these members happen to be oriented in their loves, affections, and economic commitments to members of their own sex.

Same-sex-loving members are fellow human beings possessing a natural right to secure adequate means of preserving themselves and their unions. This is an adequate basis for grounding the commitment of black religious leaders to support their litigations for fair opportunities in employment, access to health insurance, pensions, social security, inheritance, and hospital access to care for their partners. Yet these very goods that heterosexual church members take for granted are denied to same-sex-loving members. The recognition of the humanity of African American gays and lesbians and their right to associate freely and form families is a sufficient, even if not a theological, basis for advocating for their liberty to be free from harassment, overinflated rents, muggings, and verbal humiliation when walking the streets either alone or with their lovers and friends, or when entering together in houses of worship to give thanks to God.

For many members of black churches and black religious leaders, advocating these human and natural goods on behalf of gay and lesbian members creates internal conflict. The conflict comes in their attempts to reconcile their moral commitments to the basic human and civil rights for the African American community—even gays and lesbians—with their inherited sexual moralities on homosexuality. This requires a balancing act that is difficult to negotiate. Yet, as a mediating center of value in the African American community, with its internal sexual-gender diversity, such conflicts of value are required in the creative exchange of the black church that is at the same time a natural community and a holy community. Still, the black church has within itself the resources for transcending the limitations of its exclusionary sexual-gender politics and contributing to the maximization of the fulfillment and flourishing of all its members. Wieman says:

> The creative event, we shall find, weaves a web of meaning between individuals and groups and between the organism and its environment. Out of disruption and conflicts which would otherwise be destructive, it creates vivifying constraints of quality if it is able to operate at all. Thus it can utilize frustration and disaster to create and weave into a web of life's meanings vivid and diversified qualities, thus adding immensely to the richness of its variety and the depth of its significant connections. This happy outcome ensues if the participant individuals provide the conditions under which the creative event can occur. One of the most important of these conditions is the self-giving of the individual himself to such transformation. In weaving the web of richer meaning, the creative event transforms the individual person so that he is more of a person. In the beginning, it creates the human person out of the living organism of the infant.

Likewise, it creates and progressively transforms human community and the course of history.[36]

From my perspective, the creative exchange and the creative event lie in the moral self-realization of the liturgy. It is in the self-realization of the welcome, the passing of the peace, the blessing, the celebration of new life at baptism and in birth. It ushers in the moral self-realization of congregational prayer where all present their thanksgivings and needs before a merciful and gracious God. In the moral self-realization of the communion table, all are welcomed not because they are straight, gay, lesbian, bisexual, transgender, or transsexual, but because all who eat and drink at the table are children of God and have intrinsic worth. Creative exchange shows itself when the right hand of fellowship extends beyond the two-hour service on Sunday to symbolize the social reality of our life together in the African American community. These liturgical activities do not only structure our black worship experience; they constitute the life of the church itself. As a human and natural community, the black church is also a spiritual community. As such, in creative exchange, it is called to be a refuge and center of value for all its members if it is to be faithful and loyal to its center, which is Christ. As bell hooks says: "Just as the church can and often does provide a platform encouraging the denigration and ostracizing of homosexuals, a liberatory house of God can alternatively be a place where all are welcome—all are recognized as worthy."[37]

CONCLUSION

To conclude, a pragmatic theology of African American religious experience has to land in the concrete actuality of those centers of value from which and through which we have our being. It is a deeply social understanding of the lived realities of our homes and families, our concrete communities of nurture, love, and faith. It is a deeply appreciative estimation of the power of these centers to enlarge the personal wholeness of its members. But the possibilities of enlargement, fulfillment, and thriving are not actualized except as these centers of value enter into creative exchange with other centers that bring the home and family into an enriching and enlarging relational web of human significance whose intentionality is the fulfillment of basic human needs and desires.

If the Beloved Community that thinkers such as Howard Thurman and Martin Luther King Jr. envisioned is concrete and not only a regulative ideal, then our particular families must enlarge themselves in creative exchange with other families and homes in which the filial bonds of kinship increase the plurality of goods connecting homes and families. This is a lesson I learned from my home and family. We were a family constituted by the tragic deaths of my parents. By adoption, my siblings and I joined a family that was already established between my grandparents and their first adopted son. Bonds between these two families were not taken for granted. They had to grow and increase; however, that growth involved internal conflicts of values, of memories, and of loyalties. My grandmother's home was also home for the many friends we made in the neighborhood. It was the home where neighbors brought their sick children for my grandmother, the neighborhood nurse, to check them out when they were feverish. She also took in abandoned and neglected children from the neighborhood and reared them with us, as if they were naturally a part of our family. So many kids from the neighborhood became a part of my family and home that my sense of home and family increased in that creative exchange. Neighborhood kids and adults referred to my grandmother as "Mama." She concretely actualized in her encounters with others the creative event that made my neighborhood an enlargement of home and family. It was an inkling of Beloved Community, a taste of it, a creative event; and it was good.

The black church is also a center of value in my pragmatic theology of African American religious experience. It is a powerful source for the increase of good. It nurtures the love and faith of its members. It is a comprehensive community in which the basic human needs and natural desires of all its members are mediated through its liturgical self-understanding as a spiritual community. As a mediating institution, the black church is constituted by the worlds of difference that are concretely actualized in the lived realities of its members. As members gather to worship, their bodily needs and desires are not negated for spiritual ones; their need for knowledge, work, and labor are not bracketed for spiritual needs; their desires to form friendships, to associate with others, to seek peace of mind and live as human beings with integrity—none of these basic human goods and desires are in reality negated for spiritual ones. They are basic needs and goods. The black church is a human and natural community and it is also a holy community. It is a community that, like the home and family, enlarges itself through creative conflicts between these two understandings of the church. Crucial to that process of creative exchange is the cultivation of humility on the part of its religious leaders and its members. It is a center of value, not the center of value.

Creative exchange makes the black church a creative event that is concretely actualized in history. When it is faithful to its center, which is Jesus Christ, the church is enlarged in its interchange with other communities that make claims on the loyalties and trusts of its members. The black church actualizes its genuine identity when it contributes maximally to the qualitative good of all other centers it meets in its encounter with the universes of difference that define its members' lived realities. The black church will be an event of Beloved Community for all its members when it is a refuge from oppression and a center that values and uplifts the vocation of called and gifted women who seek ordination to the preaching and pastoral offices. When the black church is a center that celebrates the loving relationship of all its members, including its same-sex-loving members and seeks to maximize those goods and desires that make life qualitatively good, fulfilled, and flourishing for all, especially the least advantaged, then it concretely actualizes, albeit fragmentarily, the creative event of Beloved Community. Beloved Community is not only a regulative ideal. It is also concretely actualized as a creative event that arises from the creative exchanges of the universes of the home, family, church, and, by enlargement, the world. Beloved Community, then, is something greatly to celebrate. Such is my conception of a pragmatic theology of African American religious experience.

> After well appreciating, in its breath and depth, the unspeakable variety of each Universe, turn to those phenomena that are of the nature of homogeneities of connectedness in each; and what a spectacle will unroll itself![38]

POSTSCRIPT

This book is a constructive theological exercise. In it, I have tried to attend to matters of African American religious experience that foregrounds modes of difference that constitute the richness of faith, hope, and love in African American experience. I hope that I have been faithful to this goal. Through the idea of creative exchange, I offer an interpretation of forms of inter-human relations that, for me, concretely actualize what is at the heart of Christian faith, namely, Beloved Community. In an important article appearing in *Jubilee* in September 1958, Martin Luther King Jr. speaks to the point at hand:

> Along the way of life, someone must have sense enough and morality enough to cut off the chain of hate. This can only be done by projecting the ethic of love to the center of our lives.
>
> In speaking of love at this point, we are not referring to some sentimental or affectionate emotion. It would be nonsense to urge men to love their oppressors in an affectionate sense. Love in this connection meaning understanding, redemptive good will. When we speak of loving those who oppose us, we refer to neither *eros* nor *philia*; we speak of a love expressed in the Greek word *agape*. *Agape* means understanding, redeeming good will for all men. It is an over-flowing love which is purely spontaneous, unmotivated, groundless, and creative. It is not set in motion by any quality or function of its object. It is the love of God operating in the human heart. . . . In the final analysis, *agape* means recognition of the fact that all life is inter-related. All humanity is involved in a single process, and all men are brothers.[1]

In my judgment, King's words are remarkably compatible with the force of creative exchange as I have developed it in this book, drawing on Henry Nelson Wieman, on whom King himself wrote his dissertation. I have written this book to free up the ethics of Beloved Community from advocates and adversaries who all too often perceive it as merely a regulative ideal or principle—the actuality of which is always open to the future of inter-human relations. Rather, throughout this book, I have tried consistently to conceptualize Beloved Community in concrete forms of relationality as we think about matters of race and identity, our sources of religious insight, our experiences of suffering and evil, our understanding of the complexities of religious experience and piety, and in our estimations of home and the black church as centers of value.

I am quite aware that the constructive task I assigned myself is fragmentary, for it is one African American philosopher and theologian's particular hold on African American religious experience; however, that it is fragmentary is no intellectual fault but a sign of finitude and limits that meet all of our intellectual activities. From my reading of American pragmatists such as James, Royce, and Dewey and empirical theologians such as Gustafson and Wieman, with them I acknowledge that all of our attempts to get a handle on human experience run up against the fragmentary character of philosophical and religious inquiry themselves. That the possibility of error hovers over all, I take for granted. Sometimes in our attempts to describe in grand narratives such things as "The African American Experience," "The Black Experience," and "The Black Church," more often than not we simplify the complexities signified by these symbols and risk charges of reductivism by essentializing or totalizing the experiences themselves. I hope that I have not fallen prey to this pitfall in my account of African American religious experience by making the symbol of difference a controlling sign. I also realize that even this symbol, difference, can be so constructed as to run the risk of narcissism, totality, and closure. Here, Beloved Community is foreclosed by totalizing politics of difference where race/ethnicity, gender, sexuality, class, and other forms of difference cut off the potentiality of creative exchange. I have also tried throughout this book to avoid this pitfall.

Throughout the various chapters of *Creative Exchange*, I employed categories of experience, ambiguity/the grotesque, pragmatic naturalism, and creative exchange as unit ideas (introduction) to construct a relational concept of race in African American experience (chapter 1), to critique our sources of religious insight (chapter 2), to grasp the structure of faith in our experiences of suffering and evil (chapter 3), to see the divine in religious experience in relation to the world and piety (chapter 4), and to understand the duplicities of care and harm within the home and the black church when they are seen as natural and human yet spiritual communities that are open to creative exchange (chapter 5).

Creative exchange is a basic logic that opens human relations to Beloved Community. As a constructive theology, some readers will find my idea of God or the divine too thin for their taste, wanting instead a thicker conception of the divine. Some may even wonder why, in this book, I want to talk about God at all. I too have mused over this. My only explanation is to say that I am compelled to evoke the languages of faith, hope, and love by my own need for Beloved Community. These languages are an inheritance from ancestors long absent in the body yet present to me in Beloved Community. Through creative exchange with them, what surplus meaning I derive from my linguistic inheritance of faith, hope, and love is mine to appreciate, actualize, and to make good of in creative exchange with others. Those with whom I am in community need not be theists in any strong sense of the word in order for creative exchange to usher in Beloved Community.

On this point, I again find communion with King, who says:

> I am quite aware of the fact that there are persons who believe firmly in nonviolence who do not believe in a personal God, but I think every person who believes in nonviolent resistance believes somehow that the universe in some form is on the side of justice. That there is something unfolding in the universe whether one speaks of it as an unconscious process or whether one speaks of it as some unmoved mover, or whether someone speaks of it as a personal God. There is something in the universe that unfolds for justice and so in Montgomery we felt somehow that as we struggled we had cosmic companionship. And this was one of the things that kept the people together, the belief that the universe is on the side of justice.
>
> God grant that as men and women all over the world struggle against evil systems they will struggle with love in their hearts, with understanding good will.[2]

These last lines are a fitting benediction to my discourse on creative exchange. They best display the passions, confidence, faith, hope, and love of Beloved Community as I have tried to substantiate it both as a regulative ideal open to the future of interhuman relations yet manifest in our concrete creative exchanges. In this book, I have tried to track its potentiality and actuality in African American religious experience.

ENDNOTES

PREFACE

1. Martin Luther King Jr., A Christmas Sermon on Peace," in *A Testament of Hope: The Essential Writings and Speeches of Martin Luther King Jr.*, ed. James Melvin Washington (New York: HarperSanFrancisco, 1986), 257–58.

INTRODUCTION: FROM HUMAN EXPERIENCE

1. William James, *A Pluralistic Universe* (Lincoln: University of Nebraska Press, 1996), 16.

2. Ibid.

3. Charles H. Long, *Significations: Signs, Symbols, Images in the Interpretation of Religion* (Minneapolis: Fortress Press, 1986).

4. Anthony B. Pinn, *Varieties of African American Religious Experience* (Minneapolis: Fortress Press, 1998).

5. Theophus H. Smith, *Conjuring Culture: Biblical Formations of Black America* (New York: Oxford University Press, 1994).

6. Tyron Inbody, *The Constructive Theology of Bernard Meland: Postliberal Empirical Realism* (Atlanta: Scholars, 1995), 232.

7. Edward Farley, *Deep Symbols: Their Postmodern Effacement and Reclamation* (Valley Forge, Pa.: Trinity International, 1996).

8. Kwame Anthony Appiah, *The Ethics of Identity* (Princeton, N.J.: Princeton University Press, 2005), 22.

9. Ibid.

10. James H. Cone, *Black Theology & Black Power*, 20th anniversary ed. (New York: HarperSanFrancisco, 1989), 117.

11. Victor Anderson, "Ontological Blackness in Theology," in *Beyond Ontological Blackness* (New York: Continuum, 1995, 1998), 91–92; reprinted in *Reflections: An Anthology of African American Philosophy*, ed. James A. Montmarquet and William H. Hardy (Belmont, Calif.: Wadsworth/Thomson Learning, 2000), pt. III, §48, 117; also *African American Religious Thought: An Anthology*, ed. Cornel West and Eddie S. Glaude, Jr. (Louisville, Ky.: Westminster John Knox, 2003), ch. 38, §7, 897.

12. W. E. B. Du Bois, *The Souls of Black Folk* (New York: Signet Classic/Penguin, 1969), 45.

13. As a post-Enlightenment and post-Romantic mode of aesthetic criticism, the grotesque has been used primarily as a site for the critique of rationalist forms of epistemology oriented toward reductionist strategies for fixing meaning within totalizing frames of interpretation based on essentialist readings of human personality, perception, and representation. It accents the unresolved ambiguities between

sensibilities and perceptions and commends a playful dance on ambiguity rather than the resolution of ambiguity. See Philip Thompson, *The Grotesque* (London: Methuen, 1972); Frederick Burwick, "The Grotesque: Illusion vs. Delusion," in *Aesthetic Illusion: Theoretical and Historical Approaches*, ed. by Frederick Burwick and Walter Pape (Essen, Ger.: De Gruyter, 1990); also Frederick Burwick, *Illusion and the Drama: Critical Theory of the Enlightenment and Romantic Era* (University Park, Pa.: Penn State University Press, 1991); Geoffrey Harpham, "The Grotesque: First Principles," *Journal of Aesthetics and Art Criticism* 34, no. 4 (Summer 1976): 461–78; Peter Fingesten, "Delimitating the Concept of the Grotesque," in *Journal of Aesthetics and Art Criticism* 42, no. 4 (Summer 1984): 419–26; James Luther Adams and Wilson Yates, eds., *The Grotesque in Art and Literature: Theological Reflections* (Grand Rapids, Mich.: Eerdmans, 1997); Elaine L. Graham, *Representations of the Post/Human: Monster, Aliens and Others in Popular Culture* (New Brunswick, N.J.: Rutgers University Press, 2002).

14. Friedrich Nietzsche, *Twilight of the Idols* (New York: Penguin, 1990), 84; The Dionysian personality functions as a trope to designate a temperament that is characterized by great, unresolved ambiguity in distinction from the Apollonian personality characterized by the heroic, steady, resolved, and well ordered temperament.

15. Thompson, *The Grotesque,* 20.

16. http://www.eyetricks.dk/brainteasers (accessed October 16, 2007).

17. Burwick, "The Grotesque," 129–30.

18. See Thompson, *The Grotesque,* 20–57.

19. Among contributors whose works have most influenced my understanding of experience are: John Locke, *An Essay Concerning Human Understanding*, Book Two, (New York: New American Library, 1964), 89–250; David Hume, *An Inquiry Concerning Human Understanding* (Indianapolis, Ind.: Bobbs-Merrill, 1955), chaps. I–VII, 15–89; William James, *Varieties of Religious Experience*, Lectures I, II, XVIII, XX, Postscript (London: Longmans, Green, 1929); John Dewey, *Art as Experience* (New York: Putnams/Perigee, [1934], 1980), chaps. I–III; *The Quest for Certainty*, vol. 4 (Carbondale: Southern Illinois University Press, [1929], 1988); *Experience and Nature*, chaps. I–II, IX (LaSalle, Ill.: Open Court, 1925); John Edwin Smith, *Purpose & Thought: The Meaning of Pragmatism* (Chicago: University of Chicago Press, 1978), chap. 3; "The Reconstruction of Experience: Peirce, James and Dewey," *Monist* 68 (1985): 539–54; and S. Morris Eames, *Pragmatic Naturalism: An Introduction,* introduction and part 1: Nature and Human Life (Carbondale: Southern Illinois University Press, 1977), xi–xxvii, 3–60.

20. William James, "The Meaning of Truth" (1909), in *William James: Writings, 1902–1910* (New York: Library of America, 1987), 861–62.

21. John Edwin Smith, *Experience and God* (New York: Oxford University Press, 1968), 27.

22. Victor Anderson, *Pragmatic Theology: Negotiating the Intersections of an American Philosophy of Religion and Public Theology* (Albany: State University of New York, 1998).

23. Maurice Blondel, *Action: Essay on a Critique of Life and a Science of Practice* (1893), trans. Oliva Blanchette (Notre Dame, Ind.: University of Notre Dame Press, 1984), 101.

24. Eugene Fontinell, *Toward a Reconstruction of Religion: A Philosophical Probe* (Garden City, N.Y.: Doubleday, 1970), 42.

25. Ibid.

26. James M. Gustafson, *Ethics from a Theocentric Perspective,* vol. 1 (Chicago: University of Chicago Press, 1981), 147–48.

27. Ibid., 116–17.

28. Ibid., 115.

29. Ibid.

30. Ibid., 199.

31. Ibid., 129.

32. Ibid., 130–33; "Spiritual Life and Moral Life," *Theology Digest* 19, no. 4 (Winter 1971): 296–307.

33. Gustafson, *Ethics from a Theocentric Perspective* (Chicago: University of Chicago Press, 1984), 2:316–17.

34. Ibid., 1:262.

35. Henry Nelson Wieman, "Creative Interchange," in *Creative Interchange,* ed. John A. Broyer and Wm. S. Minor (Carbondale: Southern Illinois University Press, 1982), 454.

36. Ibid., 457.

37. Ibid., 458.

38. See Harlan R. Beckley and Charles M. Swezey, *James M. Gustafson's Theocentric Ethics: Interpretations and Assessments* (Macon, Ga.: Mercer University Press, 1988); and *Journal of Religious Ethics* 13, no. 1 (Spring 1985).

39. For example see Stanley Hauerwas, "Time and History in Theological Ethics: The Work of James M. Gustafson," in *Journal of Religious Ethics* 13, no. 1 (Spring 1985): 3–21.

40. Victor Anderson, "James M. Gustafson: Social Pragmatism, Historical Realism, and Communicative Praxis in Theological Ethics," chap. 6 of *The Legacy of Pragmatism in the Theologies of D. C. MacIntosh, H. Richard Niebuhr, and James M. Gustafson* (Ann Arbor, Mich.: U.M.I. Dissertation Services, 1995), 168–201.

41. The strongest criticism has come from Lisa Sowle Cahill who thinks that Gustafson's position is overly optimistic and somewhat naïve about the historical debates and limitations from within the scientific communities themselves. She invokes Stephen Toulmin when she writes: "Generalizations and universalizations from scientific areas of natural scientific study to the cosmos are, he thinks, extremely difficult to warrant." See "Consent in the Time of Affliction: The Ethics of a Circumspect Theist," *Journal of Religious Ethics* 13, no. 1 (Spring 1985): 22–36; quotation is from p. 28. Toulmin, whom Cahill invokes, sees the connections that Gustafson attempts among the empirical sciences, theology, and ethics more as a challenge than as a fault. See Stephen Toulmin, "Nature and Nature's God" in *Journal of Religious Ethics* 13, no. 1 (Spring 1985): 37–51; quotation is from p. 48.

42. Anderson, *Legacy of Pragmatism,* 186–90.

43. H. Richard Niebuhr, "Religious Realism in the Twentieth-Century," in *Religious Realism,* ed. D. C. MacIntosh (New York: Macmillan, 1931), 427; also see Anderson, *Legacy of Pragmstism,* 143–47.

44. Niebuhr, "Religious Realism," 427.

45. Victor Anderson, "A Relational Concept of Race in African American Religious Thought," Nova Religio Symposium on Charles H. Long, in *Nova Religio: The Journal of Alternative and Emergent Religions* 7, no. 1 (July 2003): 28–43.

46. Victor Anderson, "We See Through a Glass Darkly: Black Narrative Theology and the Opacity of African American Religious Thought," in *The Ties That Bind: African American and Hispanic American/Latino/a Theologies in Dialogue*, ed. Anthony B. Pinn and Benjamin Valentin (New York: Continuum, 2001), 78–93.

CHAPTER 1: BEYOND DICHOTOMIES

1. Stuart Hall, "What Is This 'Black' in Black Popular Culture?" in *Black Popular Culture*, ed. Gina Dent (Seattle: Bay, 1992), 21.

2. Gayraud S. Wilmore and James H. Cone, *Black Theology: A Documentary History, 1966–1979* (Maryknoll, N.Y.: Orbis, 1979); James H. Cone and Gayraud S. Wilmore, *Black Theology: A Documentary History, Volume Two: 1980–1992* (Maryknoll, N.Y.: Orbis, 1993).

3. "Philosophy and the Black Experience," *Philosophical Forum* 9, nos. 2-3 (Winter/Spring 1977–1978).

4. See Lewis R. Gordon's "Black Existential Philosophy," in *Existence in Black: An Anthology of Black Existential Philosophy*, ed. Lewis R. Gordon (New York: Routledge, 1997), 1–10.

5. See James M. Washington, "Martin Luther King Jr., Martyred Prophet for a Global Community of Justice, Faith, and Hope," in *A Testament of Hope: The Essential Writings and Speeches of Martin Luther King Jr.*, ed. James M. Washington (New York: HarperCollins, 1986), xi–xxvii; Lewis V. Baldwin, *Toward the Beloved Community: Martin Luther King Jr. and South Africa* (Cleveland, Ohio: Pilgrim, 1995); Howard Thurman, *The Search for Common Ground* (Richmond, Ind.: Friends United, 1986); and Walter E. Fluker, *They Searched for a City: A Comparative Analysis of the Ideal of Community in the Thought of Howard Thurman and Martin Luther King Jr.* (Lanham, Md.: University Press of America, 1989).

6. Cornel West, "The New Cultural Politics of Difference," in *The Cornel West Reader* (New York: Basic Civitas, 1999), 119.

7. Kwame Anthony Appiah, *The Ethics of Identity* (Princeton, N.J.: Princeton University Press, 2005), xvi.

8. Martin Luther King Jr., "Conversation with Martin Luther King," in Washington, *Testament of Hope,* 676.

9. Edward Farley, *Deep Symbols: Their Postmodern Effacement and Reclamation* (Valley Forge, Pa.: Trinity International, 1996).

10. Ibid., x.

11. Ibid., xi, 3.

12. Ibid., 3–12.

13. Ibid., 3.

14. Ibid.

15. Ibid., 23.

16. Ibid., 24.

17. Ibid., 8.

18. Jerome A. Stone, *The Minimalist Vision of Transcendence: A Naturalist Philosophy of Religion* (Albany: State University of New York Press, 1992), 83.

19. G. P. Baker and P. M. S. Hacker, *Essays on the Philosophical Investigations: Wittgenstein, Meaning, and Understanding* (Chicago, Ill.: University of Chicago Press, 1980, 1983), 280.

20. See "Philosophy and the Black Experience," *Philosophical Forum.*

21. See Richard Popkins, "Hume's Racism," in ibid., 211–26; David Theo Goldberg, *Racist Culture: Philosophy and the Politics of Meaning,* (Oxford, UK: Blackwell, 1993), 4–6.

22. Cited in Victor Anderson, *Beyond Ontological Blackness* (New York: Continuum, 1995, 1998), 54; Immanuel Kant, *Observations on the Beautiful and Sublime* (Berkeley: University of California Press, 1960), 110–11.

23. Cited in Anderson, *Beyond Ontological Blackness,* 56.

24. For strong theories of race, see Gerald Early, *Lure and Loathing: Twenty Black Intellectuals Address W. E. B. Du Bois's Dilemma of the Double-Consciousness of African Americans* (New York: Penguin, 1993); Lewis R. Gordon, *Existence in Black: An Anthology of Black Existential Philosophy* (New York: Routledge, 1997); Henry Louis Gates Jr. and Cornel West, *The Future of the Race* (New York: Knopf, 1996); Lucius T. Outlaw Jr., *On Race and Philosophy* (New York: Routledge, 1996); Cornel West, *Race Matters* (Boston: Beacon, 1993); Michael Eric Dyson, *Race Rules: Navigating the Color Line* (New York: Addison-Wesley, 1996).

25. For weak theories of race, see Kwame Anthony Appiah, *In My Father's House: Africa in the Philosophy of Culture* (New York: Oxford University Press, 1992); Debra J. Dickerson, *The End of Blackness* (New York: Pantheon, 2004); Paul Gilroy, *Against Race: Imagining Political Culture Beyond the Color Line* (Cambridge: Harvard University Press, 2000); Kobena Mercer, *Welcome to the Jungle: New Positions in Black Cultural Studies* (New York: Routledge, 1994).

26. Appiah, *In My Father's House,* 174.

27. Ibid., 18.

28. Ibid., 180.

29. Lucius T. Outlaw, *On Race and Philosophy* (New York: Routledge, 1996), xxii.

30. Ibid., xxiii.

31. Ibid., 1.

32. Ibid.

33. Ibid., 13.

34. Ibid.

35. Ibid., 157.

36. From a conversation with Edward Farley in Fall 1997.

37. Outlaw, *On Race and Philosophy,* 30.

38. Ibid.

39. Appiah, *In My Father's House,* 176.

40. Charles H. Long, *Significations: Signs, Symbols, Images in the Interpretation of Religion* (Philadelphia: Fortress Press, 1986), 84.

41. Ibid., 90–91.

42. Ibid., 92.

43. Ibid., 51.

44. The Earl of Shaftsbury, "Sensus Communis: An Essay on the Freedom of Wit and Humour," in *Moral Philosophy from Montaigne to Kant: An Anthology,* vol. II, ed. J. B. Schneewind (Cambridge: Cambridge University Press, 1990), 485.

45. Hans-Georg Gadamer, *Truth and Method* (New York: Continuum, 1993), 24.

46. Benjamin C. Ray, "African Religion: An Overview," in *The Encyclopedia of Religion,* Vol. 1, ed. Mircea Eliade (New York: Macmillan, 1977), 64.

47. Ibid.

48. Jan Knappert, *Bantu Myths and Other Tales* (Leiden, The Netherlands: Brill, 1977), 108.

49. Ibid., 63.

50. Harold Courlander, *A Treasury of African Folklore: The Oral Literature, Traditions, Recollections, Legends, Tales, Songs, Religious Beliefs, Customs, Sayings, and Humor of Africa,* 2d ed. (New York: Marlowe, 1992), 510–11.

51. Ray, "African Religion," 70.

52. Courlander, 472–73.

53. Elaine Haglund, "Moral Education in a Third World Society: Southeastern Nigeria," *Curriculum Inquiry* 12, no. 4 (1982): 378.

54. Alice Walker, "Womanish," in her book *In Search of Our Mother's Garden: Womanist Prose* (San Diego: Harcourt Brace Jovanovich, 1983), xi–xii.

55. Barbara A. Holmes, *Race and Cosmos* (Harrisburg, Pa.: Trinity International, 2002), 82.

56. Karen Baker-Fletcher, *Sisters of Dust, Sisters of Spirit: Womanist Wordings on God and Creation* (Minneapolis: Fortress Press, 1998), 34.

57. Ibid., 35.

CHAPTER 2: WE SEE THROUGH A GLASS DARKLY

1. Dwight N. Hopkins and George Cummings, eds., *Cut Loose Your Stammering Tongue: Black Theology in the Slave Narratives* (hereafter *CLST1*) (Maryknoll, N.Y.: Orbis, 1991); the second edition (2002; hereafter *CLST2*) contains a new introduction by Will Coleman and three added essays by Joan Martin, David Emmanuel Goatley, and M. Shawn Copeland.

2. Alistair Kee, *The Rise and Demise of Black Theology* (Burlington, Vt.: Ashgate, 2006), vii–viii.

3. James H. Cone, *God of the Oppressed,* rev. ed. (Maryknoll, N.Y.: Orbis, 1997 [1975]), 5, 14.

4. Ibid., 13.

5. Hopkins, "Introduction," in *CLST1,* xx.

6. Mark L. Chapman has given a great deal of attention to this third line of criticism in *Christianity on Trial: African-American Religious Thought Before and After Black Power* (Maryknoll, N.Y.: Orbis, 1996).

7. Cone, *God of the Oppressed,* x–xi.

8. James H. Cone, *The Spirituals and the Blues: An Interpretation* (New York: Seabury, 1972); *God of the Oppressed*; and the essays "Christian Theology and Scripture as the Expression of God's Liberating Activity for the Poor" and "Sanctification and

Liberation in the Black Religious Tradition, with Special Reference to Black Worship," in *Speaking the Truth: Ecumenism, Liberation, and Black Theology* (Grand Rapids, Mich.: Eerdmans, 1986), 4–34.

9. Anthony B. Pinn, *Why Lord? Suffering and Evil in Black Theology* (New York: Continuum, 1995), 21–48.

10. James H. Cone, "Black Theology and the Black Church," in *What Does It Mean to Be Black and Christian: Pulpit, Pew, and Academy in Dialogue*, ed. Forrest E. Harris, et al. (Nashville: Townsend, 1995), 57; the conference was funded by Lilly Endowment Inc. and Pew Charitable Trust.

11. The "Not on My Watch Rally" was held on May 22, 2004 in Arlington, Texas, and was sponsored by a coalition of black evangelical leaders to oppose gay marriage and the association of gay rights with the civil rights movement. The "Reigniting the Legacy March" was held December 11, 2004, and was led by Bishop Eddie Long and Bernice King, the daughter of Martin Luther King Jr., to oppose gay marriage and support the "protection of marriage" within black America.

12. James H. Evans, *We Have Been Believers: An African-American Systematic Theology* (Minneapolis: Fortress Press, 1992), 1.

13. Ibid., 5–6.

14. Dwight N. Hopkins, *Down, Up and Over: Slave Religion and Black Theology,* (Minneapolis: Fortress Press, 2000), 254.

15. Cheryl Jeanne Sanders, *Slavery and Conversion: An Analysis of Ex-Slave Testimony* (Ann Arbor: U.M.I., [1985], 1987), 2.

16. Cheryl J. Sanders, *Empowerment Ethics for a Liberated People* (Minneapolis: Fortress Press, 1995), 22.

17. Will Coleman, *Tribal Talk: Black Theology, Hermeneutics, and African/American ways of "Telling the Story"* (University Park: Pennsylvania State University, 2000), 163.

18. Joan Martin, "By Perseverance and Unwearied Industry" in *CLST2*, 128.

19. Coleman offers a highly digested examination of the debate surrounding the collection and the authenticity of the slave narratives. His account is balanced, and I find his conclusion on the debate mostly persuasive. See part 2, chapter 5, "Speaking Out: the Origin and Development of the Slave Narrative Collection," in ibid., 137–52.

20. George Cummings, "Slave Narratives, Black Theology of Liberation (USA), and The Future," in *CLST2,* 97–98.

21. Hopkins, "Slave Theology," in *CLST2*, 31.

22. Hopkins, *Down, Up and Over*, 157.

23. Will Coleman, "Coming Through 'Legion': Metaphor in Non-Christian and Christian Experiences with the Spirit(s) in African American Slave Narratives," in *CLST2,* 47.

24. Ibid.

25. Dwight N. Hopkins, *Shoes That Fit Our Feet: Sources for a Constructive Black Theology* (Maryknoll, N.Y.: Orbis, 1993), 47.

26. Ibid., 48.

27. David Emmanuel Goatley, "Godforsakenness in African American Spirituals," in *CLST2,* 131.

28. Ibid., 156.

29. M. Shawn Copeland, "Wading through Many Sorrows: Toward a Theology of Suffering in Womanist Perspective," in *CLST2,* 159; reprinted from *A Troubling in My Soul: Womanist Perspectives on Evil & Suffering,* ed. Emilie M. Townes (Maryknoll, N.Y.: Orbis, 1993), 109–29.

30. Ibid., 170.

31. Ibid., 167.

32. Ibid., 170.

33. Ibid., 168.

34. Ibid., 170.

35. Ibid., 168.

36. Ibid., 170.

37. Ibid., 171.

38. Ibid.

39. Ibid., 170.

40. Coleman, "Coming Through 'Legion'" in *CLST2,* 67.

41. Cheryl J. Sanders, "Liberation Ethics in the Ex-Slave Interviews," in *CLST2,* 73.

42. Ibid., 74.

43. Ibid., 81.

44. Ibid., 86ff.

45. Ibid., 88–89.

46. Ibid., 93.

47. Sanders, *Empowerment Ethics.*

48. Ibid., 25.

49. Hopkins, "Slave Theology," in *CLST2,* 2.

50. Ibid.

51. Hopkins, "Introduction," in *CLST1,* ix.

52. Ibid., x.

53. Hopkins, *Down, Up, and Over,* 6–10.

54. I refer readers interested in African retentions in African American religion to chaps. 2, 3, and 6 of Coleman, *Tribal Talk.*

55. John W. Blassingame, ed., *Slave Testimony: Two Centuries of Letters, Speeches, Interviews, and Autobiographies* (Baton Rouge: Louisiana State University Press, 1977), xliii.

56. Ibid., xliv.

57. Ibid., xlv.

58. Ibid., xlviii.

59. Ibid., l.

60. Ibid., li.

61. Hopkins, *Shoes That Fit Our Feet,* 22.

62. Speech by James H. Cone at the Society for the Study of Black Religion Annual Meeting, March 2006, Brite Divinity School, Ft. Worth, Texas.

63. Franz Von Brentano, "Mental and Physical Phenomena," in *The Phenomenology Reader,* ed. Dermot Moral and Timothy Mooney (New York: Routledge, 2004), 39.

64. Charles H. Long, *Significations: Signs, Symbols, Images in the Interpretation of Religion* (Philadelphia: Fortress Press, 1986), 9.

65. Ibid., 55.

66. Ibid.

67. Ibid., 61.

68. Ibid.

69. Ibid., 58.

70. Ibid., 190.

71. See introduction, 9.

72. Ibid., 196.

73. Long, 197.

74. Victor Anderson, *Beyond Ontological Blackness* (New York: Continuum, 1995, 1998), 161.

75. Coleman, *Tribal Talk*, vii.

CHAPTER 3: FAITH ON EARTH

1. Although my discussion is based on Pinn's initial critique of redemptive suffering in *Why Lord? Suffering and Evil in Black Theology* (New York: Continuum, 1995), in other books, Pinn has strengthened his argument on the relevance of redemptive suffering in African American accounts of evil and suffering and for black humanism as an alternative tradition within African American religious traditions. However, his critique of redemptive suffering in *Why Lord?* remains the clearest, most succinct statement of the problem. See Anthony B. Pinn, *Varieties of African American Religious Experience* (Minneapolis: Fortress Press, 1998); *By These Hands: A Documentary History of African American Humanism* (New York: New York University Press, 2001); *Moral Evil and Redemptive Suffering: A History of Theodicy in African American Religious Thought* (Gainesville: University Press of Florida, 2002); and *African-American Humanist Principles: Living and Thinking like the Children of Nimrod* (New York: Palgrave/Macmillan, 2004).

2. See Emilie M. Townes, *A Troubling in My Soul: Womanist Perspectives on Evil and Suffering* (Maryknoll, N.Y.: Orbis, 1993).

3. See pp. 16–17.

4. See John Hick, *Evil and the God of Love* (Thetford, Norfolk, UK: Lowe & Brydone, 1968); David Ray Griffin, *God, Power, and Evil: A Process Theodicy* (Philadelphia: Westminster, 1976); Alvin Plantinga, *God, Freedom, and Evil* (Grand Rapids, Mich.: Eerdmans, 1974); Edward Farley, *Good and Evil: Interpreting a Human Condition* (Minneapolis: Fortress Press, 1990); Wendy Farley, *Tragic Vision and Divine Compassion: A Contemporary Theodicy* (Louisville, Ky.: Westminster John Knox, 1990); Jennifer L. Geddes, ed., *Evil after Postmodernism: Histories, Narratives And Ethics* (New York: Routledge, 2001); Susan Neiman, *Evil in Modern Thought: An Alternative History of Theology* (Princeton, N.J.: Princeton Univerity Press, 2002).

5. Alasdair MacIntyre, "Is Understanding Religion Compatible with Believing?" in *Rationality*, ed. Bryan R. Wilson (Worcester, UK: Basil Blackwell, 1970), 73.

6. Kenneth Surin, *Theology and the Problem of Evil* (Oxford: Blackwell, 1986), 10–11.

7. Richard H. Popkin, *The History of Scepticism from Erasmus to Spinoza* (Berkeley: University of California Press, 1979), xviii–xix.

8. Farley, *Good and Evil*, 221–26.

9. Benedict de Spinoza, *Improvement of the Understanding, The Ethics, Correspondence*, trans. R. H. M. Elwes (New York: Dover, 1955), Def. I-VI, 1; Prop. XXIV-XL, 104–14.

10. Ibid,. Prop. XXIX-XXXVII, 206–11.

11. David Hume, "Concerning Natural Religion," in *The English Philosophers from Bacon to Mill*, ed. Edwin A. Burtt (New York: Random House, 1967).

12. Ibid., 739.

13. Ibid., 741.

14. Ibid., 746.

15. Ibid., 750–51.

16. Delores S. Williams, *Sisters in the Wilderness: Womanist God-Talk* (Maryknoll, N.Y.: Orbis, 1992),60.

17. Ibid., 161–62.

18. Williams, *Sisters in the Wilderness*, 203.

19. Ibid.

20. Ibid., 167.

21. Ibid., 174.

22. Ibid., 238.

23. Pinn, *Why Lord?*, 10.

24. Ibid., 17.

25. Ibid., 17–18.

26. Ibid., 13.

27. Ibid., 111.

28. Ibid., 158.

29. Ibid., 17–18.

30. Karl Barth, *Learning Jesus Christ through the Heidelberg Catechism*, trans. Shirley C. Guthrie (Grand Rapids, Mich.: Eerdmans, 1964), 29–30.

31. My position is in large part based on H. Richard Niebuhr's *The Responsible Self: An Essay in Christian Moral Philosophy* (New York: Harper & Row, 1963).

32. H. Richard Niebuhr, *Faith on Earth: An Inquiry into the Structure of Human Faith* (New Haven, Conn.: Yale University Press, 1989), 1.

33. Ibid.

34. See pp. 15–16.

35. Stanley Hauerwas, *Suffering Presence: Theological Reflection on Medicine, the Mentally Handicapped, and the Church* (Notre Dame: University of Notre Dame Press, 1986), 28.

36. H. Richard Niebuhr, "Faith as Confidence and Fidelity," in *Radical Monotheism and Western Culture* (Louisville, Ky.: Westminster John Knox, 1960), 16.

37. Ibid.

38. Ibid.

39. Ibid.

40. Tyron Inbody, *The Faith of the Christian Church: An Introduction to Theology* (Grand Rapids, Mich.: Eerdmans, 2005), 74.

41. Niebuhr, *Faith on Earth*, 30.

42. Howard Thurman, *The Creative Encounter: An Interpretation of Religion and the Social Witness* (Richmond, Ind.: Friends United, 1972, [1954]), 48.

43. Ibid., 49.

44. Ibid.

45. Ibid.

46. Ibid., 49–50.

47. Ibid., 51.

48. Ibid., 52.

49. Ibid., 52–53.

50. Ibid., 54.

51. Phillip Hallie, *Tales of Good and Evil, Help and Harm* (New York: HarperCollins, 1997), 4.

52. Hauerwas, *Suffering Presence*, 26.

CHAPTER 4: THE SMELL OF LIFE

1. Edward Khmara, *Ladyhawke* (1985), movie screenplay transcript available at http://www.fable.com/transcript.html (accessed November 13, 2007).

2. Gordon Kaufman, *In Face of Mystery: A Constructive Theology* (Cambridge, Mass.: Harvard University Press, 1993), 274–75.

3. Howard Thurman, *The Creative Encounter* (Richmond, Ind.: Friends United, 1954), 19.

4. See Gary Dorrien, "The Real Is the Personal: Albert C. Knudson, Francis J. McConnell, Edgar S. Brightman, and the Boston Personalist School," in *The Making of American Liberal Theology: Idealism, Realism & Modernity, 1900–1950* (Louisville, Ky.: Westminster John Knox, 2003), 286–355.

5. Edgar Sheffield Brightman, "Personality as a Metaphysical Principle," in *Personalism in Theology: Essays in Honor of Albert Cornelius Knudson*, ed. Edgar Sheffield Brightman (Boston: Boston University Press, 1943), 40–41.

6. Thurman, *The Creative Encounter*, 19.

7. Dorrien, *The Making of American Liberal Theology*, 353.

8. Thurman, *The Creative Encounter*, 20.

9. Ibid.

10. Brightman, *Personalism in Theology*, 47.

11. Thurman, *The Creative Encounter*, 22–23.

12. Ibid., 21.

13. Ibid., 22.

14. Ibid., 24.

15. Ibid.

16. Ibid., 27.

17. For a fuller account of representational epistemology, see "Pragmatism and Religious Realism," in my *Pragmatic Theology: Negotiating the Intersections of an American Philosophy of Religion and Public Theology*, Religion and American Public Life (Albany: State University of New York Press, 1998), 73–76.

18. Thurman, *The Creative Encounter*, 28.

19. Ibid., 29.

20. Ibid., 30.

21. Ibid., 31.

22. Ibid., 32; my emphasis.

23. Ibid., 33.

24. Ibid., 38.

25. In the previous chapter, I discussed Thurman's account of suffering as a preparatory discipline for religious experience, and at the end of this chapter, I will take up Thurman on prayer as a spiritual discipline.

26. Ibid, 40.

27. John B. Cobb Jr., *Living Options in Protestant Theology: A Survey of Method* (Philadelphia: Westminister, 1962), 88–89.

28. William James, *The Meaning of Truth*, introduction by A. J. Ayer (Cambridge, Mass.: Harvard University Press, 1975, [1978]), 232–33.

29. John Dewey, *Art as Experience* (New York: Perigee, 1934), 19.

30. Howard Thurman, "The Negro Spirituals Speak of Life and Death," in *African American Religious Thought: An Anthology*, ed. Cornel West and Eddie S. Glaude (Louisville, Ky.: Westminster John Knox, 2003), 41.

31. Wieman, "Theocentric Religion," in *The Chicago School of Theology—Pioneers in Religious Inquiry*, Vol.1, *The Later Chicago School, 1919–1988*, ed. W. Creighton Peden and Jerome A. Stone (Lewiston, N.Y.: Edwin Mellen, 1996), 65–65.

32. Ibid.

33. Ibid., 66.

34. Josiah Royce, *The Philosophy of Loyalty* (Indianapolis, Ind.: Hackett, 1982), 330.

35. Howard Thurman, *The Search for Common Ground* (Richmond, Ind.: Friends United Press, 1986), 74.

36. Royce, *The Philosophy of Loyalty*, 330.

37. Nancy Frankenberry, *Religion and Radical Empiricism* (Albany: State University of New York Press, 1987), 191.

38. Ibid.

39. James M. Gustafson, *Ethics from a Theocentric Perspective*, vol. 1 (Chicago, Ill.: University of Chicago Press, 1981), 236–51.

40. Ibid., 246.

41. Ibid. 112-113.

42. Robert Corrington, *Nature & Spirit* (New York: Fordham University Press, 1992), 81.

43. Howard Thurman, "Knowledge . . . Shall Vanish Away," in *For the Inward Journey: The Writings of Howard Thurman*, ed. Anne Spencer Thurman (Richmond, Ind.: Friends United, 1984), 11.

44. Gustafson, *Ethics from a Theocentric Perspective*, 1:312.

45. Ibid., 1:313.

46. Ibid., 1:314.

47. Ibid., 1:314–15.

48. Ibid., 1:317.

49. Ibid., 318.

50. Ibid.

51. Ibid., 1:319.

52. Thurman, "Prayer for a Friendly World," in *For the Inward Journey,* 297.

53. Renita J. Weems, *Listening for God: A Minister's Journey Through Silence and Doubt* (New York: Touchstone, 1999), 146.

54. Ibid., 148–49.

55. Andrew P. Watson, "Negro Primitive Religious Services," in *God Struck Me Dead: Voices of Ex-Slaves*, ed. Clifton H. Johnson (Cleveland: Pilgrim, 1993 [1969]), 3–4.

CHAPTER 5: HOME AND THE BLACK CHURCH

1. Frank Barbour Coffin, "God Sees," in *Standing in the Need of Prayer: A Celebration of Black Prayer* (New York: Free, 2003), 74.

2. Henry Nelson Wieman, "The Source of Human Good," in *The Chicago School of Theology—Pioneers in Religious Inquiry*, Vol. II, ed. W. Creighton Penden and Jerome A. Stone (Lewiston, N.Y.: Edwin Mellon, 1996), 91.

3. Ibid., 87.

4. Ibid.

5. Stephen Mitchell, *Can Love Last? The Fate of Romance over Time* (New York: Norton, 2002), 36.

6. Robert Coles, *The Ongoing Journey: Awakening Spiritual Life in at Risk Youth* (Boys Town, Neb.: Boys Town, 1995), 1.

7. Because of the sensitive nature of the incident in the lives of people most affected by the incident, I have changed the actual name of the victim to protect his anonymity.

8. Peter J. Paris, *The Social Teaching of the Black Churches* (Philadelphia: Fortress Press, 1985), 9.

9. C. Eric Lincoln, *The Black Church Since Frazier* (New York: Schocken, 1963), 116.

10. Ibid, 115–16.

11. Victor Anderson, "Explicating and Displacing Ontological Blackness: The Heroic and Grotesque in African American Cultural and Religious Criticism," in *Beyond Ontological Blackness* (New York: Continuum, 1995, 1998), 120–32.

12. C. Eric Lincoln and Lawrence H. Mamiya, *The Black Church in the African American Experience* (Durham, N.C.: Duke University Press, 1991), 8.

13. Adolph L. Reed Jr., *The Jesse Jackson Phenomenon: The Crisis of Purpose in African American Politics* (New Haven, Conn.: Yale University Press, 1986), 59–60.

14. Ibid., 45, 51, 57.

15. Ibid., 48.

16. Ibid., 51.

17. Lincoln and Mamiya, *The Black Church in the African American Experience,* 274.

18. Ibid.

19. Ibid., 294–96.

20. Marcia Riggs, *Plenty Good Room: Women versus Male Power in the Black Church* (Cleveland, Ohio: Pilgrim, 2003), 80.

21. Ibid., 68.

22. Horace Griffin, "Their Own Revived Them Not: African American Lesbians and Gays in Black Churches," in *The Greatest Taboo: Homosexuality in Black Communities*, ed. Delroy Constantine-Simms (Los Angeles: Alyson, 2000), 110.

23. Ibid., 114.

24. Don Lattin, "Black clergy gathering to fight gay matrimony," *San Francisco Chronicle*, May 15, 2004, http://www.sfgate.com/cgi-bin/article.cgi?f=/c/a/2004/05/15/MNGUP6M3ON1.DTL&hw=Lattin&sn=001&sc=1000 (accessed November 15, 2007).

25. Ibid.

26. Ibid.

27. Dyana Bagby and Laura Douglas-Brown, "Atlanta 'mega church' leads march against gay marriage," December 10, 2004, http://www.sovo.com/2004/12-10/news/localnews/mega.cfm (accessed December 31, 2007).

28. "About Operation: Rebirth," http://www.operationrebirth.com/aboutus.html (accessed November 15, 2007).

29. "Affirming Churches," http://www.operationrebirth.com/affirmingchurches.html (accessed November 15, 2007).

30. "Who we are: The Unity Fellowship Church Movement, Mission," http://www.unityfellowshipchurch.org/history.html (accessed November 15, 2007).

31. Equal Partners in Faith, "An Open Letter to MLK Jr.," January 20, 2005, http://www.witherspoonsociety.org/2005/letter_to_mlk.htm (accessed November 15, 2007).

32. James M. Gustafson, *Treasure in Earthen Vessels: The Church as a Human Community* (Chicago, Ill.: University of Chicago Press, 1961), 3.

33. Ibid., 5.

34. Ibid., 21.

35. Victor Anderson, "Deadly Silence: Reflections on Homosexuality and the Black Church," in *Sexual Orientation and Human Rights in American Religious Discourse*, Saul M. Olyan and Martha C. Nussbaum, eds. (New York: Oxford University Press, 1998), 195.

36. Ibid., 92.

37. bell hooks, *Salvation: Black People and Love* (New York: HarperCollins, 2001), 192–93.

38. Charles Sanders Peirce, *A Neglected Argument* in *Values in a Universe of Chance: Selected Writings of Charles S. Peirce (1839–1914)*, ed. Philip P. Wiener (Garden City, N.Y.: Doubleday, 1958), 363–64.

POSTSCRIPT

1. Martin Luther King Jr. "An Experiment in Love," in *A Testament of Love: Essential Wrings and Speeches of Martin Luther King, Jr.*, ed. James Melvin Washington (New York: HarperCollins, 1986), 19–20.

2. Martin Luther King Jr., "The Power of Nonviolence," in Washington, *A Testament of Hope*, 13–14.

INDEX

African American religious experience, 4, 7–13, 129–130; home and church as centers of value in, 143–171; reductivist accounts of, 7–9; 78; and social differentiation, 59; and sources of religious insight, 141–142. *See also* pragmatic theology

Appiah, Kwame Anthony, 6, 34–42; and conservation of African cultures, 36–37; on Du Bois, 35; on politics of difference, 29; on race (weak conception of), 35–40

Augustine, 137

autobiographical impulse, 4–7

Baker-Fletcher, Karen, 49–50

Beloved Community, XIII, XIV–XVI, 3–4, 23–24, 28, 48–49, 131, 145, 169–174

black church, 143–171; as (ambiguous) center of value, 144–145, 151–171, 173; gender, 156–160, 162–163; heroic depictions of, 153–156; as a natural human community, 163–169; and same-sex marriage, 159–163; and sexuality (homosexuality), 151–153, 159–163, 166–169; as source of religious insight, 153–156, 163

black liberation theology, 7–8, 89–99; alienation from black churches and culture, 54–61, 92–93; and class differentiation, 58–59; and hermeneutics of narrative return, 54, 60–72; and methodological challenges, 54–79; and problem of equivocation, 68–72; and sources of religious insight, 55. *See also* theological method; womanist theology

black philosophy and race, 33–43

Blassingame, John W., 69–71

Blondel, Maurice, 13

Brightman, Edgar S., 116–118

Burwick, Frederick, 11

Cobb, John, 124

Coleman, Will, 53, 56, 61, 63, 78, 181–182n19

Coles, Robert, 149

Cone, James H., 7–8, 55–58, 71, 97

Copeland, M. Shawn, 64–66

Corrington, Robert, 134

creative exchange, XIII, XV–XVI, 3–4, 16–21, 73, 111, 165–174; and ambiguities of home and church, 144; between black theology and philosophy, 27–28; as God, 144; and grace, 134–135; and race, 39–40; and redemptive suffering, 82, 100–110; and sources of religious insight, 77–79; and *World*, 48–52

Cummings, George, 56, 62, 64

deep symbols, 4; and race, 30–33, 48, 50–51

Dewey, John, XII, 126, 129, 138

Du Bois, W.E.B., 9, 35, 37–39

Evans, James H., 60

evil and suffering. *See* redemptive suffering experience, XII, 3; and the grotesque, 10–13; and narrative, 6–7; and pragmatic naturalism, 12–16; as aesthetic, 126. *See also* African American religious experience

faith. *See under* redemptive suffering

Farley, Edward, 4, 30–33, 85

Fontinell, Eugene, 13–14

Frankenberry, Nancy, 133

Frazier, E. Franklin, 28

Gadamer, Hans-Georg, 43–44

gender. *See under* black church

Goatley, David Emmanuel, 64

God, 99–109, 112–115, 118–125, 130–142; belief in, 173–174; as creative exchange, 144; and moral agency, 83–89, 92–98; in Wieman's theology, 17, 19; as world in pragmatic naturalism, 14, 132–137, 142

Griffin, Horace, 159

grotesque, 10–13, 73, 75–76, 108, 152, 173, 175n13; and the church, 164; and Gustafson (experience), 15; and race, 32

Gustafson, James M., XIII, XIV, 18–21; on the church as human community, 163–164; on consent 19; on experience, 14–16; on God, 133, 177n41; on piety, 14–16, 136–137

Hallie, Phillip, 80, 109

Hauerwas, Stanley, 102–103, 109–110

Holmes, Barbara, 49

home (family): as ambiguous center of value, 144–151, 163–171, 173; as deep symbol, 146

Hopkins, Dwight N., 56, 60, 62–63, 67–68, 71

Hume, David, 86–89, 99

Hurston, Zora Neale, 49

Inbody, Tyron, 3, 104

James, William, XII, 2, 12, 117, 125–126

Jefferson, Thomas, 34

Kant, Immanuel, 34

Kaufman, Gordon, 111–112

Kee, Alistair, 55

King, Martin Luther, Jr., XIV–XV, 28–30, 172; "Open Letter to MLK, Jr.," 161–162

Ladyhawke, 112–115, 149–150

Lincoln, C. Eric, 153–155, 157, 163